LE MAYA Q'ATZIJ / OUR MAYA WORD

INDIGENOUS AMERICAS

Robert Warrior, Series Editor

Le Maya Q'atzij / Our Maya Word

· · · ·

Poetics of Resistance in Guatemala

Emil' Keme

Indigenous Americas

University of Minnesota Press
Minneapolis
London

Portions of chapter 2 originally appeared as "The Discursive Economy of
Maya Culturales in Guatemala," *Hispanofila* 157 (December 2009): 25–39.
Portions of chapter 3 are adapted from "State Violence, History, and Maya Literature in
Guatemala," in *Sources and Methods in Indigenous Studies* (2016), edited by Jean O'Brien
and Chris Andersen; reprinted by permission of Routledge, a division of Taylor &
Francis. Portions of chapter 3 are also adapted from "Contemporary Maya Literature and
the Question of Modernity: Xib'alb'a as Allegory of Globalization," in *Violence and
Endurance: Representations
of War and Peace in Post-War Central American Narratives* (2016), edited by Astvaldur
Astvaldsson; reprinted by permission of NOVA Publishers.

All poetry excerpts are reprinted with permission from the poets.

Published by the University of Minnesota Press
111 Third Avenue South, Suite 290
Minneapolis, MN 55401–2520
http://www.upress.umn.edu

ISBN 978-1-5179-0807-2 (hc)
ISBN 978-1-5179-0808-9 (pb)
Library of Congress record available at https://lccn.loc.gov/2020058444.

Printed in the United States of America on acid-free paper

The University of Minnesota is an equal-opportunity educator and employer.

I dedicate this book to the memory of
Jakelin Caal Maquin (Maya Q'eqchi'),
Felipe Gómez Alonzo (Maya Chuj),
Juan León Gutiérrez (Maya Ch'orti'),
Wilmer Josué Ramírez (Maya Ch'orti'),
Carlos Hernández (Maya Achí),
Claudia Patricia Gómez González (Maya Mam),
and all the Indigenous Maya children whose dreams
for a better life could not flourish in Turtle Island.

Contents

Introduction

Iximulew's/Guatemala's Indigenous Poetry since 1960

THE *POPOL WUJ* (also written as *Popol Vuh* and *Pop Wuj*), the "Book of the Community," was written between 1554 and 1558 and is one of the most important K'iche' Maya books in the history of the Mayab' region.[1] Some scholars believe that the authors of the text were three K'iche' Maya young men whose ages ranged between fourteen to eighteen years. Two of the writers are thought to be Don Juan de Rojas and Don Juan Cortés, descendants of the kings of the city of *Q'umarkaj* (The Big House), *Oxib-Quej* (Three Deer), and *Belejeb-Tzi* (Nine Dog), who had been burned alive by the Spanish invader Pedro de Alvarado on his arrival to their city.[2] The other young man, it has been suggested, was Cristóbal Velasco, a *Nim choq'oj* or "Master of the Word" of this period, who lived in the same K'iche' city.[3] His work was to recite historical accounts, stories, and the names of old warriors during festivities and important events. Despite the uncertainty about the authors of the text, most scholars agree that the book was authored by at least three writers.

During the colonization of Q'umarkaj in March 1524, the K'iche' people witnessed the destruction of their temples and historical records, the torture and death of their leaders, sexual violence against women, and the beginning of enslavement of yet another Maya Nation; Alvarado, with the help of thousands of Indigenous allies, had already conquered other sectors of the K'iche' Maya kingdom in what is today Quetzaltenango. The Spanish colonial onslaught in Q'umarkaj included the imposition of Christianity on people who were being instructed as *ajtz'ib' ajk'ot* (scribes, or framers of the word) and political leaders. Young Indigenous literate youths were targeted because, as noted by Friar Bartolomé de las Casas, they

had news about the origins of all things, those related to religion
and gods and their cults; about how their towns and cities were
founded, how their kings and lords and lordships began, and the
types of their elections and successions; about how many and
which lord had ruled and their work and achievements and
memorable events, good and bad; of how well and badly they
governed; of great men and good and strong and brave captains;
of wars that they had and how in them they gave assignments . . .
these chroniclers had knowledge of the days, months and years,
and even though they did not have writing like ours, they nonetheless had figures and characters of all things that they want to
signify. (qtd. in Van Akkeren 2007, 86)

The Spanish priests who accompanied Pedro de Alvarado during
the conquest of the Mexica or Aztec Empire had learned important lessons. "Peaceful" efforts to impose Christianity through dialogues with
Mexica leaders, priests, and wise elders had failed, because they persistently
defended their Indigenous spiritual values. In response to their "stubborn-
ness," the Spanish tortured and later executed them when they questioned
the Christian faith. It was thus concluded that it was better to evangelize
and educate the children and young Indigenous people by forcibly sepa-
rating them from their families and imposing on them new memories and
knowledges. Initially, Indigenous children were sent to Spain to obtain an
education, after which they were expected to come back to their places of
origin and be the ones to spread the new Western knowledge to their
peoples. However, most of them died on their journey to the peninsula.
Therefore, the Spanish changed their strategy: instead of sending Indigenous children to Spain, they educated the youngsters in the new churches
established in the recently colonized territories. Pedro de Gante, one of
the figures in the crafting of Indigenous literacy and Christian instruction,
details some of these strategies in the "New World" in a letter he sent to
Phillip II in 1529:

Approximately one thousand children were gathered together, and
we kept them locked up day and night in our house, and they were
forbidden any conversation with their fathers and even less with
their mothers, with the only exception of those who served them
and brought them food; and the reason for this was so that they

might neglect their excessive idolatries and their excessive sacrifices, from which the devil had secured countless souls. (qtd. in
Mignolo 1989, 67)

Knowing of the important moral, spiritual, and political authority represented by the K'iche' authors of the *Popol Wuj*, the Spanish priests kidnapped and locked them up in churches to start the processes of evangeli-
zation and the imposition of Spanish values. They introduced the Christian
Bible as the new epistemological referent regarding the "true origins" of
humanity and the universe; the priests taught the young men to speak,
read, and write in *kaxlan tzij* (Castilian Spanish) and to use the Latin alphabet instead of the ancestral Maya pictographic and hieroglyphic writing
system. However, in their efforts to make these Indigenous framers of
the word ignore "their excessive idolatries and their excessive sacrifices,"
the Spanish priests underestimated the young men they sought to evangelize. Naively, the European invaders believed that these Indigenous scribes
would suddenly set aside their "excessive idolatries" and incorrect beliefs
to openly embrace and adopt Christianity and what Spain offered them.
On the contrary, the contents of the *Popol Wuj* reveal the K'iche' authors'
sagacity and creativity in their struggle to defend the memories, knowledge, and values of their people tenaciously.

What rhetorical exchanges occurred between the K'iche' authors and
their Christian teachers? What ideas and reflections did they develop
when they heard the bishops' teachings? How much punishment did
they endure when challenging the "new" knowledge? What complicit
gazes and silences did they patiently exchange in the rooms where they
were being instructed about Christianity? What discussions did they hold
in whispers about the new concepts and the stories coming from the European peninsula? What exchanges might have occurred among them in
solitary rooms or in the darkness of caves in the middle of the night? What
patience might they have had to absorb the "new" knowledge, perhaps bit-
ing their tongues, knowing that their words did not have an audience
under the new colonial reality? In what spaces did they reflect on the strategies they would use to inscribe their millenarian legacy in the "new" books
written in the Latin alphabet?

We will never know the exact answer to these questions, nor will we
know the dynamics and cultural exchanges between the K'iche' young
men and the Spanish priests while they received instruction in Western

knowledge. Nevertheless, despite the full context of colonial violence they were exposed to and the immense and traumatic ideological pressure they were surely subjected to during the height of the Inquisition,[4] as well as their experiencing constant punishment, aggressions, and persecution, these K'iche' Maya authors found the courage to challenge the colonizers by dignifying the spiritual Maya seeds that their parents and grandparents had planted in their minds and hearts. They soon became aware of the great usefulness of the Latin alphabet in affirming the K'iche' language and their native histories. They employed it subversively to rewrite history as their first discursive exercise of "intellectual sovereignty" (Warrior 2014) to recover lost political authority, challenging the religious knowledge coming from Europe. This is why in the first pages of the K'iche' Maya sacred text they wrote, "Wa'e xchiqatz'ib'aj chi upam chik, uch'ab'al Dios, pa christianoil chik. Xchiqelesaj rumal maja b'i chik ilb'al re *Popol Wuj*, ilb'al saq petenaq ch'aqa palo utzijoxik qamujib'al, ilb'al saq k'aslem'; chu-cha' xik" (This account we shall now write under the law of God and Christianity. We shall bring it forth because there is no longer the means whereby the *Popol Vuh* may be seen, the means of seeing clearly that had come from across the sea—the account of our obscurity, and the means of seeing life clearly, as it is said. The original book exists that was written anciently, but its witnesses and those who ponder it hide their faces; qtd. in Christenson 2007, 64).[5]

The authors of the *Popol Wuj* proceeded to present a Maya worldview where humanity and the universe are the result not of the actions of a single god, but of a divine council that gathers to create the world and the humanity who will inhabit it. The council members learn from their mistakes. First, they create the seas, the earth, and the forests and then the animals. They then proceed to create humans out of mud, but these creatures are later destroyed when the gods send rain to earth. After this misstep, the divine council frames humans out of wood; however, they are destroyed when they do not express their gratitude for their creation to the framers. They consequently are turned into monkeys. In a final attempt, the gods create the men of maize, the human creation who now inhabits the world.[6]

I begin *Le Maya Q'atzij / Our Maya Word: Poetics of Resistance in Guate-mala* by invoking the story of the *Popol Wuj* and its authors, because hundreds of years after the book was written, the experience of Maya writers resisting colonialism in the modern period is incredibly similar. The Maya people in *Iximulew* (land of corn, the ancestral Maya name of what is today

Guatemala) have recently survived a new colonial assault orchestrated by the Guatemalan nation-state in complicity with the U.S. government. Indeed, in June 1954, four years after the country saw its first democratic regime with the popular election of President Jacobo Árbenz Guzmán, a group of Guatemalan ex-soldiers led by General Carlos Castillo Armas, supported by the U.S. Central Intelligence Agency (CIA), engineered a coup d'état because the actions of the democratic government were harming the economic interests of the United Fruit Company (UFCO). With the establishment of the Castillo Armas dictatorship, its counterrevolutionary actions included repeal of the agrarian reform and the democratic constitution that had been created in 1945: the peasants were forced to return their newly acquired land, which the government then granted to the landowners and the UFCO. The Guatemala's Workers Party (PGT)—the communist political party in the country—became illegal, and the activities of the workers' union were forbidden. Social programs that favored Indigenous peasants and the working class were also suspended. Congress was dissolved, and the military government began a hostile relationship with the University of San Carlos, imposing censorship and the "anticommunist" persecution of professors, university students, and leftist intellectuals who criticized the new military government.[7]

These repressive measures and the growing role of the United States in Guatemalan politics soon provoked social discontent, which led to a rebellion in 1960 by a group of army officers who declared war against the nation-state and U.S. imperialism. That armed conflict would last for nearly thirty-six years. During this period, the Guatemalan state implemented repressive military strategies that were justified by its quest to eliminate the "communist" opposition. Toward the end of the 1970s, such measures became state terrorism and included military attacks aimed at the physical elimination of Maya communities in the rural areas of the country. The Guatemalan Army literally erased more than six hundred Indigenous communities. After the signing of the Peace Accords in 1996 and the approval of neoliberal economic programs like the Central American and Dominican Republic Free Trade Agreement (CAFTA-DR), it became clear that such counterinsurgent tactics had ulterior motives: it is in these Maya ancestral territories where today many transnational companies operate, extracting and exploiting Guatemala's natural resources. The end results of the internal armed conflict, according to the Truth and Reconciliation Commission, established in 1994, were the forcible displacement of 1.5 million people from their territories, the disappearance of more than 40,000, and the assassination of more than 200,000 individuals. Official reports conclude that the majority of these killings constituted "acts of genocide" against the Maya peoples.[8]

This is the historical context that serves as a social referent to analyze the decolonizing efforts of a contemporary Maya intelligentsia who, like the authors of the *Popol Wuj*, employ the poetic word as an agent of resistance, change, and emancipation. As in the past, theirs is an effort to validate and dignify our ancestral origins, as well as our diverse Maya identities and experiences in a present marked by a new colonial violence, now wielded under the banner of neoliberal globalization. Before proceeding, I wish to mention the personal dimension of this project, which in turn informs my reading of contemporary Maya literatures. The reader will notice that my position is not merely academic when I employ "I," "us," and "we" in the book. I am K'iche' Maya from Iximulew, and I migrated to the United States when I was nineteen because of the internal armed conflict and the economic poverty that my family and community experienced. This study explores in greater depth some of the existential issues—problems of liberty, anguish, horror, responsibility, agency, sociability, and emancipation—that have defined my own journey, experience, and trajectory, as well as my interpretation of the poetic works I analyze.

This book offers a critical analysis of the literature written by ten contemporary Maya writers who represent five Maya linguistic communities—K'iche', Kaqchikel, Q'eqchi', Q'anjob'al, and Pop'ti; it explores how these authors and their respective literary works, through the appropriation of the literary register, develop and negotiate their cultural identities and Indigenous rights. I divide the book into three parts that represent three sociohistorical moments of Maya literary insurgency, beginning with the initiation of the armed conflict in 1960 and concluding on December 21, 2012, the date that marks the closing of a long cycle in the Maya calendar known as the *Oxlajuj* (Thirteen) *B'aktun*, a period of resurgence.[9] The first chapter, which presents the first phase of contemporary Maya literary insurgency, focuses on the poetic works of Kaqchikel Maya authors Francisco Morales Santos and Luis de Lión (1939–1984). I analyze Morales Santos's composition "We Will Be Kaqchikel Again," included in his book of poetry, *Agua en el silencio* (Water in the Silence, 1961), and his lyrical poem "Madre, nosotros también somos historia" (Mother, We Too Are History, 1988). Then I examine Lión's *Los poemas del volcán de agua*.

Los poemas míos (Poems from Water Volcano. My Own Poems), a book of poetry written toward the end of the 1970s but published posthumously in 1994. I demonstrate how the poetic works, which were originally published in kaxlan tzij / Castilian Spanish, develop a process of dignifying Kaqchikel Maya identity within the context of the late twentieth-century armed conflict. With their affirmation of Indigenous identity, these authors respond not only to the oppressive politics of the nation-state but also to the Guatemalan Left that interprets the Indigenous world as a "problem" because of its cultural and linguistic specificities. In this context, ladino, or non-Indigenous intellectuals,[10] propose policies of "ladinoization" or cultural assimilation to "incorporate" Maya peoples into the revolutionary movements and their project of "modern" nationhood. Their poetry speaks of revolution and socialism while at the same time discussing Maya nationalist vindication. In this sense, these poetic works not only define an Indigenous literary continuance in the present with their Maya predecessors but also challenge the hegemonic register through—in Frantz Fanon's 1961 terms—an Indigenous "national liberation" in its own right.

In the second chapter of the book, I examine what I consider a second phase of Maya literary insurgency between 1978 and 1984, when the nation-state increases political repression in the country, turning its counterinsurgent policies into state terrorism that directly affects Maya people in the rural areas of the country. In contrast to Morales Santos and Lión, authors in this second literary phase highlight various elements of their Indigenous cultural identity, particularly their spiritual values, cultural specificities, the material culture, and Maya languages as important literary vehicles of artistic expression and creativity. The chapter concentrates on *El animalero / Animal Gathering* ([1990] 2008) by Humberto Ak'abal (K'iche'), *Piedras Labradas / Sculpted Stones* (1995) by Victor Montejo (Pop'ti'), and *The Dry Season: Q'anjob'al Maya Poems* (2001) by Gaspar Pedro González (Q'anjob'al). To better understand these authors' literary and political proposals, I complement my literary-critical analysis with a discussion of the authors' essayistic works. I show that these Maya writers employ "strategic essentialism" (Spivak 1988)—the conscious use of essentialism to "authenticate" their linguistic and cultural differences—in order to articulate a vision of the Maya world based on its relationship to the rural world, spirituality, the ancestral material legacy, and Indigenous languages. This is how these authors in the second phase respond to colonial power, indicating to the authorities that they have failed in their attempt to physically and culturally eliminate Indigenous peoples. But although I celebrate these efforts, I also point to some dangers of the Maya strategic essentialism that these authors endorse: their constructions of Mayaness end up marginalizing other Indigenous subjectivities, particularly those that emerge in the urban sphere and gender-nonconforming Maya identities.

In the third phase of Maya literary insurgency, presented in chapters 3 and 4, I examine poetic works published in the postwar period; that is, after the ending of the internal armed conflict formalized with the signing of the Peace Agreements in 1996. A new generation of Maya writers takes advantage of the global juncture to authorize their perspectives and subjectivities. In chapter 3, I analyze *Casa solitaria* (Solitary House, 2005) by Rosa Chávez (Kaqchikel/K'iche'), *Song from the Underworld / B'ixonik tzij kech juk'ulaj kaminaqib' / Canto palabra de una pareja de muertos* (2014, 2009) by Pablo García (K'iche'), and *Gemido de huellas / Sq'aqaw yechel aqanej* (Moan of the Footprints, 2007) by Sabino Esteban Francisco (Q'anjob'al). These writers, like those I study in chapter 2, produce works in both kaxlan tzij / Castilian Spanish and Maya languages and continue the debate about the Mayaness of their literary predecessors. Through the metaphor of the journey, these poetic works discuss forced displacement, and migration in the rural and urban spheres, as well as the violent and traumatic legacy of the internal armed conflict and genocide. By narrating experiences of violence, chaos, and pain, I argue, these authors diagnose the neoliberal present as a reactivation of the repressive colonial policies of the past. In this sense, these authors and their works "resuscitate" and memorialize the Maya social body as an exercise to enable reflection on our political vindication in a somber present.

In chapter 4, I focus on the poetic works of Q'eq'chi writer Maya Cu Choc—in particular, her poems "Poesía de lo propio" (Poetry of My Own, in "Poemaya," 1997), "Ix Tzib'" ("Woman Scribe"), and "Otro ¡Zaz!" ("Another Zaz!")—and *Gay(o)* (2011) by K'iche' Maya artist M anuel Tzoc. In contrast to those discussed in earlier chapters, these poetic works develop the struggle to affirm their authors' cultural, gender, and dissident sexual identities in the urban sphere. Through an appropriation of modernist aesthetics and autobiographical modes of narration, Cu Choc and Tzoc write in Spanish and underscore the political prominence of Indigenous women and queer subjects. In doing so, they challenge patriarchy and heteronormativity and make visible the struggles and experiences of

Maya women and queer subjects. I also develop a critique of some of these two authors' assumptions. For example, I complement my discussion of Tzoc's work with that of K'iche' Maya sociologist Dorotea Gómez Grijalva (2014), who interrogates some of the queer narratives that emerge in Guatemala City.

I selected the literary works and authors I discuss in this book not because they represent a Maya poetic-literary totality, but because they exemplify how Indigenous poetics carries out various processes of decolonization. It is well known that, within the context of Iximulew, there has been a powerful cultural boom in Indigenous literary and artistic production: hundreds of poetic, theatrical, and narrative works have been written. By adding Maya musical and visual works, we have an incredible and complex artistic corpus.[11] Despite the necessary omissions, the contribution made by my study shows how a contemporary Maya intelligentsia interrogates the structures of colonial power while also vindicating the complexity that the Maya world represents through their works.

The title of this volume, *Le Maya Q'atzij / Our Maya Word*, was inspired by the work of Q'anjob'al writer Gaspar Pedro González and his book, *Kotz'ib' / Nuestra literatura maya* (Our Maya Literature, 1997), which authorizes Indigenous literary voices through a dialogue with Western literary traditions. Although "kotz'ib'" is the Q'anjob'al term for "our word" or "literature," I use the corresponding K'iche' Maya term, "Q'atzij," which can be translated literally as "our tongue" or "our word." I emphasize the idea of "word" rather than literature as a gesture to emulate the writers of the *Popol Wuj*, who stress the value of the "word" as a carrier of knowledge and wisdom in the creation of the universe and humanity. The allusions to Iximulew, as well as to K'iche' Maya words and phrases that emerge in the book, are also intended as a gesture to authorize the epistemological references commonly used in our Indigenous communities and by Maya writers themselves.

In a moment during which many may see the study of literature—particularly poetry—as a devalued enterprise, what can a study about Maya literature from Iximulew offer? Why bother producing a Maya literary history based on a critical analysis of poetic cultural production? Why privilege the specific role of poetry instead of other cultural media like the novel or narrative or the visual arts? What can Maya poetics tell us and offer us during these times of neoliberal globalization?

First, a critical analysis of Maya poetry directly places us in a decisive moment regarding the role that literature plays in processes of linguistic, cultural, political, and social decolonization. Following the assumptions of the African American activist Angela Davis, we must understand that in the present the

> revolutionary struggle has been re-signified. For decades social movements have drawn standards of what it means to be a revolutionary. However, today we can do this in many ways. . . . The people can be revolutionary from the cultural world because art can see the future in ways that the rest cannot see; it can express what has not yet been expressed. If we want to create a new world, we must be capable of imagining it. Because of that, political activists and intellectuals must recognize the role of the artists because they develop a radical and revolutionary consciousness. Nevertheless, art cannot do it alone. Nor can the activists and intellectuals. All of us, as a collective, are creators of change. (qtd. in Yañez 2016)

In light of this reflection, Maya literature allows us the possibility not only of "imagining" a new world but also materializing it, because this textual production offers a glimpse of the tireless work of the Maya movement and its diverse cultural, social, and political manifestations.

It is important to underscore here that all the Maya writers whom I discuss in this book have been or are activists and, in addition to their literary works, have tirelessly contributed and continue to contribute to the vindication of their culture with their poetics and performance: they either actively participate in public protests, teach Indigenous languages at schools or in the community, develop literary and cultural workshops, guide young Indigenous peoples in the affirmation of their culture, or support others in the publication of their literary works. The Guatemalan writer Dante Liano, for example, in his book *Visión crítica de la literatura guatemalteca* (Critical Perspectives on Guatemalan Literature, 1997), notes how the Kaqchikel writer Luis de Lión stood on street corners in Guatemala City during the 1980s reciting his poetry in public while he handed out communist propaganda (301–2). The theatrical works *Awas* (2015) and *El jardín de los infantes locos* (Garden of the Crazy Children, 2013) by Rosa Chávez and Manuel Tzoc, respectively, combine poetry and theatrical performance. These works have been presented in various public spaces in the city and Indigenous communities, freely accessible to the general public. In this way, these artists transmit and maintain the Maya word and, in doing so, nourish the dignity of our trampled cultural identity. Their texts and activism develop ways to imagine a world where we can live free of racism and exclusion, as well as from the sexist and homophobic oppression that defines much of our daily experiences.

Yet we live in a period characterized by an explosion of information, transmitted rapidly through television, radio, and the internet. In this context, poetry, with its brevity and dynamism, lends itself to awakening the interest of readers. It is an art whose form often does not demand the time that a novel or a testimonial account requires. It is a genre that also adds the component of performance and public display—cultural aspects that, from a Maya perspective, can also be associated with and continue ancestral spiritual traditions. We know, for example, of the performative aspect of Indigenous prayers, songs, and rituals that are realized in public or communal contexts and are associated with human sacrifices or key dates in the Maya calendar related to the harvest or the movements of Venus, a planet tied to *Q'uq'umatz'* or the "plumed serpent."[12] Many ceremonies carried out by *A'j K'amal B'e,* or "spiritual guides," similarly involve elements of performance and ceremonial chants dedicated to the annual harvest or recognition of our ancestors. These elements, as we see, characterize much of contemporary Maya literary production. Poetry is an accessible medium whose aesthetics can be distributed easily and effectively through weekly periodicals in the community, posters, and social media.

In the last several decades we have witnessed an explosion of Indigenous literature, which makes it important to offer a critical assessment of the growing literary and cultural agency of Maya writers. We need to make this literary tradition visible; speak about its nature and its various aesthetic, cultural, and political functions; and offer a more nuanced understanding of the complexity of these poetic works and the invoked Maya epistemological references in them. For these authors, poetry becomes a vehicle to explore the intellectual, psychological, and social isolation in which the recent fratricidal experience has placed us. Following Lewis Gordon's (2000) reflections, these poetic works highlight how the Maya intelligentsia confronts the "existential reality of the day-to-day situation of their denied humanity and the historical irony of their emergence in a world that denied their historicity" (2). In doing so, these literary works represent "existential philosophies" that address "problems of freedom, anguish, dread, responsibility, embodied agency, sociality, and liberation; it addresses these problems through a focus on the human condition" (7). The themes explored by these Maya authors not only tell us about their existential concerns and their struggle for a collective well-being; they also offer important diagnoses about how colonial power operates in its quest to legitimate the expropriation of our ancestral territories and of our cultural specificities and, in turn, the cultural and political elements that characterize Maya decolonial resistance in Iximulew.

Indeed, from the Indigenous perspective represented in the Maya poetic register, what is today Guatemala represents a continuation of a colonial project that began to structure itself with the first European invasion in 1524. Such experience has been re-signified in the present with the governmental implementation of neoliberal economic, extractivist policies based on a new expropriation and exploitation of our ancestral territories. In this sense, the nation-state and its policies embody the history of the powerful and the benefits enjoyed until today by those in power through the permanent colonization of Indigenous peoples (Smith 1999, 34). While colonial violence for us has meant permanent dispossession and slow ethnocidal destruction, it has benefited non-Indigenous sectors (ladinos or *criollo-mestizos*[13]) in material, economic, social, legal, cultural, and political ways. Indigenous peoples who are politically conscious and fight against colonial violence are criminalized, incarcerated, and even assassinated. Hence, one cannot understand the history of the modern Guatemalan nation-state without giving an account of its continuous colonialist practices against Indigenous peoples, because, as proven by the recent history of the armed conflict, the country was founded and established on the basis of a massive genocide and the continuous desire to destroy Indigenous ways of life. These experiences lead us to define our decolonial struggles as constant interruptions and challenges to hegemonic sectors that established cultural and economic Western regimes, whose principal characteristics entail creating a racial ideal of whiteness. This racial ideal, which is reinforced by Christianity and other Western religions, values Castilian Spanish and English more than Maya languages; maintains and justifies violence against Mother Earth in favor of capitalist consumerism; and supports a heterosexual and heteronormative patriarchal regime that sustains and justifies itself in the domination of women, particularly Indigenous women, and queer people. Mayaness—with our linguistic and multinational diversity, gender and sexual difference, and our ancestral spiritual practices that also involve a defense of Mother Earth and its natural resources—is seen as a "problem" for the nation-state and its hegemonic institutions, because it is a threat to its Eurocentric principles and values.

The Maya literature I study here, like that of the colonial period represented by the *Popol Wuj*, develops rigorous critiques of these hegemonic ideals and principles. It instead advocates for the restitution of our territorial sovereignties and of all those elements of our Indigenous lives that have been denied to us by internal and external colonialism. The literary-poetic register represents an important vehicle that better allows us to understand some of these decolonial processes, as well as the emancipation sought out by the Maya movement.

This brings me to the idea of contemporary Maya literature. I do not intend to limit this book to a certain type of language or the representation of certain cultural specificities. Neither is this a study that privileges and understands Indigenous literatures as those that are merely written and produced in Indigenous languages. On the contrary, my study interrogates and problematizes such limited assertions in order to favor a more dynamic and heterogeneous notion of Maya and, more broadly, Indigenous literatures. In so doing, my critical reading of these poetic works also challenges the hegemonic *Indigenista* discourse; that is, literature or artistic production about the Indigenous world written and produced by non-Indigenous writers and artists. Since the early twentieth century, *Indigenismo*, with its affirmation of *mestizaje* (racial mixing) and Latinamericanism, has represented a project to redeem Indigenous peoples; however, with the Indigenous and Afro-descendant movements, these narratives and their "liberatory" missions obviously no longer make sense.[14] In other words, "mestizaje" is not the only exceptional cultural and political project in an entire multilingual and multiethnic region. Thus, contrary to the Latinamericanism and the idea of mestizaje, much of the literature written and produced by Maya writers now seeks to validate their own point of view through the construction of Indigenous selfhood. Given that much of the knowledge about Indigenous peoples still depends on what non-Indigenous people have said about us,[15] it should be no surprise then that one of the primary tasks of the majority of Maya writers is to break away from any type of discursive mediation and establish their own Maya literary agency. This operation is exemplified by the Q'anjob'al writer Gaspar

Pedro González—whose work I discuss in chapter 2—who, in his testimonial novel *The Return of the Maya,* states,

> This time I want to speak for myself. I am tired of others, the charlatans, speaking for me. I am tired of others using my name to falsify my image, to distort my true history, to profit from my misfortune and my pain. . . . This time, please allow me to speak, even though this language isn't mine. Nonetheless, I will take it and use it. (1988b, 2)

By speaking for himself, even in a language that is not "his," and by challenging the "charlatans" (Indigenismo), González simultaneously proposes his own self-representation and Indigenous literary agency by removing non-Indigenous mediation. In this way, the Q'anjob'al author establishes his own discursive authority to narrate and rewrite history within his own interpretive parameters. In a broader critical perspective, what González expresses, and what is presented in this book, manifests what Māori scholar Linda Tuhiwai Smith states about our struggles for the historical record:

> Indigenous peoples want to tell our own stories, write our own versions, in our own ways, for our own purposes. It is not simply about giving an oral account or a genealogical naming of the land and the events which raged over it, but a very powerful need to give testimony to and restore a spirit, to bring back into existence a world fragmented and dying. (1999, 29–30)

By speaking for themselves and appropriating the word, contemporary Maya writers have improved their writing and nurtured themselves from the lessons taught not only by their Maya precursors but also, ironically, by Indigenismo itself. In the poetic production I analyze, a new effort to materialize "intellectual sovereignty" (Warrior 2014) resides: it is an effort to recover and rewrite history, to affirm and celebrate our cultures, and to recover and defend our ancestral territories. Thus, the Maya literature I employ in this book privileges, first of all, the Maya origins to which the authors themselves adhere to. Many of the authors in this study, as a result of linguistic colonial policies, do not speak or write in their Maya languages and therefore write and produce their work in kaxlan tzij / Castilian

Spanish. Here, it is also important to underscore that the contemporary Maya intelligentsia, similar to that of the colonial period, has emerged from the same "lettered cities" (Rama 1984) and the modern educational institutions designed to "civilize" Indigenous peoples. As Maya Kaqchikel sociologist Aura Cumes indicates, this Maya intelligentsia represents a "group of political and intellectual activists who have educational, economic, and social conditions different from those of the great majority of Indigenous peoples, even though their initial status may have been similar to the majority" (Bastos and Cumes 2007, 89). This characterization "is not about making a negative valuation about such status, but rather understanding how and in what context these struggles have been made possible" (89). As with our educated ancestors in the colonial period, the contemporary Maya intelligentsia is politically conscious of the value of the word as a principal weapon of resistance and survival. To use it means not only to transmit our thoughts but also to spread and share the content of our culture, keeping it alive. Through the word they not only aim to rewrite their historical prominence in the dominant historical register but also share their anguish, daily life, frustrations, passions, illusions, and hopes in order to pave paths for new generations that can continue dignifying our rich ancestral history. They employ the Latin alphabet and other technologies we have inherited from European colonialisms to continue empowering our peoples, knowledge, and memories.

More than privileging the formal aspects of the poetic works, I focus on the contents and millenarian epistemological referents invoked by the authors.[16] Here, I adhere to Barbara Harlow's notion of "resistance literature." For Harlow,

poetry is capable not only of serving as a means for the expression of personal identity or even nationalist sentiment. Poetry, as part of the cultural institutions and historical existence of a people, is itself an arena of struggle. That struggle, as it is taking place, culturally as well as politically and militarily, today in various of the countries of the Third World . . . has been dramatically conditioned by the modern history of colonialism and the imperialist project of the west, of Europe and the United States. (1987, 33)

Because the context under which these literary works emerge is one marked by the struggles of liberation against military dictatorships that later transformed their counterinsurgent strategies into state terrorism, it is important to read Maya poetics critically as resistance literature with clear emancipatory intentions. Indeed, the Maya poetry I analyze should be interpreted as a social body that exemplifies urgency and impulse. In other words, although poetry often is seen as the mere result of creative imagination, my analysis deepens its conceptual, physical, historical, material, and political potentialities. I argue that contemporary Maya poetry is the result of concrete experiences that in turn articulate decolonial processes similar to those established by our ancestors and presented in fundamental texts such as the already mentioned *Popol Wuj*, *The Kaqchikel Chronicles*, *The Rabinal Achí*, and *The Totonicapán Title*.

Contemporary Maya textual production represents a continuation of literary traditions that date back at least 2,000 years before the European invasion of our ancestral territories. As I discussed earlier with the *Popol Wuj*, after the Spanish invasion we had to accommodate ourselves to the new social, religious, technological, and linguistic models imposed by the conquerors. The Spanish invasion meant the beginning of a tenacious political struggle that took place not only in the public sphere through rebellions and "daily passive resistances" (Scott 1985) but also in the symbolic terrain of language. European conquest inaugurated a battle for memory where certain colonized sectors sought to rescue and restore the sovereignty that was attacked and repressed with violent and ferocious military and religious campaigns. In this context of repression, our ancestors appropriated the tools of the colonizer, such as the Latin alphabet, to develop and communicate new resistances and to keep our millenarian historical memory alive. Contemporary Maya textual production continues these decolonizing efforts that begun in the colonial period by addressing and responding to the genocidal policies of the modern Guatemalan nation-state and its adoption of extractivist, neoliberal economic policies. For these Maya writers, the Indigenous cultural and textual legacies function as raw material in the discursive construction of an Indigenous nationalism that represents the cornerstone of political unification by articulating decolonizing policies.

I am not suggesting that our decolonizing processes and projects should be understood as struggles between the good (Indigenous peoples) and bad (settlers), but rather as complex plots or "colonial entanglements" in which, as indicated by Osage scholar Jean Dennison, Indigenous nations "have long understood the colonial process as at once devastating and full of potential" (2012, 7). As we see in the following chapters, a critical approach to Indigenous literatures necessarily involves highlighting some of its discursive limitations, contradictions, and ambiguities. We must show how contemporary Maya textual production, while it develops attractive emancipatory proposals, also articulates attitudes that exclude other Indigenous subjects who may not fit within the model of Mayaness being proposed; for example, Maya peoples who live in the urban sphere, Maya women who interrogate Indigenous and colonial patriarchy, or Maya queer subjects. Thus, it is important to make visible the diverse forms that Maya writers create and how they negotiate their identities, histories, and nationalities as a broad creative rhetorical exercise in contexts marked by the colonial experience. This poetry, in this sense, contributes to challenging assumptions that conclude that our experience as Indigenous peoples is constituted by homogeneity.

To arrive at a better understanding of contemporary Maya poetry and its decolonizing challenges during and after the internal armed conflict, my study is complemented by and at the same time engages in dialogues with existing historical, sociological, and anthropological works about the Maya movement and Indigenous literature.[17] Such studies rarely analyze Indigenous poetic-artistic contributions; there is not yet an exhaustive critical analysis that accounts for the origins of this Maya poetic movement and that displays the complexity and artistic depth of these literary works in the contemporary period.[18] Moreover, the Maya movement and its demands have not yet been read from diverse poetic perspectives. Developing a critical analysis of the poetic works written and produced by Mayas around the period of the war and its aftermath will offer an important dimension that privileges the artistic creativity of the contemporary generation of Maya writers.

My methodology has required detailed readings and interpretations of the literary texts. One of the biggest limitations of my study is my lack of fluency in Maya languages. Like many of the writers discussed in this book, I did not learn my native language (K'iche'). Although my father is a fluent speaker of K'iche, he thought the best way for me to survive in a racist context like Guatemala was to learn the dominant language, kaxlan tzij. After I became conscious of my origins and reencountered my K'iche' umbilical cord in Momostenango-Quetzaltenango, I began to take classes in K'iche' Maya as a way to affirm that important aspect of my identity. Although I have acquired a basic level of the language, I do not consider it sufficient to develop a rigorous critical analysis of the works in K'iche' or other Maya languages. Instead, my critical analyses and conclusions focus on the works in kaxlan tzij.

Even though I reference and analyze specific poetic compositions—this is the case in my discussion of Maya Cu Choc's work in chapter 4—my study concentrates on analyzing individual books of poems that from my perspective effectively articulate and explore the themes of Indigeneity, decolonization, and cultural vindication that I propose to problematize. In doing so, I follow Hugo Achugar's approach to the social dimensions of Hispanic poetry. According to Achugar (1988), when considering the political force of poetry, it is fundamental to produce an analysis of an entire poetry book instead of individual poems. Such an analysis must not only include discussions of the poems themselves but also critically consider other elements in the book such as its "title, epigraphs, date, place of publication, visual design and choice of typography, illustrations, and printer's mark" (652). All of these elements, according to Achugar, are important in considering the aesthetic and ideological enunciations that determine the social meaning of a book of poetry (652). In addition to these elements, I read the Maya books of poetry in dialogue with one another, thereby showing their discursive similarities and differences in their aesthetic, social, and cultural dimensions within national and international contexts.

Theoretically, this book is informed by Indigenous, decolonial, and African American studies. These fields have made important contributions to debates about colonialism, Eurocentrism, class, race, ethnicity, gender, culture, and the place that the subaltern (Indigenous in our case) occupies in societies in the past and present.[19] These theoretical frameworks have emphasized the operations of colonialism and how it has been recycled and influential in contemporary societies and economies, as well as how the subaltern has appropriated hegemonic tools to give voice and agency to our struggles and to challenge systems of domination and representation. In short, these schools of thought offer a better understanding about the world from the perspective of those of us who have experienced colonization firsthand. Given that my objective is to read the world from diverse Maya perspectives and, specifically, to show how Maya writers, through their works, have responded to the fratricidal experience that we have faced—particularly since the 1960s—these frameworks have been extremely valuable in exploring my assumptions. Nevertheless, I do not intend merely to "apply" these theoretical frameworks to my critical analysis but rather to expand them by showing how Maya literatures allow us to open new avenues of critical inquiry about decolonizing methodologies. My study aims to be both broad and specific. As such, I have the intention of contributing to the current debates about decolonization in Iximulew with the understanding that our struggles for emancipation are part of a larger, trans-hemispheric Indigenous decolonization project. Indeed, readers familiar with discussions of Indigenous agency and decolonization will become aware of how the histories and experiences narrated by these Maya authors echo struggles against colonialism carried out by Indigenous sisters and brothers in other parts of the planet; for example, the struggles of Idle No More and the Water Protectors in Standing Rock, North Dakota, in Turtle Island (or what is today North America); the Zapatista movement and its struggle against neoliberal extractivism in Chiapas, Mexico; the struggles for sovereignty of the Mapuche in the *Wallmapu* (Chile and Argentina); or the struggles for the defense of the Amazonian region in *Pindorama* (Brazil). Because our discussions about the defense of Indigenous rights and our ancestral territories are similar to these struggles, I place my study within the Indigenous project of Abiayala.

As I have argued elsewhere, Abiayala or "land in full maturity" in the Guna language, is the name that the Guna nation in Guna Yala (the land of the Guna in what is today Panama) uses to refer to the American continent as a whole.[20] From their perspective, categories like "America," "Latin America," "Hispanism," or "Latinity" affirm civilizational projects that have been constitutive of Eurocentrism and colonialism, because through the idea of "mestizaje" or blood quantum narratives, they endorse the political aspirations of White and *criollo-mestizo* or ladino populations. Moreover, these ideas and civilizational projects contribute to eclipsing the existing ancestral categories that continue to be used by Indigenous nations to affirm and justify our origins and our struggles for self-determination. In this sense, ideas of "America," "Latin America," or "Latinity" are not merely innocent categories, but rather geopolitical projects that embody and affirm the historical and lasting regimes of colonialism in the region. Only by renouncing our ancestral lands, languages, and cultural and spiritual specificities can Indigenous peoples be part of these projects. In contrast, Abiayala represents the possibility of developing political alliances with non-Indigenous allies and other Indigenous nations and forming a historical bloc at the national, continental, and international levels. Such alliances can lead to developing more egalitarian intercultural projects.

These are the processes that *Le Maya Q'atzij* aims to elucidate with the objective of showing, through the poetic register, our continued efforts to recover and defend our ancestral territories, as well as to restitute our linguistic, cultural, and spiritual specificities, efforts that fall short when studied from Latin Americanist, Latino, or American studies perspectives. In this sense, we need to understand and address our emancipations by developing dialogues, first with other Indigenous nations that through their art invite us to think about the world and its emancipatory potentials. Our positioning as Maya subjects, and as Indigenous in general, allows not only for the hegemonic articulation of our demands but also for negotiations with non-Indigenous peoples in the constitution of national models that are more inclusive. My study, in this sense, can be read as analogous to other discussions of Indigenous rights and decolonization that are currently taking place in Iximulew and other parts of the planet.

CHAPTER 1

Kaqchikel Maya Identity

Francisco Morales Santos and Luis de Lión

But now he [the leftist] discovers there is no connection between the liberation of the colonized and the application of a left-wing program. And that, in fact, he is perhaps aiding the birth of a social order in which there is no room for a leftist as such, at least in the near future.

—Albert Memmi, *The Colonizer and the Colonized*

IN THIS CHAPTER I offer a critical analysis of the poetic works of Kaqchikel writers Francisco Morales Santos and José Luis de León Díaz, better known by his pen name Luis de Lión. I suggest that the contemporary Maya literary movement from the 1960s on responds to the experience of armed struggle and the political and economic marginalization of Indigenous peoples. I divide the chapter into three sections. In the first one, I focus on Morales Santos's first book of poetry *Agua en el silencio* (Water in the Silence) published in 1961. I analyze his poem "Volveremos" (We Will Return), which, I argue, represents a Maya literary manifesto that anticipates Maya literature in the second and third phases I study in the later chapters. Then, I analyze the epic poem *Madre, nosotros también somos historia* (Mother, We Too Are History, 1988) in which Morales Santos vindicates the Maya world through a symbolic narrative that proposes a return to our ancestral origins. In the second section, I focus on Luis de Lión's literary works, particularly his book of poetry *Poemas del volcán de agua. los poemas míos* (Poems from Water Volcano. My Own Poems, 1994), which displays an Indigenous revolutionary political consciousness emphasizing Indigenous peoples' defense of their ancestral territories and sovereignty. Lión's work, I also argue, is organically tied to his participation in the armed movement through his collaboration with the Guatemala's Workers Party (PGT), the Guatemalan Communist Party. In the final section,

I discuss the appropriation and representation of the figure of the Indigenous mother in their poetic works. Although the mother, for these authors,
symbolizes the conditions of possibility for imagining a Maya cultural and
political vindication, her representation may also eclipse the prominent
and political role of Indigenous women who have contributed to Indigenous human rights.

Some critics may wonder why I selected Morales Santos and Lión as
pioneers of the contemporary Maya literary movement in Iximulew, given
that their works have been written and published primarily in Spanish;
nor, as far as I know, did either grow up speaking Kaqchikel Maya. In addition, their education and literary development occurred in urban settings,
particularly in Antigua and Guatemala City, not in a rural context. Some
critics argue that such hybrid or transcultural experiences limit an authentic Indigenous experience.[1] These discussions of Maya authenticity are
addressed substantively in the next chapter, in which I analyze the works
of Humberto Ak'abal (K'iche'), Victor Montejo (Pop'ti), and Gaspar Pedro
González (Q'anjob'al). For now, it is enough to say that, far from being
associated with ladino culture, Morales Santos's and Lión's works display a
strong historical, cultural, and political affiliation to Maya culture.

The fact that these authors produced their works in Spanish, not in the
Kaqchikel language, does not diminish their Mayaness. As Kaqchikel
Maya sociologist Aura Cumes reminds us,

> the forms of domination that at the local levels the great majority
> of Indigenous peoples experience, obliges them to organize
> struggles against forced labor, land expropriation, or "ladino"
> domination in whose hands, in many instances, economic and
> political power rested. This struggle was carried out by people who
> became convinced that only through assimilation—adopting
> Spanish, knowing how to read and write, and educating
> themselves—they could have the same "weapons" to fight against
> those who oppressed them. (Bastos and Cumes 2007, 189–90)

Thus, the works of Morales Santos and Lión show a continuance of Maya
tradition similar to that in my discussion of the *Popol Wuj* in the introduction. In our efforts to emancipate ourselves, using literature as a weapon
has served to dignify our Indigenous identity at the individual and collective levels. Moreover, the literary works of these authors offer a register

that reinforces our contemporary efforts to authorize the use of the Maya voice to challenge and break away from dominant literary traditions like Indigenismo (e.g., Miguel Ángel Asturias, Cardoza y Aragón, and so on).

Francisco Morales Santos and Decolonial Maya Poetics

Francisco Morales Santos recalls that when he was a child, he would go to school while his mother Magdalena Santos sold fruits and vegetables in the public market in Antigua, Guatemala, and his father Martín Morales Pérez worked as a farmer. After they began to go to the city, Francisco's parents encouraged him to get an education so he could succeed in the dominant society, in which one must learn to speak kaxlan tzij and adopt ladino ways of life. By pursuing an education—even a "ladino education"— their young Kaqchikel boy could have better opportunities than the ones they had. This survival strategy was intended to help their son avoid the verbal and physical violence charged with racism that the Native child faces daily in Guatemalan society. At elementary school, his schoolteacher and mentor Fidencio Méndez introduced Morales Santos to literature; many of his lessons included reading, discussing, and writing poetry. Encouraged by his mentor, he entered a poetry contest that he won with his poem "Oda a Centro América" ("Ode to Central America"). His prize was a literary anthology of poetry that introduced him to the works of "modernista" writers like José Martí, Rubén Darío, and Julián del Casal, among others. The book was significant in spurring Morales Santos's interest in literature, leading him to read and explore other national and international writers who in turn helped him develop his own artistic originality. These authors included Miguel Ángel Asturias, Federico García Lorca, Pablo Neruda, Roque Dalton, Miguel Hernández, and Cesar Vallejo. Later in life, after Morales Santos moved to Guatemala City, he began to engage in local literary circles and developed a close friendship with the ladino writers José Manuel Arce y Valladares and Cesar Brañas, who gave him indispensable access to the literary world. Toward the end of the 1950s, Morales Santos completed his first book of poetry, *Agua en el silencio* (Water in the Silence), and Arce y Valladares and Cesar Brañas encouraged him to publish it, though he would have to finance some of the cost. To come up with the needed funds, his father sold some of his land. In 1961, the Kaqchikel poet saw the publication of the book, whose first edition only numbered three hundred copies. Morales Santos was twenty-one at the time.[2]

Since then, Morales Santos has published more than a hundred poetic works, essays, and children's stories that have made him one of the most prolific Kaqchikel Maya writers in Iximulew.[3] He has also won numerous literary awards, including the prestigious Guatemalan Miguel Ángel Asturias National Literary Prize in 1998. However, despite his numerous publications and national and international recognition, he has gone practically unnoticed within the debates related to the Maya social and literary movement in Guatemala, and his works have not received the critical attention they deserve.[4] I suggest that his lack of recognition is because Morales Santos's experience has been urban, not rural. His literary formation, unlike other Maya writers, has occurred mostly in the hegemonic realm, as he generates dialogues primarily with ladino writers. Moreover, unlike his Maya contemporaries, this Kaqchikel author has developed themes that go beyond ethnic politics.[5] Yet underneath his literary works that may appear to be "Western" lies an Indigenous epistemological antecedent; it is recognizable especially by readers who are familiar with or come from the Indigenous world and who relate to the author's own experience. The representation and affirmation of the rural world, as we see in our discussion of *Mother, We Too Are History* (1988), organically tie Morales Santos to his Maya contemporaries, because it legitimizes an Indigenous imagination that aims to universalize its difference.

Morales Santos's work illustrates a profound concern for form that is interwoven with diverse aspects of Indigenous life in various social settings. His works explain and make visible situations that relate to the nation-state's violence against the subaltern. In addition, works like *Mother* are profound meditations on the effects that mercantilist economic policies have had on certain subaltern sectors, producing alienation (in the Marxist sense) of the subject from its social relations. Hence, this Kaqchikel author's early work references the Maya past in order to vindicate and affirm it. In this way, he aims to restore not only a negated Indigenous subjectivity in urban settings but also other forms of connection with our identity in contexts marked by the violence of a modernity that promotes mercantilist and individual capitalist values.

With publications such as *Agua en el silencio, Ciudades en el llanto* (Cities in Tears, 1963), and *Nimayá* (1968), Morales Santos starts a renaissance of modern Maya literature in Iximulew.[6] In these poetic works, he gives testimony to a complex Guatemalan reality defined by the repressive social context created by the government's fight against communism. In poems like "Momoxco," which opens *Nimayá,* the poetic voice concludes with the following rhetorical question: "From what branch / will I grasp resin / to light up my time?" (4). These verses implicitly highlight a time of adversity in which literature represents a force of hope that can allow us to imagine other alternatives to the ones experienced in a repressive society. He later became a founding member of the literary collective *Nuevo Signo* (New Sign), which emerged toward the end of the 1960s in response to the terrible reality of the country during this time of armed conflict. Poets in the group, according to Otto-Raúl González, were "witnesses and sometimes protagonists of the national pain; they respond[ed], dutifully and truly, to this painful reality" (1978, 175). The literary group's life was subsequently disrupted by the disappearance and killing of one of its members, Roberto Obregón, who was assassinated by a paramilitary group at the Guatemalan and Salvadoran border in July 1970.[7] Despite the political and repressive adversities that the group faced during this period, most of the members continued publishing their works following the ideals of New Sign; that is, they used poetry to denounce the painful injustices and realities that they witnessed and experienced firsthand, especially after the Guatemalan government adopted state terrorism as a military strategy to defeat the opposition.

Injustice and violence are some of the concerns that characterize poetry like *Agua en el silencio* and *Nimayá.* Thus, Morales Santos's works, given his Kaqchikel Maya perspective in its diverse aesthetic-social dimensions, not only read as Indigenous interpretations of Guatemala's social history since the 1960s but also open up the contemporary Maya canon in Iximulew. Morales Santos thereby continues previous literary traditions while also addressing some of the most pressing issues that Indigenous peoples face within the context of the armed conflict.[8] This Kaqchikel Maya author articulates an autonomous point of view similar to what Osage scholar Robert Warrior refers to as "intellectual sovereignty"; that is, the development of a textual production that centers itself in Indigenous traditions while at the same time nourishing itself on *other* perspectives and experiences to establish an Indigenous sovereign status.

Morales Santos's poem "Volveremos a ser Caqchikeles"[9] (We Will Be Kaqchikel Again), included in *Agua en el silencio,* not only inaugurates a Maya literary resurgence that would find its prominence in the 1990s but also represents the first political-literary Maya manifesto in Guatemala's contemporary period. It vindicates a Kaqchikel Maya social and political consciousness as having profound cultural ancestral roots. In doing so, the poem articulates what Gerald Postema (1991) calls "prophetic memory" by imagining a Maya future emancipated from the chains of colonialism. Here is the entire poem:

> We will be Caqchikel again
> in the clearing of the destroyed temple,
> and we will come back blue
> from the green ocean,
> dragged by the brain and the lead weight of our children.
>
> We are below. In the shadow
> of a floral hymn that Gucumatz safeguards,
> listening to the harangue of the return
> in the swollen mouth
> of the monolith conqueror of time.
>
> In Tikal and Zaculeu one hundred flames
> of blood are pounding and one hundred palpitations
> are uniting us so that we build
> the temple of our people
> for every absent brother.
>
> We will return with tattooed arms
> through the furrows of the maize field,
> in the smile of an ear of corn
> that will again conquer
> the naked heart.
>
> We will be Caqchikel again:
> whistles, marimbas, *chirimías,* tunes . . .
> placed before the sun to warm up the song! (13)

The poem is structured in five stanzas and written in free verse. It gives the impression that the speaker walks in Maya cities like Tikal or Zaculeu, two of the most important city-states in Mesoamerica, occupied by the Itza' and Mam Peoples for thousands of years. The poetic voice reacquires its creativity after observing the "monolith conqueror of time," or a Maya stela. The cities and the Indigenous world have been "destroyed." The Kaqchikel peoples find themselves "below." Nevertheless, amid adversity and from the "destroyed temples," an emancipatory and political project emerges. In the middle of the rain forest, safeguarded by Gucumatz,[10] or the Plumed Serpent, the Kaqchikel plan their collective return. In Tikal and Zaculeu, "one hundred flames of blood are pounding and one hundred palpitations" are uniting this Indigenous nation, which begins a journey toward reconstructing a new world. Through the anaphor "we will be Caqchikel again," the poetic voice affirms and celebrates the return with "whistles, marimbas, *chirimías,* tunes . . . placed before the sun to warm up the song!" The Kaqchikel will "again return blue from the green ocean," through the "maize fields" and with "tattooed arms" "dragged by the brain and the lead weight of our children," to conquer the naked heart.

The poem invokes significant epistemological references associated with the Maya world. For example, by indicating that the Kaqchikels will return "blue from the green ocean," the poetic voice recalls the importance of ancient purification rituals conducted before offering a sacrifice. The color blue in the Maya cosmogony is also associated with agriculture, directly linked to the rain god Chac; it also is associated with rain and the planting of corn. The celebration of the return of the Kaqchikel described by Morales Santos also reminds us of scenes of rebirth like those represented in the "The Procession of Musicians," a mural in Bonanpack, Chiapas, that includes imagery of musicians with trumpets and zoomorphic masks against a blue background.

Taking into consideration the social context in which the poem was written, published, and read as political theory, "We Will Be Kaqchikel Again" offers a response to the Indigenista policies and discourses of the conservative and progressive ladino or white elites of the period, who were debating ways to address the so-called Indian problem. Morales Santos's poem raises important questions in the context of these debates: Why do the Kaqchikel have to be Kaqchikel *again*? What stops them from affirming their cultural and political identity within the context of Guatemala at this time? Why are they "below," and why is there a need to build a "temple of our people for every absent brother"?

In the 1950s, the context referenced in the poem, the Guatemalan Congress was discussing how to incorporate Indigenous peoples into society after a long period of political, cultural, and economic segregation under the regime of Jorge Ubico (1931–1944). According to Claudia Dary, "in

1945, various Indigenista writers debated as to whether or not the new Republican Constitution should include special laws to protect and support Indigenous populations" (2013, 109). During the so-called October Revolution (1944–1954), the regimes of Juan José Arévalo and Jacobo Árbenz Guzmán developed government reforms that included educational campaigns to teach Spanish, the prohibition of forced labor, and a proposed land allocation policy to benefit peasants in the rural areas of the country. More conservative politicians and thinkers, for their part, doubted these policies would be effective and instead proposed *estatutos de tutela* (guardianship programs) that demanded that "Indians" be "civilized" by, among other things, forcing them to speak Spanish instead of Maya languages, outlawing the wearing of *traje* (Mayan dress), and banning traditional spiritual rituals. Moreover, conservatives argued that prohibiting forced labor would leave the country without a workforce.

With the overthrow of Árbenz Guzmán in 1954, the military regimes that took power undid the reforms and implemented anticommunist policies. The state reined in its civilizing agenda and reviewed the laws of Indigenous inclusion. Consequently, the Guatemalan state reestablished policies of segregation that separated the "Indian" from the nation and the possibility of Guatemalan citizenship, reenacting a regime of apartheid that sought to prevent the Indigenous peoples from influencing political decisions made within the nation-state.

What is important to emphasize in these processes and debates— whether they were "progressive" or "conservative"—is that they not only evidenced strategies of ladinoizacion or "de-Indianization" but they also emanated "from the White and mestizo [ladino] elites that were worried about the political and socioeconomic situation of their societies and their immediate future, where the Indian was a sort of thorn in their side" (Arturo Taracena 1999, 109). In contrast to those perspectives, Morales Santos's poem announces the development of a Kaqchikel social consciousness to defend, dignify, and nurture the vindication of Indigenous peoples' ancestral identities. Moreover, "We Will Be Kaqchikel Again" proposes to rebuild the Indigenous world and reconquer the "naked heart," suggesting the modernization processes during the period that privileged and aimed to replace collective values with individualistic ones.

Within a broader social internationalist context, Morales Santos's poem can also be placed in dialogue with debates and political struggles for Indigenous rights occurring outside Guatemala. Indeed, "We Will Be

Kaqchikel Again" anticipates the Indigenous literary and social movements in other parts of Abiayala or the Americas; one example is the rise
of "Indianismo" through the international Indigenous summits in Barba-
dos in 1971 and 1978, where Indigenous and non-Indigenous intellectuals
discussed alternative policies to recognize and materialize the rights of
Indigenous peoples in various countries of the hemisphere. These summits coincided with and engaged in other debates and political processes
that emanated from dependency theory (Cardozo and Faletto 1979), liberation theology (Gutiérrez 1971), "internal colonialism" theory (González
Casanova 1963; Stavenhagen 1968), and prominent social movements
toward the end of the 1970s; for example, the anticolonial movements of
Négritude, feminism, the Mothers of the Plaza de Mayo, and the African-
American, Chicano, and American Indian movements in the United States.
The debates that grew out of the struggles of these social movements
proposed pan-ethnic categories that challenged colonialism and their
epistemological legacies. With regard to Indigenous peoples, activists and
scholars contested the category "Indian" as a colonialist social construct
that eclipsed the ethnic, linguistic, and cultural diversity of the continent's
Indigenous peoples. Native intellectuals instead proposed recognition based
on linguistic, cultural, or geopolitical ancestral origins; that is, as Aymara,
Quechua, Cherokee, K'iche' Maya, Nahua, and so on. With its reference
to vindicating a Kaqchikel Maya identity, Morales Santos's poem can be
inscribed within these debates as establishing and proposing his own
political nationalist project. He centralizes the preoccupation of Indigenous political affirmation from his Kaqchikel Maya perspective, negating
the projects of assimilation advanced by non-Indigenous elites who saw
and interpreted Indigenous peoples as a problem not only in Guatemala
but also at the continental level.

Similar concerns about Indigenous vindications emerge in much of
Morales Santos's literary works. His discursive textual production, in particular that published between 1961 and 1990, reads the Guatemalan social
context from his Kaqchikel Maya perspective. He proposes the development of a contemporary Indigenous "lettered city" (to use Ángel Rama's
[1984] concept) that acquires a power to narrate alternative views of Guatemalan history, including highlighting Indigenous and non-Indigenous
relationships within dominant literary circles. Indeed, in his current role
as director of the Minister of Guatemala's *Editorial Cultura* (Culture Press),
a press run under the auspices of the Guatemalan government, he has

endeavored to generate spaces for other Maya writers such as Luis de Lión (Kaqchikel), Humberto Ak'abal (K'iche'), Maya Cu Choc (Q'eq'chi), Rosa Chávez (K'iche'-Kaqchikel), Calixta Gabriel (Kaqchikel), Sabino Esteban Francisco (Q'anjob'al), and Daniel Caño (Q'anjob'al). Thus, in addition to being a poet, Morales Santos is also a cultural broker who has immensely contributed to developing a platform for contemporary Maya literature in Iximulew.

Let us now turn to a critical analysis of Morales Santos's *Madre, nosotros también somos historia* (Mother, We Too Are History). According to Morales Santos, *this book of poetry* defines his poetic wisdom and is "notably distinct from what I have written before" (qtd. in Montenegro 2009). The book has been published in various editions, including a K'iche' Maya / Spanish bilingual 2001 publication by the prestigious Fondo de Cultura Económica. The K'iche' translation of the book was done by the poet Humberto Ak'abal, whose work I analyze in the next chapter. In this book, the journey to the ancestral Indigenous origins of the poetic voice expresses a critique of Western modernity and its hegemonic narratives, specifically official history and capitalism. I argue that Morales Santos validates the knowledge produced by Indigenous peoples in the rural areas of the country. In doing so, the poetic voice authorizes a subaltern and collective Indigenous locus of enunciation as a condition of possibility for an anti-capitalist resistance and a process of de-alienation of the narrator.

The poem *Madre* in many ways represents a "testimony" (Nájera 1988, 3) that denounces the social injustices against Indigenous peoples who have been subalternized by Western modernity; it thus becomes "resistance literature" (Harlow 1987) that proposes a utopian socialist project permeated by the Maya worldview. The title of the poem has a double meaning. First, it manifests the conversation between a son and his mother in which he indicates that they, too, are "history." The primary experiences of the invoked subjects, mother and son, are underscored here as their daily activities acquire value within their particular social context. Interpreted allegorically, the title also suggests a direct interpellation to the Nation, understood by the noun "mother." Read in this way, the title is a call for the unrecognized children of history to be included in hegemonic discourses of nationhood. Unlike other poems written by this Kaqchikel Maya author, which display a careful use of form and various literary-rhetoric devices, *Madre* has a more testimonial dimension. The poem, as Francisco Nájera indicates, "is composed of 191 verses, divided in 28 stanzas, organized in four parts. It is written in conversational form, with a simple and direct language" (1988, 3).[11] The poetic voice, the son, invokes the figure of the mother as, after a long workday, he returns home on the public bus on a winter afternoon. He closes the book he is reading and starts "to think copiously" and to retrieve memories about his mother (29).[12] Such memories detail not only his mother's "domestic daily tasks" but also "the time that corresponds to both of them" (30).

The first part of the poem, the longest, is composed of fourteen stanzas that have a celebratory tone when presenting the figure of the mother. She is described as a woman with a humble appearance who is small, kind, caring, fragile, and poor; she goes unnoticed in the public sphere. Nevertheless, in contrast to these adjectives, the poetic voice distinguishes her for her authority. She is hardworking, persistent, and optimistic, yet she is someone who operates in the "shadows." In "hard times," the poetic voice remembers her as walking "with heavy workloads, down long paths / and obligated sweat" (30). On the days she works at the market, she is "a soft fatherland, barefoot and fearless" (31). In the second part of the poem, comprising three stanzas, the narrator contextualizes the mother's sociopolitical situation. She has experienced extreme poverty, marked by labor exploitation and abuse by "cruel godparents." Phrases like "I cannot live only by quarrels" and "intransigent hate" (33) express a tone of resentment. Nevertheless, instead of centralizing the bitterness, the son celebrates his mother for "her heroic gestures in the face of life" (33). In the five stanzas of the third part of the poem, the poetic voice continues to underscore the mother's tenacity as, to encourage her son, she remembers and relates to him her own childhood. Her memories are traumatic and consist of a short childhood, "amputated at eleven years of age" by "tremendously cruel godparents" (36). Despite pain and adversity, the mother always maintains her optimism. In the last part of the poem, composed of five stanzas, the narrator reflects on his own present situation. His mother's memories feed his spirit, allowing him to "drag through the times" (37) that he now confronts.

Although at a certain interpretive level the poem appears to be a song that underscores the tenacity of the figure of the mother, it also lends itself to a sociocritical interpretation. Both the double meaning of the poem's title and its allegorical content in relation to the mother point toward a critique of modernity, specifically the dominant historical discourse and capitalism as an economic model that has generated institutional violence against Indigenous peoples in rural areas. This critique becomes evident through binary discursive constructions—light/darkness, city/rural, and writing/orality—throughout the poem.

When the bus that transports the protagonist travels away from the city and he "closes the book" he reads to "hear the voices" (29) that narrate his mother's memories, the son begins a journey to his ancestral origins in a process of mental de-alienation and individual decolonization. In distancing himself from the city, the narrator authorizes and validates the rural world through his memories; that is, the figure of the mother. That space, throughout the poem, becomes a locus of enunciation with meanings associated with the perseverance to transcend adverse experiences.

The city represents the space of work, bustle, chaos, viciousness, darkness, and "radioactive rains" (34). These surroundings, coupled with an individual experience marked by injustice and adversity for the poetic voice, do not encourage creative reflection. He states, "I don't want to speak of irritating noises / under which my heart goes through the daily and persistent challenges of instability" (30). The city, with all its noises, as represented in the book he reads in the bus, are opposed to the rural world where "the public lighting was the fireflies" (31). In the countryside, the mother's voice is "more powerful / than all the sounds" (30). Except for her, "No one here used to say: 'Once upon a time . . .'" (31); she is "a weaver of affable conversations / for tired eyes and gray hearts" (32); her "words had a glow of fireworks, / they brightened everything, / they lulled everything" (35). In addition to her voice, the poetic "I" similarly associates the mother with luminous environmental elements that suggest hope, tenacity, and optimism. These meanings are in contrast to the darkness and "gloominess" (31) that suggest fatality. She is "the sun" (29, 32) and "a light in a lighthouse" (30). Her presence is "more luminous than all the stars" (30). She possesses "an unreachable light" that extends like a mantle (35). Her richness comes from "the land just like her beauty" (37). She is a "spring one stores in a basket" (31), an "enormous river in the geography of affect" (32), "an alphabet / made out of bees and sparrows" (30).

Both the activities of the mother and her associations with light-filled natural imagery elevate her to ancestral mythic dimensions. Her prominence begins not with the present in which she lives, but rather stems from her "previous lives" and "the fire of centuries that stopped the hunger so our lives would have a future" (32). In her association with the rural world and with orality, the figure of the mother displays a universe of primordial meanings that project her as a source of another history: she spreads knowledge and continues to articulate an ancestral cultural identity. In this way, the present and past are woven together through recurring imagery of an rich primordial world. The mother acquires a symbolic dimension as the source of life that, like Mother Earth, contrasts the experiences and significance of urban life.

The representation of the mother as a symbol of origins and creation can be associated with the figure of Xmucane, whose name translates as "She Who Buries, She Who Plants." She is one of the Maya goddesses who participates in the creation of humanity and the universe in the K'iche' Maya text the *Popol Wuj*. After the creation and consequent destruction of the men of wood, Xmucane and her complementary god Xpiyacoc take charge of the new creation. When Xpiyacoc dies, Xmucane increases her power as the matriarch on earth. She takes care of her sons and grandsons, the divine twins, who consequently go to Xib'alb'a, the Place of Fear—the Maya underworld—to defeat the Lords of Death and darkness. In the underworld, the divine twins Hunahpu and Xbalanque plant the first seed of corn that will give life to the first maize harvest. The corn will later be used by Xmucane to create the new humanity, the women and men of maize. Similar to Xmucane, the mother in Morales Santos's poem is one of the selected ones "to open with fury / the breasts of earth" (32), acquiring both a mythic-symbolic figurative dimension ("a fire of centuries") and a literal one, as manifested through her daily experiences. Both dimensions underscore her tenacity within a world characterized by adversity, including labor exploitation and extreme poverty. She is a "heroine in the face of life" (33) and has the "prodigious gift to re-invent hope" (32).

It is no accident that Morales Santos develops these double mythic and literal significations of the figure of the mother. As becomes evident, the Kaqchikel Maya author aims to vindicate and dignify a marginal experience. The poem is, indeed, a rewriting of history that recognizes what the mother allegorizes—local experience, daily life, orality, nature, ancestral origins—as aspects that modernity has repressed or relegated to the margins. Colonial oppression has reduced these aspects of the Indigenous world in order to impose new forms of sociability that aim to erase and trample down the cultural development of the continent's First Peoples. Nevertheless, as *Madre* seeks to argue, colonial oppression has not been successful in stopping the expression of such values and primordial experiences.

Through the journey to the poetic voice's origins, the son activates repressed memories. Thus the poem alludes to the mother's tenacity in transcending adverse experiences, her leadership in the "face of life," and her association with ancestral imagery. However, highlighting the tenacity of the mother does not negate the colonial experience. The memories of the mother and the adversities that she experiences are parallel to those that the son perceives in the urban context he invokes. The narrator implicitly also expresses marginalization and subjugation similar to that experienced by the mother. This becomes evident when the work talks about "the poem's fate":

It was born in the worst moment
but, have we had an appropriate epoch
to say: mother, come, sit down and enjoy
since in your honor I have written poetry?
It was born when radioactive hails
replaced orchestral rains,
it was born where death left woes spread
that we gather today,
it was born in the worst moment
discarded from the popular circumstances
dismissed, relegated to the margins;
it was born outside the walls of pure lyricism
and, nevertheless . . . (34)

What does the poetic voice mean by "the worst moment"? Why are the circumstances that the narrator and his mother experience not "appropriate"? What are the causes of the "radioactive rains" that leave "woes spread"? Instead of setting aside the social circumstances under which the poem was written (it was born "outside the walls of pure lyricism"), this stanza instead aims to confront them. It is precisely because the conditions that make the poem possible correspond to a "worse moment" that it is necessary to speak out. Morales Santos's stance, in this sense, is associated with what Edward Said proposes: "Texts are worldly, to some degree they are events, and, even when they appear to deny it, they are nevertheless a part of the social world, human life, and of course the historical moments in which they are located and interpreted" (2000, 222).

Following this line of thinking, the reference to an "appropriate epoch" in the stanza can be associated with the ongoing colonial experience manifested through the daily lives of the mother and the poetic voice. The "worst moment" obliges the poet to re-signify the role of poetry—not merely to roll "out poetic words" or "pure lyricism," but to give testimony to the hostile experiences of the characters and what occurs within the society of which they are a part. The replacement of "orchestral" for "radioactive" rains suggests a process of transition from an artistic celebration to one characterized by technological violence: the "radioactive hails" refer to new technologies that have brought destruction, where death now leaves dispersed "woes." Moreover, the stanza makes reference to a "discarded" "popular circumstance" that has been relegated to the margins, which makes us think of struggle and resistance. Implicitly, the stanza is also informed by the armed conflict of the early 1980s, when the "diminished popular circumstance" was being repressed by the Guatemalan Army.

The 1980s in Guatemala were characterized by an intense and repressive political climate that affected the majority of the people, particularly the Indigenous peoples in rural areas. State terrorism became institutionalized with military campaigns led by General Efraín Ríos Montt, who used "scorched earth" and "beans and bullets" strategies to "exterminate the guerrillas, their collaborators and sympathizers" (Sanford 2003b, 33).[13] Under the pretense of eliminating only the resistance fighters, these campaigns actually became genocidal military interventions directed against Maya peoples in the rural areas. In his short tenure as president between 1982 and 1983, Ríos Montt literally disappeared more than 400 communities from the Guatemalan map, murdered more than 70,000 people, and sent thousands more into exile. The actions of the death squads in the city, along with the "Self-Defense Civil Patrols" (PAC) in the rural areas, contributed to the popularization of the adjective "disappeared," which inundated the headlines of national and international newspapers and was part of conversations behind closed doors.

The terror that characterized the Guatemalan state was accompanied by economic programs that, through the forced displacement of Indigenous peoples from their communities of origin, gradually allowed transnational companies to set up shop and impose capitalist extractivism. We can reference here the massacre of Panzos in 1978 or of Baja Verapaz in 1982. In 1978, the World Bank and the Inter-American Development Bank supported the construction of a hydroelectric dam near the Río Negro community that, during its construction in 1982, caused flooding that forced the displacement of the Achi Maya community in the region. Because the Maya resisted the project through peaceful protests and demonstrations, the state revoked their land titles and publicly accused protestors of being "communist agitators" who collaborated with the guerrilla fighters. The Guatemalan Army thus justified its indiscriminate intervention in the region and murdered more than 500 people.[14]

The imposition of these "modern" social and economic measures took on a colonial dimension for Indigenous peoples through land dispossession and the negation of their historic development through the repressive usurpation of their creative and productive forces. The genocidal campaigns that took place during this period were evidence that Indigenous peoples and peasants in the rural areas did not respond passively to those measures. In addition to the resistance of the Río Negro community, other strategies of resistance were developed, like the ones led by the Committee of Peasant Unity (CUC) and the Guatemala's Workers Party (PGT): thousands of Indigenous peasants decided to join the revolutionary movements as a last-ditch effort to fight for social and political vindication.

Given this context for Morales Santos's *Madre*, the reference to the "worst moment," the "radioactive rains," and the places where "death left woes spread" reflect campaigns against settler colonialism, waged to bring about the "diminished popular circumstance"; through the "logic of elimination" of "Indians," the state seeks to access and appropriate their land. As Patrick Wolfe writes, "Territoriality is settler colonialism's specific, irreducible element" (Wolfe 2006, 388). Similarly, Carlos Guzmán Böckler states, "It is in the struggle for land that the amalgam [of] all beliefs and resentment ultimately leads to the outbreak of rebellions. The killings of Indians have to do, always, directly or indirectly with issues related to land" (1986, 53). The poem *Madre* provides testimony to these experiences of dispossession and, at the same time, through the metaphor of the mother, offers optimism about the ability to transcend new forms of colonialism experienced at the time the poem was written.

If we read the figure of the mother in the poem as allegorizing ancestral origins, tenacity, hope, and so on, the verse "and nevertheless . . ." that closes the stanza suggests the perseverance of those who survive modernity from a subaltern position. It is no accident that the mother (the Indigenous world) embodies the attributes of tenacity and resistance that began not in the 1980s but centuries before — "have we had an appropriate epoch." Morales Santos aims to make us understand that Indigenous cultures represent viable alternatives in the construction of political projects that are concerned with our survival. Despite all the colonial assaults we have endured, Indigenous peoples have always found a way to survive and continue. Therefore, we hold the key to collective survival by managing to transcend the most extreme conditions of physical and material deprivation. The daily experience of the mother, who has transcended adversity, attests to this. The son reactivates her memory to feed his own spirit in a moment characterized by experiences of violence and marginalization.

In the poem, the figure of the mother becomes re-signified to underscore meaning beyond Iximulew. Her perseverance and tenacity acquire a revolutionary dimension, permeated with a socialist ideology articulated by a "diminished popular circumstance" during this period. This becomes clear through the references to Ernesto "Che" Guevara (33) and the song, "Que saco rogar al cielo" (What Do I Get from Begging Heaven?) by Victor Jara (35).[15] Jara's song is cited in the verse "If there is a spike in the field," which is organically tied to the figure of the mother, whose perseverance and tenacity (she transforms "her sorrow into a sword" [32]) are symbolized in the "red spike" invoked in the following stanza:

a spike so tall it gives relief to the horizon,
a spike that never cuts deals with hurricanes
and it is a red spike,
that no one should doubt you are
that it does not matter if you show your cheeks
impregnated by the fire and the sun from March to May. (35)

The "red spike" that will never "cut deals with hurricanes" symbolizes the mother's strength, perseverance, and resistance. Moreover, it is associated with luminous symbols like the sun, fire, and a light that suggest an utopian ideal that goes against the "hurricane," or the repressive conditions embodied in the institutional violence orchestrated by the nation-state.

It is important to note that the political commitment associated with the figure of the mother in the poem *Madre* illustrates much of Morales Santos's literary production after he developed and participated in the New Sign collective. In an interview, he speaks about his work: "All of my literary work has been aligned with just causes. . . . I have always supported such causes and my poetry goes in that line as well, denouncing, giving testimony, and vowing for these intentions" (qtd. in Martínez 2007). His literature, in this sense, can be understood in terms of Barbara Harlow's ideas of "resistance literature"; that is, it develops "a struggle for the historical and cultural record" (1987, 7). For Morales Santos, it is about not only recording "just causes" represented by the daily activities of marginal subjects invoked in *Madre* but also counteracting the hegemonic archive by inscribing other histories, "denouncing, giving testimony, and vowing" for just causes. *Madre* develops an anti-capitalist and decolonial perspective that is related to the experience of exploited people. Indeed, the narrator's experience in the city manifests alienation as a definitive characteristic of capitalism.

Karl Marx's theory of alienation proposes that under capitalist industrial societies the essential aspects of the individual's human nature are separated or antagonized through the imposition of bourgeois society's rules. Members of the proletariat lose control of their lives and of themselves when they no longer have control over their work or their creativity. Workers lose their autonomy and full realization as social subjects, becoming a sort of merchandise or instrument that operates on the basis of capitalist reproductive demands, industry, and private property. According to Marx, "the worker sinks to the level of a commodity and becomes indeed the most wretched of commodities . . . the wretchedness of the worker is in inverse proportion to the power and magnitude of his production . . . the necessary result of competition is the accumulation of capital in a few hands, and thus the restoration of monopoly in a more terrible form" (1964, 106). From this perspective, capitalism, with its voracious advancement, aims to control and feed not only on natural resources but also on labor: it creates the appearance that when we work for others we create wealth, but in reality such wealth accumulates in the hands of the few. This illusion blinds us to the fact that capitalism progressively destroys the basis of our existence and survival, in the sense that its trajectory deepens economic and social inequality and destroys Nature. One need only call to mind the current debates about climate change to become aware of these effects of capitalism.

Through a gradual physical distancing from the city and his place of work and a growing proximity to the rural world, the narrator in *Madre* evokes memories of his mother and, thus, his ancestral origins and Nature. In doing so, a process of de-alienation—in Warren Frederick Morris's sense—takes place. De-alienation becomes a telos that moves the alien-ated subject toward "a perfect completed whole" (2002, 234). This process involves "an existential process of self-identification, self-projection, and self-realization. . . . Within this process, being is revealed, and even created. What is true meaning and normative is a continuous result of revealing being with an indeterminate horizon" (235).

Morales Santos, through this journey to origins, proposes a process of liberation characterized by a full restitution of social, historical, individual, and collective aspects—the "We Too Are History" from the title. In this poem, the author reimagines and reinvents a world and its social relations without the exploitative chains imposed by capitalism and state terrorism, a world where individuals develop and grow fully and creatively, as exem-plified by the mother, who transmits knowledge through orality. In the city, where the narrator realizes that his daily labor is creating alienation, going through "the most persistent trials of insensibility" (30), he has lost the fundamental connections to his ancestral past and his own full indi-vidual and social creativity. Moreover, affected by the "radioactive" hails— that is, the state terrorism that during this period sought to eliminate Indigenous peoples—the speaker is inspired to transcend the most diffi-cult adversities. He invokes the memory of his mother when he activates his "self-projection" and "self-identification" to begin his reconversion toward a more self-realized and full subjectivity. The memory of his mother returns "the sun" to his mind, allowing him "to see his present and future more clearly, like when in your hand I have read my past; that is, my childhood and the subsequent years" (29). The poem acquires a symbolic dimension that suggests a journey to the future. This in turn allows the reader to better understand Morales Santos's poetics: the vindication of the past as a political-discursive exercise to recover lost sovereignty.

In a digression, it is important to underscore here that the literary trope of the journey to the past is a recurring theme in the works of Kaqchikel Maya writer Luis de Lión and the K'iche' Maya poet Humberto Ak'abal, whose work I address in chapter 2. It is also a prominent theme in other contemporary Indigenous literatures in Abiayala. As Morales Santos's poem *Madre* shows, this theme is frequently played out with characters represented in situations of adversity within social contexts marked by colonialism. Such situations force these characters—or the poetic voice in the case of poetry—to reflect on their ancestral origins, to begin a journey to an imaginary past, and to invoke it for the purpose of reactivating ancestral elements—cultural values, political strategies, and so on—that can be used to transcend the colonial experience lived in the present. This literary modality becomes apparent in Lión's *Time Commences in Xibalbá* ([1985] 2012). This novel features an Indigenous community that develops a political consciousness after the people begin "to walk backwards, ass first to run into their memories" (50). In this imaginary voyage "backward," the community arrives at a precolonial past during which the people become aware of elements that dignify their subjectivity. Consequently, they develop a collective political consciousness that allows them to confront their oppressors: "and when they remembered, they all began to walk forward, to bump into everything that they had wished for" (50). To walk forward and "crash against everything" in the novel marks the beginning of a decolonizing process that symbolically suggests ways to destroy the non-Indigenous or criollo-mestizo / ladino world. The community is vindicated when it destroys the wooden image of the Virgin of Concepción, the only non-Indigenous woman in the town, and replaces it with an Indigenous virgin that gives the people "eternal happiness" (75). Similarly, in his poem "Tz'olq'omin b'e" (I Walk Backward), Humberto Ak'abal uses the poetics of brevity to invert the linear narrative of modernity. He proposes to "walk backward" as a way to remember. The poetic voice concludes, "We xat intukel kinbin cho nuwach / kinkuwin ne ri' kinb'ij chawe / jas ri', ri ucholaj ri sachib'al" (If I only walked forward, I could tell you about forgetting, 1996a, 43). The idea of "progress" that characterizes Western modernity, symbolized in the idea of "walking forward," suggests "forgetting" as a principle of existence. Instead, to walk backward, for the poetic voice, means to explore the ancestral past, to not forget who we are, where we come from, and where we are going.

The literary modality of activating the ancestral past also characterizes other Indigenous literary works, such as *House Made of Dawn* (1968) by Kiowa writer N. Scott Momaday. In the novel, the main character, Abel, returns to his New Mexico Pueblo town after fighting in World War II and battles alcoholism and posttraumatic stress disorder. However, once he begins to invoke the memory of his ancestors, he starts to recover essential elements for his healing. Hence, for Indigenous authors, the journey to the past allegorizes processes of recovering Indigenous cultures that help dignify not only the ancestral past but also, most importantly, the present struggles of Indigenous peoples against colonialism.

It is also important to emphasize that the journey to the origins in *Madre* and in Indigenous literatures in general does not signify a nostalgic, literal return to an ancestral past, nor does it mean a literal reproduction of that ancestral past in the present, as has been argued by some prominent critics.[16] Rather, we should understand these literary representations as a rhetoric-discursive strategy to affirm an autonomous locus of enunciation and intellectual sovereignty (Warrior 2014) that allows Native writers to reinterpret and rewrite, or re-*right*, history, like *Madre* does. Indigenous literary voices have been silenced or marginalized within hegemonic discourses. Morales Santos is perfectly aware of this silencing; he understands that the past is not a reservoir where one deposits and leaves ideas. Rather, the past is a stage where intense discursive and conceptual struggles take place that involve rewritings and reinterpretations of that past, which at every moment has involved political-discursive auto-modernizations to regenerate the Maya world. The contemporary period has not been immune to these processes: we have recently survived a new fratricidal experience that required a reevaluation and rewriting of history, especially from those whose voices were consciously relegated to the margins by hegemonic sectors.

Read in this way, the journey to the origins in *Madre* advocates, at the same time, a return to and a powerful vindication of the figure of the mother and its multiple epistemological meanings: orality, tradition, local history, contemporaneity, resistance, and nature. These elements deserve social renditions, because they can enable us to harvest a more enriched present-future: we need not only to inscribe the prominence of peasant communities (Indigenous and non-Indigenous ones) from the rural areas in the hegemonic historical register of the "mother-nation" but also to propose such narratives as an alternative. In other words, the journey to the origins manifests a decolonial process that recalls what Bissau-Gunean activist and intellectual Amílcar Cabral has in mind when he writes:

Study of the history of liberation struggles shows that they have generally been preceded by an upsurge of cultural manifestations, which progressively harden into an attempt, successful or not, to assert the cultural personality of the dominated people by an act of denial of the culture of the oppressor. Whatever the conditions of subjugation of a people to foreign domination and the influence of

economic, political and social factors in the exercise of this
domination, it is generally within the cultural factor that we find
the germ of challenge which leads to the structuring and development of the liberation movement. (1979, 142–43)

By emphasizing the recovery and vindication of the past in an obscure and
dangerous present, the symbolic association between the mother and the
rural natural world does not merely aim to validate the importance of the
land and ancestral origins but also to legitimize and empower "structuring
and development" as alternatives in the "struggle for liberation." By not
specifying the Indigenous subject in the poem, Morales Santos allows the
"we" from the title to refer to a collective well-being. That is, he opens the
door of his political proposal not only to Indigenous peoples but also to
those who have been placed in a position of subalternity by capitalism and
state terrorism. He aims to make his proposal about Indigeneity universal
to establish the conditions of possibility for a collective emancipation.

Furthermore, the representation of socialism as a utopian possibility
reveals not a simple reproduction of such ideology, but instead a recon-
ceptualization of it from an Indigenous perspective. In its vindication of
an ancestral past, *Madre* permeates class consciousness with an Indigenous
social imagination in order to establish possible conditions that would de-
alienate a subaltern collective subject. In doing so, the poem ties together
ethnic and class politics to challenge and disarticulate the capitalist
mode of production and state terrorism by inscribing a Maya cosmogony in the hegemonic historical record. In addition, by highlighting the
mother's resistance, the poem also authorizes the memory and prominence of Indigenous peoples. In this sense, through the metaphor of the
journey to the origins, the poem shows how official history has marginalized female, collective subaltern subjects including Indigenous peasants
and their daily local experiences. But in an inversion of this dynamic, the
poem suggests that dominant narratives of the modern nation-state have
been constituted by the heroic sacrifices and contributions of marginalized subjects like the mother invoked by Morales Santos. The poetic voice
underscores this point in the conclusion of the poem: "Whether it is or is
not recognized, your daily acts have been the grout that has edified this
country, damn it!; / a country made out of simply and human acts that, /
in the end, is what matters, / because we, mother, are also history" (38).
Hence, the poem inscribes the Indigenous historical prominence in the

dominant narrative and recognizes the "human and simple daily acts" of those who contribute to the life of the nation-state. By challenging racism and labor exploitation with the mother's tenacity, we are offered not only another history but also alternative perspectives from which we can understand the nation-state's foundation.

Thus, Morales Santos's poetic production underscores the efforts needed to articulate a critique of Western modernity and its capitalist, economic tendencies, as well as a critique of state terrorism. For this Kaqchikel Maya author, the discursive construction of an individual or collective Maya voice can serve as an alternative in the struggles against colonialism. In Indigenous knowledges, it is suggested, we will find lessons on how to build more just intercultural societies.

Luis de Lión: The Angry Imagination

Just before his forced disappearance on May 15, 1984, José Luis de León Díaz, better known by his pen name Luis de Lión, placed many of his literary manuscripts in a small box. This cache included a novel, three collections of short stories, three books of poetry, children's books, and a compilation of poems written by his students at a literary workshop at the José Clemente Chavarria school where he taught. For several weeks before, León Díaz had received anonymous death threats. One day, he told his wife María Tula that if anything were to happen to him, she should take the small box with his writings to the Kaqchikel poet Francisco Morales Santos, who would know what to do with his manuscripts. The writers were close friends and regularly met at coffee shops to read and discuss their literary works (Arias 2017, 43).

On May 15, León Díaz left his home in the community of San Juan del Obispo and traveled to Guatemala City, where he was to meet with members of the PGT, the country's Communist Party. He failed to return home, and his whereabouts were unknown until 1999, three years after the signing of the Peace Accords that formally ended the thirty-six-year armed conflict in Guatemala. As part of the process of reconciliation of the Peace Accords, the Guatemalan Army and the police force were obligated to make public many of their records compiled during the dirty war. Among these documents was a report from the police force that included a list with 135 names and photographs of people who had been detained and disappeared during the month of May 1984. León Díaz appears in this report as number 132. Three days after León Díaz was captured, the code "300" in the document indicates that he was executed.

Since these official reports came to light, Lión's family members have tirelessly petitioned the Guatemalan government to provide information about his remains. The government has ignored them and refused to offer any information.[17] Yet Lión's memory and sacrifice will never be forgotten; they remain alive today through his writings. Furthermore, thanks to the efforts of his daughter Mayarí de León and with the help of students from Loyola University in New Orleans, Project Luis de Lión has been created at the author's home in San Juan del Obispo. This cultural project, which works closely with the public schools in the town, promotes art, a public library, and a museum that displays information about Lión's life and the history of the community. According to its website, the aim of Project Luis de Lión is "to vindicate Luis de Lión's ideals through concrete actions to help in the education of young people in the rural areas of the country."[18] We owe the publication of Lión's texts, in great measure, to the work of his wife María Tula, his daughter Mayarí, and his friend Morales Santos.

This literature is living testimony of a period filled not only with uncertainty but also with hope for many Maya and non-Maya intellectuals, who were committed to armed struggle and a socialist utopia as a political alternative after the 1954 coup d'etat. This literature inscribes an Indigenous consciousness into debates about the best ways to integrate Indigenous peoples into the armed struggle—whether through assimilation, ladinoization, or native sovereignty.[19]

Lión's work can be placed in dialogue within these discussions precisely because it not only offers a dignified view of Indigenous peoples but also proposes a Maya nationalism founded on Indigenous memory. Throughout his work, Lión considers political emancipation a form of "Indigenous sovereignty" (Warrior 2014) and an opportunity to recover and affirm ancestral values by revisiting the past and gathering elements that can help build a new present-future. For Lión, this involves a confrontation with the hegemonic system and with those who give themselves the authority to speak for and about Indigenous peoples. The Guatemalan writer Mario Roberto Morales, for example, talks about Lión's dissident personality as expressed through his strong opposition to Indigenismo, or literature about Indigenous peoples written and produced by non-Indigenous authors. Lión, according to Morales, proposed to "kill" Guatemala's 1967

Nobel literary laureate Miguel Ángel Asturias by reading him more, mean-ing that for Lión it was important to understand Asturias's literary repre-sentation of Maya people in order to criticize him. After Morales (who is non-Indigenous) shared with Lión some short stories of his own with Indigenous protagonists, the Kaqchikel writer told him, "It would be best if you left Indians to me. You're better off dedicating your time to your ladinos" (M. R. Morales 2012). These reactions show how Lión was fully conscious that literature represented an indispensable register not only for inscribing Indigenous memory and prominence within the major narra-tives of modernity but was also a powerful weapon to imagine another world—a world in which it is possible to articulate new projects to recover our sovereignty.

Consider Lión's short story, "Los hijos del padre" (The Sons of the Same Father), included in his book *La puerta del cielo y otras puertas* (The Door to Heaven and Other Doors, 1999), which presents the need to confront a hegemonic system and underscores the revolutionary role of Indigenous peoples. This story tells of a community with two "principal" Christian saints, sons of the same father: one performs miracles for the ladinos, and the other takes care of the Indigenous peoples, "the poor rabble of the community" (13). On Good Friday, the two groups are car-rying their respective saints in procession when they encounter each other on a street. When the ladinos demand that the Indigenous people turn back and carry their saint on a different route, they refuse to do so. The Indigenous peoples, with the approval of their saint, "[raise] their head and, without measuring, without estimating the others, [begin] to walk forward, with the drum and the whistle sounding of war. The time had come" (15). This scene is defined by confrontation and struggle. After cen-turies of exhaustion and desperation owing to conditions of subordination, Lión envisions the beginnings of an "Enough is enough!" or a decolonial project that must inevitably confront and destabilize the established hege-monic system.[20]

It is important to underscore here that, for Lión, these challenges were not merely relegated to the literary realm. The Kaqchikel Maya author knew full well that, to bring about substantial changes for Indigenous peo-ples in Iximulew, political action was also essential. He became involved with the PGT, and his activism directly resulted in his forced disappear-ance. His writings, in this sense, must be thought of as a *performance* that represent his political ideals: he wrote the way he thought, and he lived the way he wrote. He was committed to political change to improve the conditions of existence for Indigenous peoples and to the revolutionary struggle to end colonialism.

Lión's novel, *El tiempo principia en Xibalbá* (Time Commences in Xibalbá, 1985), has been the primary subject of critical literary analysis, with his poetry, short stories, and children's literature remaining at the margins of rigorous criticism.[21] To fill some of these analytical gaps, in this section I explore Lión's book of poetry *Poemas del volcán de agua. los poemas míos* (Poems from Water Volcano. My Own Poems), completed in 1981 but not published until 1994. Much as Morales Santos does in *Madre*, Lión invokes the maternal figure to represent the advent of a nationalist revolutionary project. Lión presents a pregnant mother who will give birth to a son who, as he grows up and becomes aware of land dispossession in his home community, develops a political social consciousness to change things.

The immediate context of Lión's literary work is his native community of San Juan del Obispo in the department of Sacatepéquez. This town, founded by Spanish bishop Francisco Marroquín in 1547, with its baroque colonial structures, is located a mile and a half from Antigua, Guatemala. The name "San Juan" comes from San Juan Bautista, the prophet who in the Christian Bible baptizes Jesus Christ. The church is a distinguishing feature of this small town, inhabited by about 7,000 people. To the west, the community faces Water Volcano, and to the east, Fire, Pacaya, and Acatenango Volcanoes are visible. Water and Fire Volcanoes, in particular, serve as a creative inspiration for Lión; he wrote not only *Poemas del Volcán de Agua* but also *Poemas del Volcán de Fuego* (Poems from Fire Volcano, 1994). His lifelong partner, María Tula, is the central character of this latter book. According to his family, there are still some literary works of his that remain unpublished because of a lack of money, though some have been published periodically in literary anthologies or newspapers. For example, in 1997 a national newspaper in Guatemala, *El Periódico*, published Lión's poetry collection, *Poemas para el correo* (Poems from the Post Office), which he completed in 1983.

Poemas del Volcán de Agua can be read as a response to "Poema al Volcán de Agua" (Poem to Water Volcano) by the nineteenth-century Guatemalan criollo / ladino poet José Batres Montúfar (1809–44). This poem, along with "Yo pienso en tí" (I Think of You) and his short stories, *Tradiciones de Guatemala* (Guatemalan Traditions), has been canonized in the country and is widely read in schools.[22] I suspect that Lión was familiar with Batres Montúfar's work and especially with this particular poem to Water Volcano. This poem—in Alexandrine verse—describes a philosopher who travels to the top of the volcano in search of inspiration. The poetic voice recognizes the majesty of the beautiful volcano as the "largest American mural"; it is "Jupiter's cradle," "strong, superb, the largest of the largest." In addition to these associations, the poet also displays a denigrating view of Indigenous peoples. The poem, for instance, includes a footnote in which the poet expresses his dislike for the name "Hunahpú," the Kaqchikel Maya name for Water Volcano.[23] According to Batres Montúfar, the natives "vulgarly call it that [Hunahpú] because of the waters stored in its crater, which in 1542 caused a flood that destroyed the then primitive city of Guatemala" (qtd. in Bran Azmitía 1978, 32). The flood that Batres Montúfar refers to actually occurred on September 10, 1541. After intense rains, a raging current destroyed the recently established city of Guatemala, originally called *Ciudad Vieja* (Old City). Many people drowned, including Beatriz de la Cueva, the wife of Pedro de Alvarado, one of the conquerors of the Maya peoples in the highlands of Guatemala.[24] After this tragic event, the officials of the town renamed the volcano "Volcán de Agua," and the city was rebuilt in what is today Antigua Guatemala (Old Antigua).[25]

Lión's poems are not written "to" but rather "from" Water Volcano. The preposition "from" and the indication that these are Lión's own poems in the title suggest a desire to establish his own literary authority. In doing so, he reappropriates and develops a history of the community that differs from and is newer than that of Batres Montúfar. Indeed, Lión's book of poetry displays an organic metonymic relationship between the poetic voice, the community, and Water Volcano. The speaker in the poem recognizes himself as part of the community and speaks from his mother's womb or, if we interpret the imagery metaphorically, from the crater of Water Volcano. The author recognizes the community of San Juan del Obispo as being more than 400 years old and adopts the name given to the volcano by the Spanish, suggesting that he confronts and recognizes a history of colonization.

Poems from Water Volcano is set in the second half of the 1970s and the early 1980s. The book comprises fourteen poems written in free verse and in a vernacular language. The first thing one notices about Lión's typescript in all the poems is the lack of capital letters, which in my view suggests the author's desire to display a sort of modesty. This interpretation is supported by the fact that the experiences narrated in the poems are of humble, poor Indigenous peasants. At first glance, in its allusions to the local church, its bell ("Poem to a Girl"), the town council ("Poem to the Town Council"), the Sumpango kite festivals ("Poem to my Kite"), and the pastoral descriptions of the village, *Poems from Water Volcano* seems to pay homage to the author's community. However, a closer reading reveals a more sophisticated decolonial discursive strategy that not only challenges Indigenismo but also issues a revolutionary call to defend and reestablish Indigenous sovereignty.

The poetry collection can be read as a *bildungsroman* that, through the metaphor of childhood, allegorizes a process of the awakening of consciousness of the community of San Juan del Obispo. The book is divided into three parts that emphasize three moments in the development of a revolutionary Indigenous consciousness in the narrator. In the first part, through the poem "Poema para el niño del volcán de agua" (Poem for the Water Volcano's Child), Lión uses personification to characterize the town of San Juan del Obispo (San Juan is the "son" of the volcano) as an ingenuous and alienated child who is dark-skinned, peaceful, and sweet. The narrator also tells us that, even though San Juan is the son of the volcano and is more than 400 years old, he is someone who "just now is becoming an adult" (7)—though he is married and has children. He has served as a soldier to the country that "oppresses him," and he "has neither a voice nor a vote on the things of the earth" (7). San Juan plants hope, but he only harvests grief. After adopting Christian values, he believes that there is no possibility of redemption on this earth, but only in heaven. Although these descriptions seem to suggest a lack of hope, reinforced by the use of ellipses, the poem anticipates a nationalist revolutionary change in its closing verses: "Now, [San Juan] still has a piece of land / under his feet; / but, tomorrow . . . / well, pretty soon everything / will be the color of this flag" (8).

In the second part of the book, Lión allegorizes the coming of revolutionary social change through the metaphor of pregnancy. The narrator switches to the first person and imagines itself as speaking from the mother's womb—invoking a primordial origin and a harmonic world without contradictions. In the poems "poema para mi cielo" (Poem for My Heaven) and "mi casa" (My Home)—dedicated to María Venancia, the author's mother—the poetic voice speaks of being "protected" (14) and "safe from capitalist exploitation" (13). In his mother's womb, he moves happily, like

a fish "in the middle of the water" (13). There, the air is soft; there are "no
hurricanes, / no storms, / no dust, / no garbage. it was the air of a country
without deforestation" (12). In his "home," the narrator is exposed to a
blue heaven made of flesh where there is "only an enduring sun, / with no
winter, / with no summer / with no fall. there is only an eternal spring" (12).
He sees hundreds of birds fly over that heaven, the leaves of trees falling,
butterflies, kites, stars, and fireworks. As he "grows more" in his mother's
womb, the sky extends to other places. It stops being an "infantile and rus-
tic" sky and becomes an "international heaven" (11). The poetic voice also
realizes that, for him to be able to live in that paradise, the owner of the
house has to "do a lot of hard work" (13). Consequently, the child gets
ready to leave his house and to "come out into this world" (14).

In the third part of the book, in "poema a mi niño" (Poem to My Child),
the reader learns that the boy has been born. While in his mother's womb,
the poetic voice felt safe from capitalist exploitation; once in this world, the
child becomes "a slave, / in his forehead / he carries the marks of the leather
strap for carrying wood / like a mark of a livestock" (27). As soon as the day
begins, he gets up and "runs behind the shadow of his mother" to go to the
volcano. They go up to pick the harvests of peaches and custard apples
from their piece of land. Later, he and his mother go down to sell them at
the city's market. From the volcano, both of them descend "like two beasts
of burden: she flattened under the weight of a big basket, / he, bent under
the weight of a heavy bundle" (28). Little by little, the boy begins to realize
the contradictions and changes that are occurring in his community. In
"poema a mi barrilete" (Poem to My Kite), the narrator speaks of how he
flies his kite "over a green carpet, / next to a grove of cypresses, amid birds
and pine trees" (16). This makes him feel like he is the owner "of all the
rainbows." His happiness turns "into a reed of string" (17). This, however,
changes when the places where he had flown his kite, and other places
where children played freely, are made off limits due to the privatization of
land. Lión explores similar themes in the poem "la alfombra" (The Carpet), which describes the places where children play, using the carpet as a
metaphor for the community. On the "carpet" there was "a ravine full of
secrets" that during "winter brought, / besides a small river, / fish from the
wilderness" (18). Its gigantic pines "always responded to our whistles as if
they were other children." But now there is an "owner" who has appropriated and privatized the land. The new owner "does not love children other
than his own." This restricts the narrator and other children from playing

where they used to play freely. When they tell the elders of the community what has happened, the boy learns from them that land dispossession has also been happening in the coastal region of the country "where the land is being divided" (19–20). The elders also talk about "a history of shame and plundering" (20). One day, the narrator tells us, this boy "will stop being a boy / and a peasant . . . and he would grow up like a tree" (29).

Poems from Water Volcano is a critical reflection on the establishment of a mercantilist economic system imposed on San Juan del Obispo and other parts of the country, as defined by the plundering of territory. In the first part the author recognizes "San Juan" as a passive subject who has assimilated the ways of life and thinking imposed by colonialism—for example, his Christian beliefs. Yet the birth of the boy and his consequent consciousness-raising suggest the advent of revolutionary change against the exploitative capitalist system. His birth could even be interpreted allegorically as a new "flood"—in relation to the historical flood that destroyed the Old City in 1541—that will allow for the construction of a new society, one similar to that evoked while the boy is in the womb, where children play freely and happily.

In addition, it is suggested that the capitalist system has been put in place with the complicity of Christianity, which works to depoliticize the community. The process of the privatization of land invoked in the book is reminiscent of the expropriation of Indigenous territories by transnational companies such as the United Fruit Company (UFCO) in Guatemala. The principal investors in this company included John and Allen Foster Dulles; occupying important political posts as directors of the CIA and Secretary of State, respectively, in the U.S. government under the Dwight Eisenhower administration. The Dulles brothers were influential in developing the foreign policies that supported intervention in Guatemalan politics and led to the overthrowing of Árbenz Guzmán in 1954. Though Lión does not make this historical context explicit, the poem suggests that Indigenous lands were given to new "owners" who consequently privatized them. But although the hegemonic system has alienated people by imposing exploitative material conditions of existence, with the birth of the child—a symbol of hope and change—Lión suggests that a new national project will be coming soon: "pretty soon everything will be the color of this flag."

The representation of volcanoes or the mountains as literary tropes of emancipation projects associated with revolutionary struggles is a modality that characterizes much of Latin American literature, particularly works influenced by the "foquismo" (focalism) ideology proposed by Ernesto "Che" Guevara and Regis Debray in the 1950s. It is in the mountains or volcanoes where those rebels developed their ideas and military strategies to bring about revolution. In Guatemala, Rodrigo Asturias (the son of the 1967 Nobel laureate, Miguel Ángel Asturias), under the nom de guerre Gaspar Ilom, founded the Revolutionary Organization of People in Arms (ORPA) in 1979, during the internal armed conflict. He tells of the time when he, along with a group of rebels, arrived in the rural areas and heard stories from community leaders that "one day, from the mountains, men would come down to liberate the People" (qtd. in Forster 2012, 227). Omar Cabezas expresses similar ideas in his famous testimonial account, *Fire from the Mountain: The Making of a Sandinista* (1982). The mountain, Cabezas states, is "power," "an unrecognized mystery" "where the force is located and even the weapons, the best men, indestructibility" (28). For her part, the author Claribel Alegría in *Cenizas de Izalco* (Ashes of Izalco, [1966] 1982) develops a vision of volcanoes very similar to Lión's. She describes a community near the dormant Izalco volcano in El Salvador, a politically inactive society that lacks a social consciousness. However, once the people become conscious of their oppression, the book suggests, the volcano will erupt.[26]

These figurative references to the importance of the landscape and, in particular, volcanoes and mountains as explosive forces of political change also emerge in Lión's work, though he uses the trope differently. His volcano disarticulates the hegemonic system, inviting us to reimagine the nation-state from the Maya worldview. It is precisely in this desire to vindicate and dignify Mayaness, as well as to forge a revolutionary utopian national project based on Maya history, where Lión's originality lies.

When we consider the metaphor of the mother's pregnancy in the second part of his book, we become aware of the organic association that Lión develops with the image of Water Volcano. In other words, the mother's pregnancy represents Mother Earth's pregnancy (represented in Water Volcano), which will lead to the birth of a boy. In turn, through these images, Lion also expresses the significance of mountains and volcanoes in the Maya worldview. In the rituals of the Q'eq'chi Maya people in what is today called Alta Verapaz, for example, ceremonies include rituals to *Tzultacaj* (the top of the hill), the god of the mountains and hills. Such rituals are celebrated in caves and include burning *copal* (resin from the

Protium copal tree) and offering food and drink to Tzultacaj. The prayers to this deity request good harvests; one says, "Oh Father! Oh Mother! Oh great Tzultacaj! You that help to clean the earth and water. Now, oh, our god, from your feet and hands will emerge our maize" (Villa Rojas 1995, 241).

This symbolic association to the spiritual meaning of Water Volcano also suggests a Maya spiritual precedent in honoring and recognizing Mother Earth. In Mesoamerican Indigenous worldviews, volcanoes have great significance: they are points of reference to determine the solstice during certain periods of time. The *ajq'ij ab* or Maya spiritual leaders interpret volcanoes as protectors of Mother Earth and people because they contain positive and negative energies. Our ancestors, before the arrival of European invaders, displayed respect for volcanoes and mountains through the architectonic constitution of their Mesoamerican pyramids. The designs of important temples such as Tikal, Chichen Itza, or Palenque were inspired by their landscape and surroundings. According to James Brady and Wendy Ashmore, Indigenous Mesoamerican nations, through the design of their temples, recognized the importance of Mother Earth and thus aim to emulate and humanize it by "bringing primordial powers more firmly into the realm of accountable human action and control" (1999, 132). "In living with the land, Maya and neighboring peoples continually re-create and renew the world; their material legacy bears witness to repeated or re-crafted strategies for acknowledging the earth, for honoring and harnessing its vital forces" (126). Moreover, strategies to "re-create" and "renovate" the world through the building of temples inspired by the mountains sought to sanctify and legitimize the city and their rulers.

It is no accident that these temples include small entrances on the very top that look like caves, which in Mesoamerican Indigenous worldviews hold particular significance for understanding ancestral origins. According to Frauke Sachse and Allen Christenson (2005), our Mesoamerican ancestors emerged from *Wuqub' Pek Wuqub' Siwan* (Seven Caves, Seven Abyss Mountains). After their birth, they began their long journey to find Tulan Siwan or "the big palace or highest house." Thus, from an Indigenous perspective, caves represent Mother Earth's womb and symbolize the entrance to or exit from the underworld—from where the origins of humanity and the universe are materialized. In the *Popol Wuj*, Xib'alb'a, or the place of fear, is where humanity is created and a new, harmonic order is established. For the Mexica people, *Mictlán* (the place of the dead) represents the underworld. It is where Quetzalcoatl (the Plumed Serpent deity) goes and finds jade bones. He cuts his penis so it bleeds and spreads blood over the bones to "populate the world." Today, Maya and Nahua priests gather at caves and *cenotes* (water deposits or small lakes) to perform religious ceremonies for spiritual renewal. Coming out of a cave, in this sense, acquires a symbolic and religious significance associated with rebirth, re-creation, and renewal.

The symbolic meaning of mountains and caves is particularly relevant for a reading of Lión's poetry. The references to the mother's pregnancy and the subsequent birth of the boy not only invoke our ancestral origins but also accommodate them to Lión's present. Indeed, Lión suggests that we currently face a new necessity to "re-create" and "renew" the world. In contrast to the past, this need arises from the colonial experience that does not allow us to be "free," as allegorized by the activities of the boy and his friends who can no longer play in the open fields and other parts of the community, now privatized. Through paradox, Lión suggests that the capitalist economic system is not only privatizing lands in his own community but also creating widespread environmental damage—the countryside has been stripped of it's trees, and the air is becoming contaminated (12).

The image of the son inside his mother's womb parallels the image of the figure inside the volcano. In his mother's womb, the boy happily navigates like a fish "amid the waters." Implicitly, he expresses a desire for emancipation. Later, such a feeling emerges after the boy is born and he is exposed to the capitalist system. In the poem "El ojo de agua" (The Eye of Water), the boy imagines himself returning to his mother's womb, or to Water Volcano. The narrator expresses his admiration for the majestic Volcano, descends the slopes and jumps "inside its waters":

> from its waters,
> I came out transparent,
> like a drop of dew
> that only needed the sun's rays
> to become a bird. (25)

The images display a cleansing ceremony—a desire to be reborn, to return to the mother's womb with the aim of, once again, feeling the freedom the boy once felt. "To become a bird" here symbolizes that utopia—of living in a world where spring is "eternal" and where one is free from the exploitative chains of capitalism.

The idea of being inside the volcano can also be associated with Brady's and Ashmore's analysis of the symbolism of mountains, water, and caves in the Maya worldview. They indicate that mountains and volcanoes are inhabited by "the Lord of the Earth," much like the Tzultacaj deity. However, the importance of volcanoes and mountains is not exclusive to Indigenous peoples in Mesoamerica: they are also essential to Indigenous knowledge in other parts of the hemisphere, in the Andean region and Turtle Island. In Andean mythology and spiritual rituals in Peru, Ecuador, Bolivia, and Colombia, the spirits of the mountains are referred to as "Apus," or gods. The Apus can sometimes also be caves or "solitary" stones, which are referred to as *huacas*, that hold spirits and have great spiritual importance for the Andean Peoples. As in religions in Mesoamerica, many Apus participate in ceremonies and offerings made by Indigenous spiritual guides or locals to request protection and good harvests.

These ideas about the significance of mountains and caves become more evident when we examine Lión's other texts. His novel *Time Commences in Xibalbá* ([1985] 2012) more explicitly recognizes the K'iche' Maya underworld as *the* place of origins. As the title of the novel suggests, for Lión, time or life begins only in the K'iche' underworld, "Xibalbá." Using the Maya worldview from the *Popol Wuj*, Lión proposes the destruction of the ladino or non-Indigenous world and the reconstruction of a new Maya order.[27] After the community destroys ladino symbols, they begin to rebuild the town. Lión invites us to reject other histories of creation, like that of the Christian Bible, and radically affirms a Maya worldview. Lión's short story "Los hijos del padre" (The Sons of the Same Father), as discussed previously, is also about a confrontation with the hegemonic ladino social order, which is inevitable in the effort to establish Maya authority and agency in the vindication of Indigeneity.

These decolonial efforts, as we can see, also appear in *Poems from Water Volcano*. For Mark Anderson, the boy in the poetry book "becomes a polyvalent symbol used to refer alternatively to Lión's own childhood, the repressed Guatemalan peasantry as a whole, and the infancy of a growing social revolution" (2011, 125). From this perspective, the boy clearly represents future emancipation because he embodies hope, change, and action. The birth of the boy and the development of his political consciousness point both toward a generational change and the vindication of an ancestral cultural identity. Through the representation of the volcano and childhood, Lión not only responds to previous literary traditions but also re-signifies the idea of the Mesoamerican cave to propose an alternative political and revolutionary project founded on the Maya worldview.

It is important to add here that Lión frequently represents childhood in his literary works, usually associating it with the potential for change. In his role as an elementary school teacher and through his children's literature, he expressed a strong commitment to dignify Indigenous identity. He felt that the cultural projects that the nation-state promoted contributed to a growing assimilation that constantly devalued Indigeneity. In his essay "Education as a Form of Assimilation" (*Conversatorio* 1991), Lión states that schools offer children "useless facts" and try to turn Indigenous children into ladino subjects. In contrast, Lión sees literature as a weapon of liberation that can develop a critical consciousness in his students. His book *Una experiencia poética: Taller de poesía infantile* (A Poetic Experience, 2007) is a compilation of children's poetry written in a workshop he organized at the school where he taught. The Kaqchikel writer also promoted his ideals in his children's literature, as seen in his poem, "Poema a los heroes" (Poem to the Heroes) and his story "El libro de los cuentos" (The Book of Tales).

Here is "Poem to the Heroes" in its entirety:

Before Superman, the man of Steel
would fly through the sky like an eagle
and Batman and Robin
would be disguised as bats;
before the Phantom
occupied the ancient Skull Cave
and that Tarzan launched his first scream
and defeated the first lion in the jungle;
before the silly Goofy and smarty Mickey
captured Pistol Pete, the delinquent
and that Scrooge McDuck saved his first penny
leaving a little boy without food;
before Bugs Bunny
stole his first carrot from Elmer [Fudd]
and that Fox from the comics
was foully tricked by the Crow;
before the Lone Ranger
became a superhero

and that Kaliman, the Incredible Man
sought to become more credible;
before all of them and others,
there were two boys, Hunahpu and Xbalanque
that in Xibalba defeated Death
two boys whose adventures don't appear
on TV, nor the radio or the press,
much less in comic books,
but they are bigger and more credible
than Superman and all his relatives;
there were two boys whose great adventures
all children should know . . . (2002, 34)

In its allusions to popular culture represented by "superheroes" like
Superman, Batman and Robin, Goofy and Mickey, Bugs Bunny, and others, Lión expresses his concern for the growing cultural imperialism that,
along with economic capitalism, has been attacking Indigenous specificities and memory.[28] These processes—as the poem suggests—affect the
future of Indigenous peoples as Disneyfication distances children from
the ancestral knowledge represented by the *Popol Wuj*. Lión then invites
his readers to learn about the achievements of the hero Maya twins,
Hunahpu and Xbalanque, who, in the underworld, "before all of them and
others," defeated the Lords of Death to plant the first seed of corn that
would give life to humanity and the universe.

Lión's stance in this poem brings to mind Ariel Dorfman and Armand
Mattelart's book *How to Read Donald Duck: Imperialist Ideology in the Disney
Comic* ([1972] 2003), which expresses their concerns about the growing
economic and cultural role of the United States in Latin America. Focusing on the role of Disney's comic books, Dorfman and Mattelart state that
the "popular" characters from this multimillion dollar media industry have
been "incorporated into every home, they hang on every wall, they deco-
rate objects of every kind; they constitute a little less than a social environment inviting us all to join the great universal Disney family" (12). Dorfman,
Mattelart, and Lión suggest that far from being innocent cultural practices
of entertainment, the "popular comic" is complicit in the justification of
imperialist economic and cultural plunder and colonial submission.

From these particular concerns, Lión developed a series of poems and
short stories for children that would cultivate a social and critical Indige-

nous consciousness and so lead to the vindication of the Maya world. Furthermore, his stories also invite social action as represented in his children's story "El libro de cuentos" (The Book of Tales, 2002). In this beautiful story, a boy receives a book titled "José from the Tales" as a birthday present. The boy, however, who expected to get toys, is disappointed about the present and puts it on a shelf. One day, his teacher asks him to copy a story and bring it to class. He then remembers the book he got as a present and, when he gets home, picks it up and opens it to choose a story. He sees that the pages are blank and that the stories have escaped. The boy then goes out in search of them. After walking for a while, he finds one of the tales in a corner, surrounded by children who are laughing and enjoying how the tale tells itself to them. The boy continues to walk and, at another corner, finds another tale that, similar to the first one, tells itself to a group of children, who laugh hearing the story. He finds the other ones in different corners, where the scene is the same. The boy then begs the tales "to return to the book, and he promises them that now he will read them" (12). Initially, they tell him that they do not want to return because they do not believe the boy, but he continues to beg. The tales finally gather together in council to take a vote and decide to return to the book as long as the boy promises that, after reading each of the tales, he will share them aloud with other children so they can enjoy them as well. The boy accepts, and "one by one, letter by letter, when the boy was asleep, the tales returned to the book, filling out, once again, its pages" (12).

Lión's story captures both his literary project and his role as an activist that through his participation in the PGT sought to change things and establish a better life for future generations. In terms of the story, on the one hand, it expresses the role of literature: it should not only be absorbed through reading but also must be transmitted and shared with others orally. Hence, Lión personifies the tales from "José from the Tales" as bearers of knowledge and entertainment. Moreover, for Lión, orality and writing are not mutually exclusive but are complementary. They feed on each other. Therefore, the knowledge we obtain from books must be shared with others.

By now it should also be clear that Lión's literature aims to dignify Indigenous identity. Similar to Morales Santos, Lión's literary works also respond to the so-called Indian problem in Guatemala. Whereas Morales Santos's "We Will Be Caqchiquel Again" is a response to the social context of the 1950s, Lión's literary works respond to debates and discussions about racism as a constitutive element of Guatemala's hegemonic society in the early 1970s—particularly, how the Left in their efforts to create a strong revolutionary movement dealt with Indigenous peoples. These discussions emerged from the growing Indigenous participation in revolutionary cells like Guatemala's Workers Party, of which Lión was a part, the Guerrilla Army of the Poor (EGP), and the Revolutionary Organization of People in Arms (ORPA). When those organizations saw a massive participation of Indigenous combatants, a group of ladino intellectuals began to debate how to deal with the diversity of Indigenous languages and of Maya ethnic groups. Prominent ladino figures—Severo Martínez Peláez, Julio Pinto Soria, Mario Payeras, Rodrigo Asturias (aka Gaspar Ilom), Mario Solórzano Foppa, Huberto Flores Alvarado, Carlos Guzmán Böckler, and Jean-Loup Herbert—motivated many revolutionary leaders to address the best ways to incorporate Indigenous peoples in the revolutionary struggle. Some of these intellectuals thought that the best way to integrate them was through "ladinoization" or assimilation; that is, the elimination of Indigenous languages and the teaching of Spanish to break down linguistic barriers. In addition, they thought "Indians" needed to adopt a Marxist-Leninist ideology, which in turn meant understanding their struggle as merely a "class" struggle. This meant that the "proletariat" or the "peasant" became the revolutionary figure. A collective embrace of this subjectivity supposedly led to change the material conditions of existence of an entire exploited "class" rather than a specifically Maya population. Conversely, other groups of intellectuals suggested that the revolutionary process should avoid "assimilation" and that the linguistic, cultural, and spiritual specificities of Indigenous peoples needed to be respected. These aspects of their identity needed to be dignified as a way to motivate more Indigenous participation in the revolutionary struggle. This is why authors like Guzmán Böckler and Jean-Loup Herbert advanced the idea of discussing Indigenous specificities against ladino ones.[29]

These debates, as suggested in *Poems from Water Volcano*, led Indigenous intellectual elites—like the one represented by Lión and Morales Santos—to question the proposals made by ladinos. Indigenous writers began to reflect on their own role within the revolutionary process. In her book, *La revolución indígena y campesina en Guatemala 1970–2000* (The Indigenous and Peasant Revolution in Guatemala 1970–2000, 2012), Cindy Forster includes testimonies of more than seventy Indigenous revolutionary militants who speak about why they decided to join movements like

EGP, PGT, and ORPA. Some were motivated to join the armed struggle to end class exploitation and the ethnic marginalization they experienced. María Lupe, for example, recounts,

We used to work from one in the morning until ten at night. Because in the fields there was no electric windmill, we had to do everything by hand. My husband made 50 cents a day, and I only worked for food. Twelve years ago we decided to go north, to Ixcán, to see if we could get some land, but things were harder there. I was pregnant with my third daughter, I got malaria during the pregnancy, and I was malnourished. The child was born after seven months. She was so small! I almost lost her [sic]. After two years of being there, the first comrades from the Guerrilla Army of the Poor arrived. They helped us build a house. It was the first time we saw collective work. We were the first families that began to collaborate with them. (Forster 2012, 356–57)

During this same period in the early 1970s, there were efforts to create a renewal of Maya culture and thereby achieve an Indigenous social vindication. For instance, 1971 to 1973 saw the creation of the Indigenous Association Pro Maya Quiche Culture and the Association of Leaders of Quiche Ideals (AFOIQUI) in the Santa Cruz del Quiché region; in 1972 the Indigenous seminars supported by Catholic Action started (Arias 1985, 70–81); and between 1977 and 1979, *Ixim Magazine* published various texts by Indianista writers such as the Aymara intellectual Fausto Reinaga and the already mentioned Amílcar Cabral. We also see the emergence of the *Cabracan* collective, which was led by various Indigenous university students who spoke about returning to our ancestral roots (Bastos and Camus 1993, 64).

Political efforts continued, including the creation of the political National Indigenous Front (FIN) and the first attempts to form the Civil Committee Xel Ju in 1972 in the city of Quetzaltenango. A few years later, in 1978, the Committee on Peasant Unity in the Quiche region emerged; around the same time, the Tojil (Fire) Movement was born. The Tojil Movement published important documents for Indigenous rights including "Guatemala: De la república burguesa centralista a la república popular federal" (Guatemala: From the Centralized Bourgeois Republic to the Popular Federal Republic). Using a class-based critique, this document criticized Mayas who focused only on cultural topics without addressing issues of poverty and exploitation, as well as Maya university students who became "comfortable" within and "uncritical" of the dominant social system.

The Tojil Movement and its publication set an important precedent— not only making a call for political involvement but also, most importantly, distancing its proponents from the Indigenista, leftist critique that rejected proposals discussing "ladinoization" or "assimilation." Instead, the movement highlighted the historical and prominent role of Indigenous peoples in the foundation of the Guatemalan nation-state and demanded a new nationalist project based on federalism. It spoke of the struggle for liberation situated within a context where colonialism was understood as "a global phenomenon based on the cultural and economic oppression, exploitation of the Indian people; a system maneuvered by the ladino sector" (MacLeod 2013, 43). Thus, the struggle for liberation should be understood as politically "simultaneous and fundamentally anti-colonialist and anti-classist" (42), based on the recognition of diverse and autonomous Maya Nations within the Guatemalan state. Guatemala needed to be decentralized to maintain "ethnic diversity within the State's unity" (43).

With its strong emphasis on dignifying Maya culture, Lión's writing aligns with the Tojil Movement and its political initiatives and proposals. As we saw, Lión rejected any efforts that led to the "ladinoization" of Maya peoples into the dominant culture. For example, Lión stated, "I cannot participate in the so-called *mestizaje* [racial mixing] precisely because Hispanism is the rejection of my language, of my culture" (qtd. in Montenegro 2004, 8). On the contrary, for Lión, the Indigenous worldview should be reactivated when discussing ideas of nationhood and citizenship. Similar to Tojil's political stand, Lión argues that what exists in Iximulew is not an Indigenous problem, as we were made to believe, but rather a ladino problem: this is because, instead of trying to solve issues from within Indigenous cultures, non-Indigenous peoples continue to seek solutions by looking to Europe and North America as models of "development" and "sociability." By offering and privileging Maya peoples' perspective, Lión not only dignifies our ancestral values but also demonstrates that, within debates about "national liberation," Indigenous revolutionaries place their faith in an Indigenous nationalism. Hence, we can conclude that for Lión and many other Mayas who became part of the revolutionary struggle, joining the Guatemala's Workers Party or the Guerrilla Army of the Poor meant an opportunity to materialize—to use the words of the Maya Ixil leader, Pablo Ceto—"a conspiracy within the conspiracy" (Arias 2017, 57). In this sense, Lión's literary proposal, as represented in *Poems from Water Volcano,* inserts itself in these cultural and political efforts to imagine an Indigenous emancipation. Through his reenactment of and allusions to the Maya millenarian past, Lión—similar to Morales Santos—registers the Maya world as a condition of possibility for imagining another present and future. Through the metaphor of childhood, Lión imagines a new Indigenous generation finally taking a stand against colonialism and for the rights of Mayas to live in a world free from racism and economic exploitation.

The Indigenous Mother, Imagined and Real

Let us now reconsider the figure of the mother in both Morales Santos's and Lión's books of poetry. Both representations vindicate the Indigenous mother as a prominent historical figure whose sacrifice has enabled and validated the role of the narrators. The poems lack a father figure; both poets emphasize the contribution of the mother as the one who bears and transmits history and who embodies a utopian ideal of a desired nationalist future project.[30] These representations of the mother differ from those we see in other works, such as those by Guatemalan Otto René Castillo, who develops the image of Guatemala as the mother fatherland in his poetry anthology, *Informe de una Injusticia: Antología poética* (Reports about Injustice, 1982). In his book, the figure of the "mother country" is a victim of military dictators who establish repressive economic-political social orders that directly affect the "proletariat" and other subaltern sectors. In poems like "Let's Go, Guatemala, Let's Walk" (135) and "Distance From Your Face," for example, we find an obedient son who will descend into the "most profound abysses," will drink the "bitter chalices," or will lose his sight so that the "mother country" has eyes to see the light. These poems show the figure of the mother as weak, passive, and in need of her sons' protection. Castillo writes such verses as "I am tired of carrying your tears with me" and I am tired of "seeing colonels that piss on your walls," refers to "little mother land of mine" and "little peasant," and describes a "loving mother" who has given birth to "vile sons" and is an "old mother in pain and suffering," portraying a submissive, sentimental, small, afflicted, and defenseless feminine figure. The tone of anger that emerges from the poetic voice displays a masculine subject—the guerrilla warrior—who needs to become the defender of the "mother country." In contrast to Castillo's perspective, the figure of the mother in *Poems from Water Volcano* and *Mother, We Too Are History* allegorizes a utopian ideal of emancipation organically associated with Nature, perseverance, tenacity, hard work, Mother Earth, the ancestral past, and the future.

That being said, although there are indeed significant differences between the mother as depicted by Kaqchikel Maya authors and by Castillo, Morales Santos's and Lión's appropriation and representation of the figure of the mother still exhibit some shortcomings. In the end, the mother is displaced to give agency to the male poetic voice—the son. The son becomes the authorized voice to speak of the mother's experience or to lead the way to a nationalist subaltern emancipation. In chapter 4, I explore these topics further in my discussion of Maya Cu Choc's poetic works, highlighting how her decolonial feminism disrupts representations like those of Morales Santos and Lión within a heteronormative dominant system. For now, it is enough to mention that, though their aim is to highlight the "simple" acts of the mother that contribute to establishing the nation-state, they also end up eclipsing her prominence, while in fact Indigenous and non-Indigenous mothers, as we saw with María Lupe's testimony above, played a significant role in the struggle for emancipation in Iximulew.

In the 1970s and 1980s, for example—the period referenced in Morales Santos's and Lión's poetry—social and human rights movements emerged that were led by women within a context of strong military repression, including the National Coordinator of Widows of Guatemala (CONAVIGUA) and Mutual Assistance Group (GAM). Activists like Kaqchikel Maya Rosalina Tuyuc, one of the founders of CONAVIGUA and leader of the Guatemalan Revolutionary National Unity (URNG), have shown how Maya women have contributed to the struggle for Indigenous human rights. Tuyuc later became a senator in Congress for the New Guatemala Democratic Front (FDNG), serving between 1996 and 2000. In Congress, she often breastfed her son or demanded Indigenous rights with her son standing next to her. Tuyuc's prominent role offers another dimension of the Maya mother imagined by Morales Santos and Lión, one in which she leads the struggle for emancipation. Indeed, much like the Mothers of Plaza de Mayo in Argentina, the protests led by Maya women like Tuyuc showcase the constant struggles of Indigenous women not only against racism and political violence but also against domestic violence and sexual abuse in their Indigenous communities. The role of Indigenous women in these movements, displaying their courage through their political actions within a social context marked by continuing political repression, laid the foundation for their current struggles against the colonial violence perpetrated by the Guatemalan modern nation-state.

In addition, many female Maya revolutionary combatants played an important role in the Guerrilla Army of the Poor (EGP), as highlighted in *Memorias rebeldes contra el olvido / Paasantzila Txums'al Ti' sotzeb' al K'u'l* (Rebellious Memories against Forgetfulness [Hernández Alarcón et al. 2008]). Testimonies indicate that many Maya women, who were active combatants and participated in the armed struggles, were also mothers. For example, one woman stated, "My first husband died in combat. I left my youngest son in care of an organizer. It hurt me a lot, but many women did the same. . . . I did not know what was going to happen. I was sent to the CPR [Communities of Population in Resistance]" (66). More recently, fifteen Maya Q'eq'chi women from Alta Verapaz, displaying courage and heroism, fought in court from 2011 to 2016 against Esteelmer Reyes Girón and Heriberto Valdez Asij, two ex-military officers from the Guatemalan Army. During the thirty-six-year armed conflict, these Maya Q'eq'chi women were systematically raped and enslaved by the military in a small community near the Sepur Zarco military outpost in the regions of Alta Verapaz and Izabal. The trial concluded with a jail sentence of 120 years for Reyes Girón and 240 years for Valdez Asij for authorizing the enslavement of the Maya women; this ruling set an important precedent in the struggle for Indigenous human rights and against sexual and domestic violence.[31]

By offering these examples, I do not aim to diminish the literary representation of the Indigenous mother in Morales Santos' and Lión's poetry, but rather to offer other dimensions of the prominent role of Indigenous women in Guatemala's social and political realm. These Maya Kaqchikel authors' works vindicate the Indigenous mother figure, which when considered alongside other representations (like the one developed by Castillo) offers us an alternative knowledge that gives authority to Maya ancestral values, in particular, those associated with environmental justice politics who have been threatened by capitalism and state-terrorism. In addition, these authors show the influence of Marxist-Leninist ideology and seek to understand it and interpret it from their own Maya perspectives. In doing so, they have developed their own nationalist/emancipatory projects to vindicate Mayaness and to question the Left's understanding of Indigeneity as a problem that can be solved through ladinoization. By speaking for a Maya/Indigenous locus of enunciation, these authors challenge the Indigenismo represented by major figures like Miguel Ángel Asturias or Batres Montúfar to authorize the Maya voice in the contemporary period. Their works set an important precedent in the struggle against colonialism, planting a seed that allows for the germination of other Maya modern voices that complement and enrich the national and international realm of the Indigenous literary canon in Abiayala.

CHAPTER 2

Strategic Essentialism against State Terrorism

Humberto Ak'abal, Victor Montejo, and Gaspar Pedro González

This is our genealogy; it will not be lost, because we know our origins and we'll not forget our ancestors.

—*Kaqchikel Chronicles*

AS SHOWN in the previous chapter, the work of Kaqchikel Maya authors Francisco Morales Santos and Luis de Lión represents contemporary Maya literature in Spanish that responds to the so-called Indian problem discussed by Guatemalan elites in the 1950s and to the leftist sectors that were ideologically influenced by Marxism-Leninism in the 1970s. Through their representation of the figure of the mother, they aim to vindicate the Maya worldview as a condition of possibility for imagining a world free of the chains of colonialism. Their literary imaginary employs the language of socialism while at the same time develops ways to advance and affirm a Maya nationalism. Both authors also present a vision of hope for Indigenous peoples that emanated from the revolutionary struggle beginning in 1960, when the insurgency challenged U.S. imperialism and the repressive policies of the Guatemalan nation-state. By 1975, we see the beginning of the "second guerrilla cycle" in which many Indigenous sectors join the revolutionary movement to achieve some of their political goals. Addressing the demands of Indigenous combatants, the Guerrilla Army of the Poor (EGP) and the Revolutionary Organization of People in Arms (ORPA) integrated Indigenous cultural elements into their strategies and actions and operated in Maya communities in the highlands (Rangel Romero 2013, 182). As mentioned, Luis de Lión would become a member of the Guatemala's Workers Party, an action that cost him his life in 1984. Nevertheless, as these Kaqchikel authors show in their literary works, revolution for Indigenous peoples represents "a necessary process to dismantle

the racist privileges in the economic, social and political spheres that benefited a minority that self-identified as ladino" (Forster 2012, 21).

As the second guerrilla cycle got under way, however, the Guatemalan
state began to adopt new military strategies to respond to the growing
Indigenous support for the opposition. According to Marta Elena Casaús
Arzú, from 1978 to 1984

> an organic crisis emanated that saw a void in power since there was
> a political tension between the local oligarchy for hegemony, while
> at the same time there was a massive incorporation of Maya
> peoples to different forms of political struggle and social vindica-
> tion. On top of this, we had a deep economic crisis due to the
> exhaustion of the agro-export model, which led to an economic
> recession that provoked aggressive and virulent reactions by the
> Guatemalan elite. (1998, 36)

The prominent and increased Indigenous participation in the revolutionary process and in movements of peaceful dissent, like the ones spearheaded by the Tojil Indian Movement and the Committee of Peasant Unity
(CUC), generated profound anxiety among Guatemalan elites and in the
nation-state governed by military dictators like Romeo Lucas García, Óscar
Humberto Mejía Victores, and Efraín Ríos Montt—particularly because
in Guatemala, Indigenous peoples make up the majority. The peaceful
march led by the CUC in Guatemala City on May 1, 1978, filled the streets
with thousands of Indigenous peasants. This event certainly provoked
uneasiness and concern in the hegemonic sectors: the CUC and other social
movements represented a threat to their political and economic interests
that needed to be neutralized. During this period, the nation-state, with
economic and logistical support from the United States and Guatemalan
elites, put into practice Maoist military and despotic strategies of "taking
the water away from the fish." In the terms of that metaphor, the nation-state
aimed to destroy the communities (the water) that supposedly supported
the insurgency (the fish) and, in this way, eliminate popular support for
the guerrillas who sought to "destroy" the state.

The Guatemalan Army focused its efforts on the rural parts of the country, which were mostly inhabited by Maya peoples and where the insurgency was largely being generated. Its military incursions were justified by
the logic that "Indians" were illiterate, stupid, and extremely poor, which

meant that they would be easily manipulated to join the revolutionary movement once the guerrilla groups introduced their discourse of class struggle and ending oppression. To prevent this mobilization from happening, the army leaders argued, future "communists" had to be eliminated. Some soldiers thus shared accounts of how they were given orders by their superiors to kill everyone, because "practically all of them were part of the guerrilla" (qtd. in Drouin 2011, 42). Another soldier indicated that the army's intention was to "kill even the seeds" (43). This military campaign, operating under a logic of elimination, began in the Panzos region, in Alta Verapaz, toward the end of 1978 when the army and landowners assassinated more than fifty Q'eq'chi women, men, and children. As was mentioned in chapter 1, in that same year, in the Rabinal region, more than four hundred Achi Maya people, who refused to relocate to allow for the construction of the Chixoy hydroelectric dam, were kidnapped, raped, and massacred by paramilitary and military officials. In January 1980, Indigenous members of CUC peacefully occupied the Spanish Embassy to denounce the government's repression of Maya peasants in the highlands. The response of the Romeo Lucas García's (1978–1982) military dictatorship was to bomb the embassy. Of the thirty-eight people who occupied the premises, only Máximo Cajal, the Spanish ambassador, survived that terrible military incursion.

The military strategies later turned into state terrorism and genocidal campaigns that found their cruelest dimension between 1982 and 1983 under the presidency of General Efraín Ríos Montt. When the general came into power, he implemented his military campaign nicknamed "beans and bullets," in which he sought to use poverty and misery as a political strategy to gain support in Indigenous communities. He gave people the choice of food (beans) or death (bullets)—that is, if you support the army, you would live and get food, but lack of support meant you were part of the opposition, which meant death. Ríos Montt's military incursions took place in areas like the "Ixil Triangle" in Nebaj, in the Quiché region, and various parts of Sololá. His military operations literally erased from Guatemala's geographic map more than four hundred Indigenous communities and resulted in a death toll of over seventy thousand people. Thousands of others were forcibly displaced and driven into exile.[1]

This is the social and historical context that serves as a referent for the second moment of Maya literary insurgency in contemporary Iximulew. In this chapter, I focus on the following literary works: *The Animal Gathering*

(1990) by K'iche' Maya poet Humberto Ak'abal; *Sculpted Stones / Piedras labradas* (1995) by Pop'ti Maya author Victor Montejo; and *The Dry Season: Q'Anjob'al Maya Poems* (2001) by Q'anjob'al Maya writer Gaspar Pedro González.[2] In addition to these authors' poetic works, I also address their essayistic textual production. Whereas the works of Kaqchikel authors Morales Santos and Lión articulate an Indigeneity that engaged with the socialist discourse and politics of the Left at the time, in this second moment of literary insurgency we see a different literary and ideological modality that distances itself from the Left to instead explore the vindication of Maya cultural identity within the context of the genocide. The poetic works I analyze develop a poetics that aims to authorize and give agency to Maya languages and Indigenous cultural specificities. With the use of Maya languages and the publication of bilingual editions, the Maya authors in this second literary wave propose a resistance to the Guatemalan state's colonial logic of elimination through literary forms that often do not use metaphor or symbolism. Rather than focusing on aesthetics, these authors, using a straightforward, vernacular language, seem to be primarily interested in expressing a message about Maya political vindication that foregrounds the importance of Maya languages as capable of articulating a literary aesthetics, which in turn asserts an intellectual and political self-determination. These bilingual poetic works challenge the hegemonic social context in which kaxlan tzij / Spanish is the dominant language. We also see songs to Nature, animals, and the ancestral material culture, as well as an exaltation of linguistic and cultural specificities, such as Mayan weaving and dress. These literary proposals make sense because these authors are responding to the fratricidal experience that Maya peoples faced between 1978 and 1984. These literary works operate as a cultural practice of "resurrection": the authors' poetics not only diagnose the reality that Maya peoples experience in Iximulew under state terrorism but also, through the use of "strategic essentialism" (Spivak 1996), seek to resurrect, restore, and dignify all the Maya cultural elements that the nation-state has sought to eliminate with its counterinsurgent military incursions.

Before proceeding to analyze the poetic works by Ak'abal, Montejo, and González, it is important to briefly discuss some literary and cultural Maya precedents in the struggle for Maya linguistic and literary rights in Iximulew. K'iche' Maya linguist Adrián Inés Chávez (1904–1987) is considered by many as "the intellectual father of the current ideas of Pan-Mayanism" (Fischer and Brown 1996, 57). In 1945, Chávez was a keen follower of then-president Juan José Arévalo, who served from 1945 to 1951, and of his "spiritual socialism." In that year, Chávez organized a gathering with Indigenous teachers in the region of Cobán, Alta Verapaz, with the objective of developing a strategy to standardize Maya languages. Four years later, he organized the First National Linguistic Congress, which was followed by the opening of the Academy of the K'iche' Maya Language in Quetzaltenango. Chávez became one of the first Maya intellectuals to support a Maya linguistic policy. He traveled to many regions in Iximulew to offer workshops about Maya history and culture as well as language rights. Later, in 1978, he published a bilingual K'iche' Maya / Spanish version of the sacred text the *Popol Wuj*, which he titled *El Pop Wuj: Poema mito histórico Ki-ché* (The Pop Wuj: Mythic-Historic K'iche' Maya Poem). The book used the standardized version of the K'iche' Maya language that Chávez developed.[3]

K'iche' writer Luis Enrique Sam Colop (1955–2011), much like Chávez, was a pioneer in this second wave of Indigenous literary insurgency and a champion of K'iche' Maya linguistic rights. Sam Colop started his literary career as a member of the collective Grupo Editorial, RIN-78 (Editorial Group, RIN-78) created by the writer Max Araujo in response to the counterinsurgency campaigns carried out by the regime of General Lucas García.[4] In addition to Sam Colop and Araujo, the collective also included non-Indigenous writers such as Luz Méndez de la Vega, Mario Alberto Carrera, Carlos García Escobar, Carmen Matute, and Dante Liano; in fact, Sam Colop was the only Indigenous writer in the group. The majority of the collective's members were university students at Rafael Landívar University, and they routinely met there to read, exchange, and comment on their literary texts. While working toward his law degree, which he completed in 1983, Sam Colop experimented with writing poetry and short stories. Through RIN-78 the K'iche' Maya author published his first two books, *Versos sin refugio* (Verses without a Home, 1980) and *La copa y la raíz* (The Cup and the Root, 1979). These two books are informed by social realism and testimonial and vernacular poetics, similar to the ones used by his contemporaries Ak'abal, Montejo, and González. What is significant about Sam Colop is that he promoted the publication of K'iche' Maya / Spanish editions of his works to encourage the use of and give agency to Maya languages, as Chávez had earlier suggested with his publication of the *Popol Wuj*.

Sam Colop later left the RIN-78 collective and became a fervent activist for Maya rights. He developed a friendship with Barbara and Denis Tedlock, professors of anthropology and literature at SUNY-Albany, and they invited him to pursue graduate studies at that university. There, with the Tedlocks as his dissertation advisers, Sam Colop completed his PhD in anthropology and linguistics, writing a dissertation titled "Mayan Poetics" in 1994. In it, the author discusses the literary "parallelism" that emerges from Maya textual production in both the colonial and contemporary periods. He discusses the *Popol Wuj*, as well as other Maya texts that include *The Rabinal Achi'*, Calixta Gabriel Xiquin's poetry, and the K'iche' Maya oral tradition from Cantel—his own native community—and Momostenango. Building on the conclusions about parallelism he developed in his dissertation and his critical approach that challenged other translations of the *Popol Wuj*, the K'iche' Maya author developed a new translation of and critical approach to the K'iche' Maya sacred text. In 1999, he published the "poetic version" of the *Popol Wuj*, using the standardized K'iche' Maya language proposed by the Academy of the Maya Languages in Guatemala. This version has become obligatory reading and a reference for the contemporary Maya intelligentsia.[5]

As the Indigenous movement in Iximulew gained increasing prominence toward the end of the 1980s and beginning of the 1990s, Sam Colop became a major cultural figure. Nonetheless, it was not his literary production that allowed him to obtain national recognition. It was through his translation of the *Popol Wuj*; his essay, "Jub'aqtun omay kuchum k'aslemal / Cinco siglos de encubrimiento" (published in English as "The Discourse of Concealment and 1992" [in Fischer and Brown 1996]), and his weekly newspaper column, "Ucha' xiq'" (His Saying), in the national newspaper *Prensa Libre* (Free Press)[6] that the K'iche' Maya author became an influence for other writers and Maya intellectuals during this period, including Ak'abal, with whom he developed a close friendship. Furthermore, Sam Colop's work, similar to Chávez's and Luis de Lión's activism, became a praxis. In the 1990s, he and his partner, the K'iche' Maya anthropologist Irma Otzoy,[7] founded the Maya Foundation for the Study and Professionalization of Young People in Guatemala, or FEPMaya. This organization offers academic fellowships to Maya students who wish to attend college in various regions in Iximulew. As of today, more than fifty Indigenous students have greatly benefited from this program.[8] Sam Colop, unfortunately, passed away in 2011, but he left an important legacy: the revitalization of the literary, linguistic, and political Maya movement in Iximulew.

Kaqchikel activist, writer, and spiritual guide Calixta Gabriel Xiquín, who began to publish her work in 1978 in the newspaper *El imparcial* (The Impartial) in Guatemala, was another important cultural and political figure in the generation of Maya writers that emerged toward the end of the 1970s. Xiquín had taken classes at the University of San Carlos de Guatemala with the ladino writer Adolfo Méndes Vides, who was a "critical mentor in helping Xiquín improve her writing in Castilian and in Kaqchikel" (Arias 2017, 70). Many of her poems would later be published in national and international literary anthologies such as *Ixok Amar-Go: Poesía de mujeres centroamericanas por la paz / Central American Women's Poetry for Peace* (Anglesey 1987) and *Voices from Silence: Guatemalan Literature of Resistance* (Zimmerman and Rojas 1998). During the armed conflict, the Guatemalan Army attacked Xiquín's community, the town Hacienda Vieja (Old Farm) in the San José Poaquil region, in Chimaltenango. Three of her brothers were kidnapped and later assassinated. The Kaqchikel Maya writer then left the country and went into exile in California, where she lived between 1981 and 1988. Her first book of poetry, *Hueso de la tierra / The Earth's Bone* (1996), was published under the pen name Caly Domitila Canek in a trilingual Spanish/English/Kaqchikel edition. It offers a testimony to that fratricidal experience and her exile. Under that same pen name, Xiquin published several essays in which she denounces the genocide in Iximulew and vows to fight for the human and political rights of Maya women. One of these essays is "Guatemala: Women's Participation in Maya History" (1990). In 2002, she published her second book of poetry, *Tejiendo los sucesos en el tiempo / Weaving Events in Time*, with Yax Te' Press,[9] and in 2008, she published an essay on Maya spirituality titled *La cosmovisión maya y las mujeres: Aportes desde el punto de vista de una ajq'il* (The Maya Cosmovision and Women: An Ajq'il's [Spiritual Guide] Perspective).[10]

In 1983, with the publication of *I, Rigoberta Menchú, an Indian Woman in Guatemala*, narrated by Rigoberta Menchú and transcribed by Venezuelan anthropologist Elizabeth Burgos, the Indigenous voice in Abiayala acquired wider prominence and cultural and political authority: this testimonial account sparked a great interest in hearing the Indigenous voice through Indigenous literatures. Many nongovernmental organizations began to provide financial support for the publication of works by Maya authors that complemented Menchú's political vindication of Maya peoples' cultural and linguistic rights and her denunciations of racism and human rights violations in Iximulew. Menchú, as is well known, was the daughter of Vicente Menchú, who was one of the founders of the CUC organization and was among those killed in the previously mentioned attacks on the Spanish Embassy in 1980. His family was subsequently harassed and perse-cuted by the Guatemalan government. Rigoberta Menchú's mother Juana Tum and her younger brother Petrocinio were kidnapped, tortured, and assassinated by the Guatemalan Army. Two of her sisters "went to the mountains. They joined the armed struggle" (Menchú, Miná, and Liano 1998, 171–72), while Menchú went into exile in Chiapas, Mexico. With the help of Bishop "Tatic" Samuel Ruíz—who in 1994 became a mediator in the armed conflict between the Zapatista Army of National Liberation (EZLN) and the Mexican government[11]—she embarked on an extensive public campaign to denounce the genocide in Guatemala. Menchú traveled to various parts of Mexico, offering public talks about her own experience as a survivor of the war and appearing in newspapers and TV news programs denouncing human rights violations in Guatemala. She soon became a major voice and spokesperson for Indigenous peoples. Her public activism during this period brought Menchú to Paris where she met Elizabeth Bur-gos. Together, they produced what would later become *I, Rigoberta Menchú, an Indian Woman in Guatemala*. The French newspaper *Le Monde* had ini-tially assigned Burgos the task of writing a newspaper article about the war in Guatemala. She decided to interview a war survivor, and members of the Guerrilla Army of the Poor in Guatemala suggested she talk to Menchú. The charisma and eloquence that Menchú displayed in their conversa-tions and the stories she told about Maya culture and spirituality, as well as her own life experiences, motivated Burgos to write more than a newspa-per article. She collected and transcribed all the recorded conversations with Menchú and realized she had enough material to produce an entire book. After putting together and editing the texts, Burgos submitted the manuscript to the prestigious Casa de las Americas Literary Prize in Cuba. In 1983, the book won under the "testimonio" category. From there, the book became a bestseller and a cultural phenomenon, obtaining global recognition after it was translated into many languages. Once it was trans-lated into English, for example, the book became required reading in vari-ous high schools in the United States. Many instructors at the university level in departments of literature, anthropology, and English also assigned the book in discussions of issues of Indigeneity in the Americas. Conse-quently, charges were made against Menchú that she included lies in her text, which generated a number of debates and controversies about the genre of *testimonio,* human rights, and the politics of truth.[12] Despite all the debates and controversies surrounding the book, no one can take away its significance in alerting various national and international political circles to the harms to Indigenous rights in Abiayala. Indeed, the book became a threat to U.S. foreign policy in various countries in Latin America.

Menchú's *testimonio* emerged at a time when conservatives and the Right were trying to discredit human rights organizations around the world, especially those that denounced U.S. economic and military assistance to armies and paramilitary groups in Latin America during the "dirty wars," such as the fight against the Contras in Nicaragua (Arias 2001, 6; Cook-Lynn 2000, 85–86). Ronald Reagan was U.S. president during this time (1981–1989). The Republican administration and its supporters legitimated this complicity by suggesting that the Central American insurgents were "Communist agitators" who were part of a global conspiracy that threatened "Western democracy." Menchú's testimonio contradicted these claims, denouncing the local militias that were murdering innocent people in the name of "freedom" and "democracy," enlightening international opinion on the consequences and injustices of these civil wars that were taking place throughout Latin America, particularly the Guatemalan one. The decision of the government to negotiate with the guerrillas was, in large part, a result of this successful moral campaign by those involved in producing Menchú's text. The impact of Menchú's work in raising public consciousness was recognized by her being awarded the Nobel Peace Prize in 1992, which, in turn, motivated her to continue her struggle for Indigenous human rights in Abiayala. Her testimonio and activism changed the ways in which the global public thinks about the Indigenous world, transforming discussions of testimonial narratives and cultural and postcolonial studies.[13]

Some, like anthropologist Kay Warren, have criticized Menchú's testimonio, arguing that the book "has over-shadowed the writings of Mayanists living in exile, who have composed powerful personal testimonies, worked with Maya refugees in Chiapas and advocated cultural revitalization rather than revolution. In the post–Cold War era, with the transition to civilian governments and the signing of the peace accords, it is particularly important to hear other voices and grammars of dissent" (1998, 116–17). In her critique Warren is referring particularly to the "silencing" of Victor Montejo's testimonial account, *Testimony: Death of a Guatemalan Village*

(1987), and his work on the ground with Maya communities in Chiapas. Montejo himself, at one point, also expressed his concern about how Menchú's testimonial account was receiving the lion's share of attention by critics.[14] Both Warren and Montejo call on critics to "listen" to Maya voices other than Menchú's.[15] Nonetheless, for better or worse, no one can dispute the immense value of Menchú's testimonial account: her prominence in the fight for Indigenous rights and the many debates that emanated from *I, Rigoberta Menchú* have strengthened the Indigenous rights movements in the continent, as well as many literary voices in Iximulew and the rest of Abiayala.[16]

Considering this historical context, as well as the tradition of testimonial writing in the region that has introduced the Maya world to a wider readership, especially non-Indigenous ones, what do the literary works of Ak'abal, Montejo, and González tell us about the contemporary Maya experience? What narratives of Maya "insurrection" do they propose to their readers? How do these authors and their works respond to the fratricidal experience they witnessed and, in many cases, physically experienced themselves? In the rest of the chapter, I explore some of the responses to these questions. I begin by critically analyzing Humberto Ak'abal's work and then move on to the poetic works by Gaspar Pedro González and Victor Montejo. These literary works were written in a context marked by a racism that became "a powerful state mechanism; a technology of power in which the state feels that it possesses the privilege and right to determine who must live or die. They give themselves the right to kill or eliminate the Other in the name of sovereignty" (Casaús Arzú 1998, 17). Within the context of the indiscriminate military counterinsurgency campaigns, I argue that Maya authors like Ak'abal, Montejo, and González developed a "strategic essentialism" (Spivak 1988, 1996) that uses literature to construct an Indigenous worldview that, though some may consider its symbolic representation to be "fundamentalist" or "absolutist," tells the Guatemalan state that it has failed in its attempt to eliminate the Maya peoples and their cultures. Indeed, these Maya authors' works follow a series of paths through complex Indigenous temporalities that express the need to reactivate and dignify the ancestral values that characterize Maya cultures. They suggest that, by doing so, we will be able to confront the state's genocidal campaigns and our own survival within Western modernity.

My reading of these texts displays ambivalence and even contradiction: I both express my profound admiration for these writers and critically analyze their writings, pointing out some of the shortcomings I see in the literary proposals surrounding ideas of Mayaness. Thus, although I offer a reading that proposes an understanding of this textual literary production based on the context under which it emerges and to which it responds, these authors—in their celebration of our spiritual values and our linguistic and cultural specificities—unconsciously penalize Indigenous identities that may not fit within the cultural Maya frameworks they propose. Hence, I aim to expand on our understanding of Maya identity so it may also account for the heterogeneity of Indigeneity in various social and political contexts; that is, Mayaness is not limited to the rural regions they imagine but rather expands to other urban and transnational realms.

Humberto Ak'abal's *The Animal Gathering:*
The Maya Environmental Imagination

Humberto Ak'abal was born in 1952 in Momostenango, Totonicapán. He was a native speaker of K'iche' Maya; his last name Ak'abal not only means "dawning"—the demarcation between darkness and sunlight—but also is one of the names of the days in the Maya calendar. Ak'abal took this meaning of his last name and its association to the Maya calendar very seriously. Indeed, Ak'abal developed an organic relationship between Nature and the cosmos, and it is from this organic relationship that he extracted his communicative creative and poetic force to produce his art, a worldview that he wants to share with his readers. In an interview, he said, "Most of my poetry has to do with Nature in general because that is practically my own world. I have grown up in Nature, and my grandparents taught me to be in harmony with it, and so I'm inserted in Nature . . . the universe that permeates my poetry is totally natural, and it goes with me wherever I go" (Ak'abal and Ollé 2004, 220). He added that his grandparents and great-grandparents were "Aj' k'amal b'e," or spiritual guides. From them he learned to "read the physical phenomena, the language of nature, the flash of lightning, thunderstorms, the wind" (211), elements that he frequently invokes in his poetic works. In addition to learning these important lessons from his family, his inclination toward literature ironically stemmed from his working as a garbage collector in Guatemala City. In the garbage cans he emptied, he found lots of books that he would later take home to read. These books opened up many imaginary worlds to him that helped him explore and expand his own imagination. Ak'abal consequently began writing, beginning a long and prolific career that came to an end when he passed away in January 2019.

Ak'abal left behind a large body of work—more than thirty books of poetry and short stories—that has made him the most famous Maya poet from Iximulew. His literary works have been translated into many languages, including English, French, German, Italian, Portuguese, Arabic, Hungarian, Scottish, and Hebrew. He has been invited to read his poetry at many universities and cultural centers in Europe, Asia, and Abiayala. In addition, Ak'abal received multiple prestigious literary awards, including the International Poetry Award, the Blaise Cendrars Poetry Award from Sweden (1997), the Continental Award, America's Song given by UNESCO in Mexico (1998), the International Pier Paolo Pasolini Poetry Award from Rome, Italy (2004), and the Chevalier de L'Ordre des Arts et des Lettres from the French government (2005). In 2003, the K'iche' Maya author was honored with Guatemala's Miguel Ángel Asturias National Prize in Literature but he declined it, because he believed that the award represented racism toward Maya peoples. Asturias, a ladino writer who wrote a good deal about Indigenous peoples, titled his 1923 master's thesis "The Indian as a Social Problem." It proposed a view of Indigenous peoples as biologically "inferior"; the Guatemalan state needed to save the degraded Indian by promoting European immigration, which would allow for racial mixing and so improve Indigenous peoples' existence. In a 2004 interview with Juan Carlos Lemus, the K'iche' Maya poet justified his decision to decline Guatemala's highest literary award: "I'll tell you the truth. When I read Miguel Ángel Asturias' thesis, *The Indian as a Social Problem,* it really hurt me. He, with that thesis, offended Indigenous peoples in Guatemala, and I am a part of those peoples; therefore, even though it may have a lot of merit, I don't feel honored in being awarded a literary prize named after the Nobel Prize winner. In many ways, that thesis was hurtful, at least for me it was."

Yet Ak'abal remains an indispensable referent in contemporary Indigenous literatures. He has perhaps exerted the most influence on other Indigenous writers in Iximulew, as becomes evident when we discuss the works of Rosa Chávez (K'iche'-Kaqchikel) and Sabino Esteban Francisco (Q'anjob'al) in the next chapter, and Daniel Caño (Q'anjob'al) below.

Ak'abal began his prolific literary career with *El animalero* (*The Animal Gathering,* 1990), the book that I discuss in this section. After this book, the K'iche' Maya author published *Guardián de la caída de agua* (The

Guardian of the Waterfall, 1993), which sold a lot of copies internationally. He then published *Hojas del árbol pajarero* (Leaves from the Bird Tree, 1995) and *Retoño salvaje* (Wild Sprout, 1997). In 1996, the author published a K'iche' Maya / Spanish anthology, *Ajkem Tzij / Tejedor de palabras* (Weaver of Words, 1996a), whose 2,000 copies sold quickly. In 1998, a second edition of this poetry book was published, sponsored by UNESCO, and as with the first edition, it became an international success. These publications were later followed by other poetry collections that include *Lluvia de luna en la cipresalada* (The Moon's Rain over the Cypress Salad, 1996c), *Hojas, solo hojas* (Leaves, Just Leaves, 1996b) and *Los cinco puntos cardinales* (The Five Cardinal Points, 1998). Moreover, Ak'abal's literary works are included in the state educational curriculum.

In 1990, when he was thirty-eight years old, *Animal Gathering* was published by the Ministry of Culture and Sports' editorial house and with the support of Guatemalan poet Luis Alfredo Arango.[17] The book had an unexpected success and, at the time, gave modest fame to Ak'abal; it has since gone through five editions. Published entirely in Spanish, this book of poetry contains two parts: "The Animal Gathering" (which I discuss in this section) and "Xalolilo lelele, A Pastoral Song." Ak'abal recounted that initially he wanted to publish the book in K'iche' Maya and Spanish, but the response of the editors was, " 'Why publish it in K'iche'? No one will read it.' I had to accept—he asserts—that the book got published only in Spanish" (Ak'abal and Ollé 2004, 213). The bilingual edition, *Ajyuq' / El animalero*, did not appear until 2004 when Cholsamaj, an editorial house run by Mayas in Iximulew, invited Ak'abal to produce a K'iche' translation of his celebrated book.[18] In 2008, Piedra Santa, another publisher in Guatemala, published an English/Spanish version that has two epilogues, one written by Luis Alfredo Arango and titled "The World of Humberto Ak'abal," which appeared in the first edition, and another by the critic Carlos Illescas titled "Humberto Ak'abal and the Doctrine of Nature." In the first epilogue, Arango states that the K'iche' Maya poet "attempts to recover the simple things that surrounded his difficult childhood, recalling them in his poems" (115). For his part, Illescas affirms that, through Ak'abal's revealing words, "color is fire or earth or nostalgia for what is lost, for what is found in a world always newly discovered by a poet who is color under his human garment" (117). These affirmations highlight and celebrate Ak'abal's environmental imagination that is organically tied to his own figurative ethics, so prominent in his literary works.

In this section, I argue that in its invocation of animals, "Animal Gathering" offers a critique of Western modernity and, more specifically, the Maya genocide in Guatemala. The destruction of the Indigenous worlds in Abiayala—Ak'abal's work suggests—has generated a profound crisis in humanity that has come to undermine our original relationship with animals, Mother Nature, and the planet as a whole; this crisis manifests itself today with climate change. Indeed, with European colonization's introduction of mercantilist logics to our hemisphere, all those traditions that previously mediated between humans and Nature were broken, leading us to the "capitolocene" (Moore 2017).[19] Ak'abal's poetry book expresses these concerns through the existential crisis of the poetic voice who, once he encounters the animals invoked, aims to reconnect with them, the natural world, and his ancestral origins. In this sense, the book proposes to recover and restore ancestral elements that characterize Maya identity within a world that through military incursions in the highlands, policies of assimilation, and the adoption of mercantilist values seeks to eliminate Indigenous peoples.

Ak'abal's "The Animal Gathering" includes fourteen artistic images or poems written in free verse. The compositions have as protagonists bats, crickets, buzzards, moths, ants, bees, hermit thrushes, roosters, blue jays, mourning doves, fireflies, ch'iw (chicks), owls, and a female coyote. These animals can be divided into three groups—birds, insects, and mammals—and they can be associated with the sky and earth, where they move. The poetic voice describes activities of these animals using the third-person perspective except in three poems—"Buzzard," "Blue Jay," and "Hermit Thrush"—where the second person is used to address these animals (I return to this point later). The book is structured as if the poetic voice were walking through his community, encountering the various animals, and reflecting on their daily activities in their natural habitats: some are active at night and others during the day. At night, for example, the narrator finds the bats, who are on their heads "when the village is on its feet" and, at the same time, are on their feet "when the village is on its head"; "Crickets" describes the "most inept musicians" who, night after night, for a long time, repeat the same old song. In the darkest night, "like a Nixtamal pot," we also find "The Owls," whose songs, though usually associated with death, on this particular night announce "the love song of the owls" (34). During the day, the narrator describes the activities of insects in "The Ants": they always walk in a hurry, carrying their food (18). In

"The Bees," these insects are "the Godmothers of the flowers; the ones that walk with their legs covered in pollen" and "Pause only / to drop little turds / and go back to their banter" (20). During the day we also hear the "Blue Jay," who, during the maize harvest, flies throughout the fields, "Leaping and flying / over stubbled fields, / over furrows" (26) to pick up and swallow each kernel—"Kernel fallen, kernel gathered . . . Down the hatch" (26). Or the "Mourning Dove," whose song stretches alongside the sunlight to untangle "bindweeds, / slips through the vines, / sprinkles eyes on the foliage / and with the softness of moss / caresses the nest" (28). The path of the poetic voice returns the reader to the night again with the poem "The Coyota," in which a boy shepherd scares away a female coyote that is getting close to a sheep corral. The boy's screams, figuratively associated to a "bull's bellow," scares away the coyote who, after her failed attempt, runs away toward the hills.

Aesthetically, Ak'abal uses various literary devices, including personification, parallelism, couplets, and chiasmus; for example, in "Bats" and "The Fireflies,"

When the village is on its feet
the bats are on their heads,
when the village is on its head
the bats are on their feet. (10)

or

The fireflies
are stars descended from the sky
and the stars are fireflies
that could not descend. (30)

As we can see, the stanza from "Bats" displays the metrical structure *abba* in which the verses are divided into eight hemistiches separated by four caesuras. Both this stanza and the one from "Fireflies" display chiasmus as a discursive strategy. These literary devices, as Luis Enrique Sam Colop, Allen Christenson, and Denis Tedlock have shown, are characteristic of the pre-Colombian Maya literatures that certainly influenced Ak'abal. The use of chiasmus, in particular, can be associated with the Maya literary tradition. In his study of chiasmus in Maya texts from the sixteenth century, including the *Popol Wuj*, *The Totonicapán Title*, and *The Rabinal Achi*, Christenson shows how much of this Maya textual production is written like a long string of words and phrases, without any intent of establishing thoughts organized by logical phrases or sentences. Instead, these books depend much more on "parallel arrangements of words and concepts to structure their ideas and assist the flow of the narrative" than on logic (2012, 318–19). According to Christenson, chiasms are used in these works as mnemonic devices to facilitate the listeners' recall of certain information. Particularly in certain stanzas, Ak'abal's literary constructions seem to have similar purposes to those of his Maya ancestors who wrote the texts studied by Christenson.

"The Animal Gathering" is also characterized by its poetics of brevity; most are poems of three, four, or five lines that each have four or five syllables, written in the vernacular or in colloquial, simplified language. According to Ak'abal, his poetics of brevity is intentional in order to enable the reader to participate in the poem, "and if something is liked, the poem can be easily memorized" (Montenegro 2002). "Vulture" is a good example: the entire poem reads, "Vulture: / dead man's coffin, / flying tomb; / all you lack is an epitaph" (14). This short poem displays parallelism but lacks complex and aesthetic language. The poem seems more like a literary snapshot that expresses a reflection about death, personified by the vulture ("dead man's coffin"). We can conclude that, with his poetics of brevity and use of literary devices like chiasmus and parallelism, Ak'abal wants his readers to participate by remembering, interpreting, and imagining the surroundings and contexts invoked by the narrator. Some Guatemalan critics like Mario Monteforte Toledo (2004, 13) and Mario Roberto Morales (1999, 254) suggest that Ak'abal's poetics of brevity resembles the Japanese art of *haiku*. It is important to note that Ak'abal is not the only poet employing a poetics of brevity or the only one to emulate ancestral Maya literary traditions in Mesoamerica. Kaqchikel authors like Francisco Morales Santos and Luis de Lión also experimented with these literary modalities, as seen in their respective poems, "Razón del heroismo" (The Reason for Heroism) and "Epitaph." The first of these poems states, "What made us go in search for death / if not the blind desire for life?" (Morales Santos 2008, 116), and "Why does death insist in vainly killing life, if the most humble seed breaks the strongest stone?" (qtd. in Valle-Escalante 2010, 47).

In "The Animal Gathering," Ak'abal underscores the importance of anthropomorphic and animistic traditions as constitutive of Indigenous cultures and, in this case, of Mesoamerican peoples. In contrast to other literary representations of animals in the textual production of this region, however, Ak'abal's animals are characterized by smallness. Many of them, like termites, crickets, and ants, often go unnoticed because they are so tiny. These small animals do not generate the aesthetic interest, respect, or admiration that other larger animals may evoke. Ak'abal's animals do not express the authority of, say, a lion, a tiger, or an eagle, animals that are usually associated with courage, strength, and power, which often makes them attractive as prey. Ak'abal's animals are not "domestic" animals, like dogs or cats that are characterized as loyal and capable of being good human companions. Neither are they ornamental birds like canaries or parrots that are frequently found in cages, decorating homes, or keeping their owners company. In sum, the majority of the animals in Ak'abal's poetry book do not represent an immediate aesthetic interest. Rather, the majority of them can be categorized as having freedom precisely because of their marginal condition or for being "invisible"; these are animals that perform their daily activities without anyone bothering them.

Yet some of the animals represented by the K'iche' Maya poet, like owls, ants, and bats, can be associated with animals represented in other Mesoamerican literary traditions, such as the *Popol Wuj* or the Aztec "Myth of the Five Suns." Ak'abal, however, does not seem interested in developing explicit connections. In the Mesoamerican literary traditions from the colonial period, personification was often used to assign essential meaning to the animals invoked. In the *Popol Wuj*, for example, a bat decapitates Hunahpu in Xib'alb'a (the Maya underworld). A pumpkin later replaces Hunahpu's head. The owl that initially serves as a messenger for the Lords of Death from Xib'alb'a later turns on them by helping save the life of the Princess Ixquik', the mother of the hero twins. The owl tricks the Lords of Death into believing that Ixquik' has died by showing them the heart of a dead deer. There is also a mosquito that helps Hunahpu and Xbalanque guess the names of the Lords of Xib'alb'a. A rat tells the divine twins where they can find the attire their parents used to wear to play the Maya ballgame. To start off the third creation of humanity attempted by the gods, the dogs lead the destruction of the wooden people who did not express their gratitude to the deities. In the Mexica tradition, after Quetzalcoatl (the Plumed Serpent, creator God) creates humanity in Mictlan (the place of the dead), the ants guide the recently created humans to the deposits of maize so they can eat. In these Maya and Mexica creation narratives, personification is used to create a powerful symbolic connection between humans and the "more than humans" (Abram 2013). There is an intrinsic relation between these beings manifested through mutual exchanges that are of equal social importance: humans and animals depend on one another in their daily lives and activities. The ethicist Peter Singer makes a similar argument that humans and the more than humans—"animals"—are equivalent and that "the ethical principle on which human equality rests requires us to extend equal considerations to animals because animals, like humans, have interests, pains and pleasures" (qtd. in Oliver 2009, 28).

Nevertheless, in the animal world invoked by Ak'abal—in contrast to other literary traditions in Mesoamerica that show a direct and imbricated connection between the human and more-than-human world (for example, Nahualism[20])—there is a demarcated distance between humans and animals. The poetic voice thus observes or hears the activities of the animals in their respective habitats without having a close relationship with them. For example, he hears the crickets' songs and observes the "termites" that "make tiny holes" (16). In some cases, their activities even provoke irritation, as do the songs of the crickets. The poetic voice also does not coexist or exchange experiences with the animals. As previously mentioned, it is only in poems like "Vulture" and "Hermit Thrush" that the reader sees a change in the perspective of the poetic voice: it moves from the third to the second person. In those poems, the narrator speaks to the animals. It tells the vulture "all you lack is an epitaph" (14) and the hermit thrush that "your song / is a rush of little stones / dropping into a spring" (22). Yet Ak'abal's poetry does not allow the vulture and hermit thrush to respond to the narrator. The absence of responses implicitly expresses a certain longing and nostalgia for a restored connection between the animal and human worlds.

The poet's journey throughout his community and his invocation of these animals reveal a quest to reconnect his subjectivity with those of the animals, as represented in the *Popol Wuj* and the "Myth of the Five Suns." It is no accident that, through his ecology of observation, Ak'abal registers the animals he invokes within a geographic and imaginative space distanced from any context associated with modernity, such as the city or cars. Instead, the narrator places them in the rural context, doing their daily activities, and so expresses a zoomorphic geography that displays the animals' habitat as a sacred place. In contrast to urban contexts—marked by chaos, noise, and uproar; a space intolerant of the activities of the animals described—Ak'abal imagines a world that is, to some extent, primordial. Ak'abal's nostalgia and yearning not only reveal our distancing from Mother Earth but also underscore our disconnection with animals, as is evident in "The Animal Gathering."

Continuing along this line of thinking, Ak'abal represents animals as the primary protagonists, which connects his works directly to the *Popol Wuj*. After creating the earth and the forests, the sacred K'iche' Maya text narrates how the gods go about peopling the earth: they proceed to create "the animals of the mountains, the guardians of the forest, and all that populate the mountains—the deer and the birds, the puma and the jaguar, the serpent and the rattlesnake, the pit viper and the guardian of the bushes" (Christenson 2007, 74). The creation of the earth and of animals precedes the consequent formation of the mud, wooden, and, finally, maize people. Ak'abal is familiar with the Maya worldview expressed through our sacred text and invokes it frequently in his work to highlight and activate the importance of Mother Earth and animals. In some poems, he invokes that relationship with a certain yearning, as in "Before": "Before, / so long ago / that the sun does not remember: / the Earth owned humanity. / Now, it is the inverse" (95). The poem implicitly references the *Popol Wuj* by reminding us how the heavens and the earth represented the very first creations of the Maya Gods. Like humanity and animals, they were also given life. Thus, by making reference to the Earth as owning humanity, because it preceded the creation of humans, the poetic voice points to humanity's dependence on the land for our survival—a knowledge that progress and modernity aim to invalidate. In other poems, Ak'abal also underscores humans' dependence on animals. In the poem "Over the Mat" (87), for example, the narrator remembers when "Sat over the mat, / on the kitchen's floor, / we would eat *tamalitos* ["corn tamale"] with salt / and drink hot coffee. / With us, the chicken, / the dogs and a pig." As becomes evident, the poem shows the harmonious coexistence between animals and humans in daily life.

By deriving his poetic creativity from the communicative force of Nature and the animals invoked, Ak'abal expresses a sentiment that is reminiscent of philosopher Kelly Oliver's (2009) interpretation of Jean Jacques Rousseau's *Discourse on Inequality* (1755). According to Oliver, Rousseau describes civilized man as the end result of an evolution from "savage hunter" to "barbarous shepherd" to "civilized peasant." In these progressive stages of "evolution," the civilized man slowly distances himself from all those elements that once constituted an existence based on a balanced relationship with Nature and animals. Such a relationship, under modernity, will later be considered "savage" and "uncivilized." Ak'abal, interestingly, seems to be conscious of the stages of "civilizational progress" described by Oliver. His composition "I Don't Know" (190) narrates the moment in which he leaves his village to go to the city, thus marking the time he stops "being a peasant" and becomes a "worker." The composition concludes, "I don't know if I progressed or moved backward." In developing these reflections about civilization, the K'iche' Maya poet underscores a marked distance between the primordial where we discover—following Friedrich Salomon Rothschild's approach to biosemiotics—that "our position that the history of subjectivity does not start with man, but that the human spirit was preceded by many preliminary states in the evolution of animals" (1962, 777). Hence Ak'abal highlights the importance of the ethical principle that demarcates our link and relationship with animals and Nature as counteracting "civilizing progress" and colonization. These later experiences, it is suggested, have disconnected us from our original spiritual values through the imposition of Western mercantilist logics.

Indeed, the Spanish invasion and consequent colonization turned our world upside down, forcibly imposing new Christian and Spanish social values that sought to erase our relationship with our own surroundings. In Iximulew, the fragmentation of our communities begins with the first Spanish invasion of the Alvarado brothers in 1524. Nevertheless, given that Ak'abal's book of poetry was published in 1990, we do not need to go that far into the past: we can also connect his work with Guatemala's shameful modern history and its implementation of state terrorism against Maya communities in the highlands of the country. When we take this context and its logic of elimination into consideration, we can better understand Ak'abal's objectives for "The Animal Gathering." In drawing the disconnect between humans and the nonhuman worlds, the K'iche' Maya poet makes the reader conscious of the destructive forces of capitalist globalized economic and cultural policies. Ak'abal invites us to reconnect to our millenary roots and to reactivate the social relationships with animals and the natural world that were interrupted by settler colonialism.

I can add here a perspective that complements Ak'abal's assumptions—that of Q'anjob'al poet Daniel Caño in his poem "Lost Sensibility" (2011):

The little boy speaks with his cat and dog,
he speaks with the butterflies, the bees,
the plants and flowers,
he speaks with the moon and the stars.

When he grows older
all of this seems ridiculous to him.

I ask myself:
How, when, and where
did he lose his sensibility? (47)

The question that closes the poem is powerful, and like "The Animal Gathering," it underscores how our ancestral values and spirituality, based on an organic and intrinsic relationship with "plants," "flowers," "the moon," "stars," and the "animals," like the "cat and the dog," have been interrupted, leading us to "lose" our original sensibility to the more-than-human worlds. Implicitly, "Lost Sensibility" references our distancing from Nature and animals, caused by the imposition of alien values: valuing material possessions over spirituality, placing more value on Western religions and education than on Indigenous culture, and so on. Both Caño's poem and Ak'abal's poetic works underscore the need to place renewed value on the human condition before modernity threatened it, so we can start processes of de-alienation like those in Francisco Morales Santos's works discussed in chapter 1.

Thus, Ak'abal expresses his desire to restore ancestral values: "If we could go back / to those times / when the land sang / with the men and women, / with the children and the elders" (18). In addition to restoring these values, he also suggests defending them against all odds. This is how we can interpret the poem "La Coyota" that closes "The Animal Gathering." As previously indicated, in this poem, a boy shepherd (an obvious alter ego of the K'iche' Maya poet) defends a flock of sheep against a female coyote that wants to eat them. Against this threat, "the young shepherd rises bravely, gulps down the night air / and with a guardian's power / blows through his horn, / sounding a bull's bellow, / menacing, defiant" (36). The young shepherd reminds us of the boy in Luis de Lión's *Poems from Water Volcano* who also develops a social consciousness about capitalist exploitation and decides to defend his ancestral territory.

In the introduction to their book *The Semiotics of Animal Representations*, Morten Tonnssen and Kadri Tüür write that "the manner in which we represent animals says a lot about who we are, or who we strive to be, and what we are conflicted about" (2014, 7). In invoking the animals in "The Animal Gathering," Ak'abal expresses his desire to have the freedom that has been denied to Indigenous peoples in Iximulew. The animals represented by Ak'abal are important to him because they operate without anyone bothering them: they are free to go about their daily activities in their own habitats without anyone intervening in their quotidian tasks. Ak'abal also expresses his desire for liberty in his book of poetry *Raqonchi'aj / El grito* (The Scream, 2004b), particularly in poems like "El estrecho" (The Stretch) in which the narrator discusses how he uses his time to do the tasks that have been given to him in life without "bothering / anyone"; "Libertad" (Freedom, 176), in which the poetic voice observes and envies birds—blackbirds, buzzards, and doves—"in full flight they shit" over cathedrals and palaces "with all their liberty" (176); and "Quisiera" (I Would Like, 158). The narrator concludes this last poem as follows: "How I would like to be a bird / and fly, fly, fly, / and sing, sing, sing, / and shit—with pleasure / on some people / and some things!" The metaphor of excrement invoked in these poems can be directly associated with the idea of freedom that the author longs for and, in many ways, envies, as exhibited by the animals he invokes in "The Animal Gathering." Thus, these poems implicitly suggest that the social context in which the poet develops his artistic poetic work is characterized by political repression, as the nation-state implements policies that aim to eliminate the native. Ak'abal, through his representation of animals, imagines a world fully autonomous and sovereign, where the freedom to be Indigenous, among other things, translates into not being afraid of one's Indigeneity. Rather, being Indigenous means being proud of our cultural and linguistic specificities, as well as of our right to activate and put into practice the original values that we have inherited from our ancestors, values that can help us restore our sovereignty.

Gaspar Pedro González and Victor Montejo: Mayaness and Strategic Essentialism

Let me now turn to the Maya literary representations developed by the Maya writers Gaspar Pedro González (Q'anjob'al) and Victor Montejo (Pop'ti'). In this section I analyze their respective poetry books, *The Dry*

Season: Qanjob'al Maya Poems and *Sculpted Stones / Piedras labradas*. In these books, these authors articulate a discursive relationship between the precolonial Maya past and the present both to legitimate a historical temporal continuity in the constitution of a Pan-Maya identity in Iximulew and to rebuild and dignify Indigenous historical and cultural memory within the context of the Guatemalan armed conflict. I compare their poetic representations of Mayaness to their essayistic works to demonstrate how such representations bear a striking resemblance to Indigenista or non-Indigenous cultural constructions of Indigeneity. In both poetry and essays I find idealized ideas of Mayaness associated with living in the rural world, speaking Indigenous languages, and wearing the Maya *traje* or dress that in turn consciously or unconsciously marginalize and obscure the political prominence and agency of Maya subjects in urban contexts. Yet, despite their efforts to affirm a Maya-specific locus of political enunciation and the pride of Indigenous peoples with a narrow view of "authentic" Indigeneity, I still find immense value in these literary constructions. I propose a decolonial interpretation that allows us to understand both their contributions and shortcomings. Indeed, when we read their works from the context of the Maya genocide and the perspective of "strategic essentialism" (Spivak 1988), we can better understand how these Maya authors respond to colonialism by emphasizing its failed attempt to eliminate Indigenous peoples.

As seen in a critical reading of Ak'abal's poetics, there is no doubt that one of the most important contributions of contemporary Maya textual production is that it effectively reconfigures and re-signifies our Indigenous historical memory in the present. We can interpret these efforts as a new stage in Indigenous struggles for self-determination. The poetic literary production of Gaspar Pedro González and Victor Montejo displays a desire to vindicate the Maya ancestral past in a historical present. Though the works by these poets differ, they represent the Maya experience similarly: both offer accounts of how colonialism operates and the urgent need to vindicate constitutive elements of Maya identity.

Gaspar Pedro González was born and raised in San Pedro Solomá, a town in Huehuetenango. He later moved to Guatemala City and obtained a bachelor's degree in education from Mariano Gálvez University. He then became a member of the Academy of Maya Languages in Guatemala and has been writing literature and essays since the 1970s. He completed the manuscript of his first novel, *A Mayan Life*, in 1978, but because of the political repression in the country at the time, he had to hide the text and wait until 1992 to publish it; first, in Spanish: *La otra cara: La vida de un maya*. The novel was later translated into English by Elaine Elliott as *A Mayan Life* and published in 1995. A year later, González published a bilingual Q'anjob'al Maya / Spanish edition of the novel *Sb'eyb'al jun naq Maya Qanjobal (La otra cara)*. (The title, though, can be translated as "The Life of a Q'anjob'al Maya.") This edition represents the first novel in a Maya language in Iximulew. González indicates that he chose to finally publish the novel in 1992 because of the active debates surrounding Indigenous popular resistance to celebrations marking "500 Years of the Discovery" of the "New World." This novel (and his literary works in general), according to González, responds to the prejudice and negative stereotypes that emerge from the Indigenista literary tradition, particularly *Men of Maize* ([1949] 1969) by Miguel Ángel Asturias. *A Mayan Life* aims "to distort these stereotypes, and present the Maya with their values, their anguish, their view of the world, and of mankind in that part of the world" ("In Our Own Words" 2006, 23). In addition to *A Mayan Life*, González has also published the novella-testimonio, *The Return of the Maya* (1998a, 1998b); the novel *The 13th B'aktun: A New Era* (2010); the books of poetry, *The Dry Season: Q'anjob'al Maya Poems* (2001) and *Xumakil / Botón en Flor / Budding* (2014), and the historical critical essay, *Kotz'ib': Nuestra literatura Maya* (Kotz'ib': Our Maya Literature, 1997).

Of particular interest to this discussion is *The Dry Season*, a book of poems that includes thirty-five compositions originally written and published in Q'anjob'al Maya and Spanish in 1998. The book was translated into English by R. McKenna Brown and published in a bilingual English/Q'anjob'al edition in 2001. The poems are written in free verse, and the author uses various literary devices, including personification ("The Word" and "The Hummingbird") and onomatopoeia ("The Chib'al" and "First Rain Storm"). For the most part, however, the reader is exposed to a testimonial language without many aesthetic literary conventions. The book, similar to the works of other Maya authors discussed, displays the strong influence of the *Popol Wuj*, Maya material culture and cosmogony. The majority of the poems are accompanied by the author's drawings and illustrations. For example, the poem "The Hummingbird" is set next to his drawing of the bird, and "The Calendar" is accompanied by a description of the twenty sacred days from the Maya calendar and their respective iconographic and hieroglyphic representations.

González's poems can be divided according to four themes. First, poems like "The Word," "The Mayas," "Maize," "The Calendar," "The Nawal," "The Hummingbird," "Worldview," "White Cities," "Over There," "Our Writing," "My World," and "The Oracle" elevate and dignify the constitutive elements that characterize Indigenous millenarian cultural identity in Iximulew. For example, in "The Word," which is the first poem in the book and serves as a preamble, the narrator invokes the figure of an ancestral Maya scribe—the "Old grandfather"—who in ancient times produced codices using Maya hieroglyphic writing: the words "with which you carved mountains of glyphs" and "with which you bound our history to stone" (3). Though that language remains alive in temples and ceramics, the poem suggests that the Spanish invasion halted the use of hieroglyphic writing. With the approval of the "Old grandfather," the narrator now must "gather up what's left" of the Word and rebuild it. Invoking memories and the influence of the Maya ancestors, the poem concludes, "to the beat of our drum / we sit on the edge of the world / to savor our word" (3).

The second theme is the invocation and reconstruction of our Indigenous ancestral memories through the Word: it is represented by poems that discuss local histories and include "The Chib'al," "Enchanted Mountains," "First Rain Storm," "Imagining," "The Dry Season," "The Fiesta of the Birds," "My Hometown," and "The War Years." "The Chib'al," for example, narrates a tradition in which young boys from the community walk up the mountains during winter when it is very cold and there is a lot of rain. There, they make a bonfire and wait for birds to fall to the ground so they can beat them with sticks. The boys then pick up the birds and "At daybreak, they come home. / How the children smile!" (21). Similarly, "Enchanted Mountains" talks about the roosters' songs that emanate from the cliffs—whose names are Yaxkanul, Tzib'aj, and Mimanwitz—and the pacts between men and the mountains. The men offer "their souls in exchange for wealth / here on earth" (37). The traditional and mythic elements in the realm of the rural community are contrasted to the atmosphere in the city in the poem "Rush Hour in the City." The narrator appreciates his surroundings in the countryside, and a "bull" with eyes that display "a calm lake" underscores the great tranquility of the rural environment, characterized by "monastic ruminating" (47) instead of races "to nowhere" in the city. The themes of the exaltation of animals and the placid context of Indigenous villages far from the city are reminiscent of those expressed in the poetic works of Ak'abal, Morales Santos, and Lión. For these poets, the city represents a realm characterized by chaotic fluidity.

A third theme, which is related to the urban context invoked in his poetry in poems like "The Laws," "Prayer of Supplication," and "False Identity," develops a critique of settler colonialism by detailing the violent processes used by those in power to dispossess Indigenous peoples of their lands and cultures. "The Laws" (58), for example, shows "certain types" of people who enjoy "prestige and power"; they manipulate laws at their will, favoring their own political and economic interests; thus, "Only those laws made by man / rot and go without will." For its part, "False Identity" critiques the new generations that have embraced the cultural baggage of globalization—"The machinery of the media / with its persuasive sprockets"—and are becoming "sleepwalk generations, / running after unreachable dreams": "they undress themselves of the cloth of their ancestors" and "set their gaze apart from themselves / tossing pieces of their soul far away / to embrace the illusion / with which they deny their being" (33).

Finally, poems like "Love," "Your Look," "One Story about the Sun and the Moon," "Not Even a Word," "A Dream," "Your Body," and "Afternoon Falls over Guatemala City" explore erotic and romantic themes in which the narrator discusses his courtship of women or his love adventures. Of these, "One Story about the Sun and the Moon" (26) and "Imagining" (45) are noteworthy because they address the Indigenous heterosexual patriarchal system. The first of these poems, through personification, tells the story of when the Sun met the Moon. The Sun wants to kiss her, but the Moon escapes and hides "behind the earth." The "pursuit" finally concludes when the Sun possesses the Moon and begins to assault her in a metaphor of a lunar eclipse. When this occurs, the narrator states that "there are fears among men and women / on earth: people shout to help our mother, they build bonfires, strength is sent, *juuuy! Hiiip!* Until father sun feels shamed and lets her go" (27). In "Imagining," after a long day in the fields, an Indigenous Maya peasant returns home and, walking down the mountains, begins to feel joy when he appreciates the landscape of his town. The man becomes even happier when thinking about how his wife will be preparing his dinner when he arrives. His "dog will be there. Waiting for me out front; / my son standing in the doorway / will take the hoe from me" (45). I do not address here the patriarchy that emerges in these poems, but I explore these issues in my critical analysis of the literary works of Q'eq'chi poet Maya Cu Choc and K'iche' Maya artist Manuel Tzoc in chapter 4. For now, I focus on González's vindication of the Maya world.

In *The Dry Season* the Q'anjob'al poet aims to give prominence to the pre-Colombian Maya and rural worlds as constitutive of Maya cultural identity. By invoking these cultural and spatial referents, González—like Ak'abal, Lión, and Morales Santos—develops discursive strategies to dignify contemporary Maya identity. These are recurring themes in his essays and fictional textual production. In *A Mayan Life*, for example, the central protagonist of the novel, Lwin, confronts hurtful and sinister attacks on his Maya identity through an epistemic violence established and legitimated through settler colonial laws and education. Similarly, *The Return of the Maya* addresses the forced displacement of Maya communities in the rural areas that, because of state terrorism, had to go into exile in Southern Mexico. Such attacks on Maya cultural identity and the forced displacements, nevertheless, have not erased the characters' strong spiritual ties to Maya culture or Indigenous cultural and linguistic specificities. These texts and their characters highlight the tenacity of Maya peoples in defending and restoring their ancestral memory and cultural values.

In *The Dry Season*, González invokes the precolonial Maya world using tones of nostalgia and longing that imagine it as free of problems and social contradictions and as a place where cultural values bring people together harmoniously. The poem "The Mayas," for example, establishes a "before" and "after" temporality that is manifested through the simple past and present tenses. In the past, Maya peoples lived "on pure gold, over there far away / behind curtains of green vines / that fell like jade streams bathed in light"; "in the shelter of walls / made of gods, / where a history was woven / on pure gold"; or they "spent their lives observing the sky where / they traced geometry among the stars, / and lowered them as stones to build their temples" (5). The Mayas also "danced to the beat of drums and rattles, / and stamped their print upon gold and stone" (5). In the poem, there are many references to Maya scientific and cultural contributions based on what we know about their advanced knowledge of astrology and architecture.

The full, harmonious Indigenous life radically changes after Europeans arrive, followed by their criollo-mestizo / ladino descendants who colonize Maya territories and trample down Maya subjectivity. Later in the same poem, Maya culture and its cultural contributions are interrupted through a euphoric scream: "And Now!" (7). From this verse on, the tone of the poem goes from celebratory to angry and anguished; the narrator denounces the devastation and destruction of Maya societies caused by colonialism:

> Their name is left buried
> where they excavated the veins of gold,
> where they uprooted the jade mines,
> in the place they looted the royal tombs.
>
> All that is left—bird songs
> which walk lonely through the forests. (9)

Moreover, the original names of the ancestors and their cities have been "buried"; the temples and millenarian cities "have been left alone / like crypts / in the loneliness of the cemetery" (73). Even though the sacred sites invoked represent a testimony of a living historical memory, they remain uninhabited, damaged, and isolated. The cities of Chichén Itzá, Tikal, and Quirigua, where "the memory of [his] people lies" (73), are associated with solitary cemeteries where "time sleeps." These lines thus conjure images of ruins, debris, graves, and wandering wounded people.

In "Over There," González again explores the themes of ancestral cities and the Mayas, as noted earlier, by describing the traumatic effects of the internal armed conflict and the consequent Peace Accords that formally ended the war in 1996. Far from mitigating the extreme poverty and lessening discrimination against Maya peoples, the same old structures of colonial power and domination have instead been perpetuated in the postwar period. In "Over There," the narrator states, "an army of naked children / sleeps on the lonely streets. / The famished fight the vultures / over garbage. / The crying doesn't cease. / The cemeteries multiply" (53). The neoliberal economic measures adopted after the war, rather than bringing prosperity, have deepened poverty. Thus, the poem denounces the irony of a modernity that, instead of producing benefits for a national collective, has recycled the same colonialist logic of the past under the banner of democracy.

For González, amid these changes history is only sleeping, waiting to be awakened. Just as the Q'anjob'al author expresses in "The Word," the role of the Indigenous writer is to rescue and give a voice to the experience of past and present harassment. The Indigenous writer also has to dignify the past, affirming and resurrecting it to mine historical and cultural elements that can strengthen Indigenous peoples in the present; such writers offer accounts about "the intrinsic nature of Maya culture as constituent of communal cohesion, and as an emotionally charged symbol of strength" (Arias 2017, 140). This is why González in "Our Writing" challenges assumptions that Maya civilization has disappeared; it concludes, "Lies! / The Maya people have not died. / Nor have they departed. / This is *kotz'ib' li:* our writing; / yesterday, today, forever" (55). González capitalizes on this idea about millenary continuity when he associates Indigenous peoples with the imagery of "roots"—"roots / in the lands of Mayab" (11)—that continue sprouting despite the destruction, dispossession, plunder, and oppression. The metaphor suggests Indigenous regeneration over time and against the weight of colonization. The relationship between writer and writing, in this sense, underscores the role of the Indigenous poet as a carrier of memory: the one in charge of keeping that memory alive through the word. This is the basis for an epistemological struggle in which, through Indigenous self-representation, the Maya voice is empowered. We can conclude that González's critique highlights the continuity of a colonial project as constitutive of modernity and, therefore, of Indigenous marginality and exclusion. Thus, it is necessary to revisit our ancestral past and our local traditions to find the elements that can come together to ensure our individual and collective survival.

The poetic works of Victor Montejo, who speaks both Pop'ti and Q'anjob'al, are characterized by many of the same concerns as González's writing. Montejo is a survivor of the armed conflict in Guatemala. In his *Testimony: Death of a Guatemalan Village* (1987), he narrates how in September 1982 a Civil Defense Patrol in the village of Tzalalá attacked a group of soldiers in the community. The patrol mistakenly thought that the army officers were guerrilla insurgent fighters trying to recruit people to their cause. This attack unleashed a deadly cycle of events in which many people were killed, including Pedro Antonio, Victor Montejo's brother. At the time, Montejo was an elementary school teacher in the village. After the attack, he was captured by the army, interrogated, and tortured. Fortunately, he escaped and immediately left the country because his life was in danger—leaving behind his people, his family, and his job. He went into exile in Chiapas, Mexico, where he met the Guatemalan writer Victor Perera and the actress Jane Alexander, who, after learning about his tragic experience, sent a petition to the U.S. government to grant Montejo and his family political refuge. The petition was granted, and once in the United States Montejo pursued an anthropology degree at Bucknell University in Pennsylvania. He then continued his graduate studies at the State University of New York, Albany, and at the University of Connecticut, where he completed his PhD in 1993. Subsequently he obtained a tenure-track position in the Native American Studies Department at the University of California, Davis, where he concluded his academic career in 2011 (Arias 2017, 177). Montejo also served as a Guatemalan governmental official, the "Secretary of Peace" (2004–2008) under the Oscar Berger government. He has written poetry, narratives, and essays and published his works in Pop'ti Maya and kaxlan tzij. His publications include *Brevísima relación testimonial de la continua destrucción del Mayab' (Guatemala)* (A Brief Testimonial Account of the Continuous Destruction of the Mayab') [Guatemala], 1992), *Sculpted Stones / Piedras labradas* (1995)—the text I discuss in this section—*El Q'anil, Man of Lightning* ([1982] 2001), *Voices from Exile: Violence and Survival in Modern Maya History* (1999), *Maya Intellectual Renaissance: Identity, Representation, and Leadership* (2005), *The Bird That Cleans the World* (2006), and his latest novel in Spanish, *Pixan, el cargador del espíritu* (Pixan, the Carrier of the Spirit, 2014).

Sculpted Stones, Montejo's second book of poetry, is divided into two parts.[21] The title itself references Maya historical memory, materialized through the sculpted glyphs in temples and stones in the cities of Tikal, Palenque, Copán, and Chichén Itzá. Thus, it recognizes that millenarian history grants the author a strength that, despite his having left the country, allows him to maintain an unbreakable connection with his homeland and his history. Montejo's book of poetry, then, illustrates a symbolic journey that starts in the Mayab' (part I) and culminates in New York (part II). The book describes the author's own journey and political commitment that vindicate and restore elements of his culture.

Part I, "1982–1986," consists of seventeen poems contextualized in the most repressive period in Iximulew, during which Montejo was forced to leave the country. They explore themes of Maya cultural vindication, much like those discussed in the works of Ak'abal and González. Through the metaphor of "sculpted stones," the poetic voice journeys through ancestral Maya sacred sites such as Tikal, Palenque, Copán, and Chichén Itzá. In these sites, through personification, the poetic voice imagines conversations with the Maya stelae with hieroglyphic inscriptions, his ancestors, "tourists," and the "Mayanists" who visit these sites. For example, in poems such as "Interrogation by Ancestors," "Remembrance," and "Useless Brujos," the narrator rhetorically asks himself what would happen if "our [Maya] ancestors came to life" (43) and returned to ask about our ancestral legacy and material culture. The answer offered by the narrator is that they would "give us, their descendants / thirteen lashes for being / sleepwalkers and conformists" (43), because we let the European invaders burn our books, dispossess us from our riches, and steal our stelae and codices. As descendants of a rich and powerful civilization, we failed to learn to "conquer the darkest of nights," and by remaining "asleep" and in "silence," we forgot the message "to struggle, build and forge ahead / so that no one's left behind" (43). The poetic voice also indicates that we have contributed to the spread of a collective amnesia that for centuries "has made us forget our names" (43) and origins. The poem "Sculpted Stones" talks about a tourist who admires the architecture of temples in the city of Tikal. He stops to appreciate and try to decipher a Maya stela that displays phrases written in round glyphs. The poetic voice imagines the response of the stela to the tourist; with a mocking smile it says, "After two thousand years, / traveler, / we're still on our feet / vigilant / among the silken / cobwebs of time" (35).

Other compositions in the first part, such as "The Five Directions," "Thunder and Lightning," and the "The Water Feast," offer accounts of Nature's communicative force; here he associates Nature with Maya spiritual values that have survived in Indigenous communities. The description of cosmological elements is offered to authorize and contrast Indigenous knowledge to Western schemas. For example, although the narrator in "The Five Directions" tells us that Westerners "see just two directions: East and West," from a Maya perspective, the world is conceived in five directions demarcated by "The red dawn of day (East), The dying black of evening (West). The white of the chilly North. / The yellow power of the South; / and in the center of the world / the intense blue-green / of the tropics" (21). In addition, by personifying the ecological elements, the poetic voice calls for us to respect Nature and recognize its destructive powers if we disrespect her. Echoing the *Popol Wuj* in the "The Water Feast," the narrator remembers the words of the rain: "Hey you, fat-faced sinners! / you assassins, you crooks, / don't forget you're nothing but tiny ants, / fragments of flesh and bone" (31). In contrast, the poems "Captive," "Vision," "The Dog," and "A Mother's Weeping" have no mythic and cosmological

elements and instead reflect social and political realities. Through testimonial accounts, these poems talk about the repressive operations of the
Guatemalan Army in various areas in Iximulew. "Captive," for example,
narrates the story of "Pilin," a deaf-mute young boy who is apolitical and
peaceful but who is forcibly apprehended by a group of Guatemalan soldiers. They torture him to try to "make him talk" and "make him denounce
the others" (66), the guerrilla fighters. Pilin, being deaf-mute, cannot say
anything; he can only smile. The soldiers consequently decide "to cut out
his tongue, / gouge his eyes out / and burn him alive" (66). The next day,
the soldiers instead declare to the news media that they have killed "one of
the top guerrilla chiefs" (66). "A Mother's Weeping"—dedicated to Pedro
Antonio, Montejo's brother who was assassinated by the army—is a heart-
breaking poem that narrates a mother's mourning after her "young plant"
is plucked. Her son has been disappeared, and every day she hopes to see
him again. The narrator consoles the mother and, one day, invites her to
see the horizon from where her disappeared son emerges: "Here comes the
son you weep for / galloping in the distance, / he's not alone, he's joined /
by the cheering crowds" (73).

The second part of the book, "1986–1992," includes only seven poems,
in which the theme of exile is explored. They include various elements
from the author's life and are contextualized in Lewisburg, Pennsylvania,
and Albany, New York, the places where Montejo lived when he settled in
the United States. In these compositions, the narrator expresses a tone of
nostalgia and longing for his country and the Maya community he left
behind. "Guatemala," the poem that opens the second part, narrates a conversation between the son who has gone into exile and his mother country.
Similar to Morales Santos's personification of the figure of the "mother"
discussed in the first chapter, the son listens as the mother grieves and
cries for "your horrendous birthing / of malignant sons / who tear out of
your womb / the malevolence of the dollar / to drive the workers / even
deeper down" (83). Despite the fact that he is far away from his mother
country, the narrator promises to continue his struggle for her well-being:
"In your name, homeland, / and in the name of your sons, / the thousands
of dispossessed, / I'll lift my head and fight / as you wanted me to" (81).
These ideas reemerge in other poems in the second part, in which the narrator confirms his political commitment even while in exile. The poem
"Umbilical" states, for instance, "And though I'm a long way / from home /
I know my undivided / heart / beats as before / and endures the distant /

melancholy" (89). It is important to emphasize that the conversational style of the poems in this part, in particular "Guatemala," bears a strong resemblance to Otto René Castillo's poem, "Let's Go, Country, Let's Walk," that I briefly discussed at the end of chapter 1. Indeed, both Montejo and Castillo emphasize the sons' commitment to defend the homeland, which has been reduced to a "sad and withered," "multinational banana tree" (1982, 81), a direct reference to the operations of the United Fruit Company in Guatemala.

Similar to Morales Santos's poem, "We Will Be Caqchiquel Again," discussed in the previous chapter, Montejo suggests the urgent need to recover Maya sovereignty through the symbolic representation of prophetic memory; that is, by announcing the return of the Maya ancestors who lead the way to empowering their contemporary descendants. In doing so, Montejo speaks of seeing "the world through a Maya prism" (21) and stresses the power of Nature to announce a utopian future when the Maya world will recover its sovereignty. These ideas are clearly expressed in the first part of the book, in the poem "The Rising Dawn," in which, after a long wait, animals and humans "on the brink of war" acquire and celebrate the revealed "secret hidden by the stones for centuries" (39). The poem states,

Everyone will feel great joy.
Bells will dissolve
in loud chimes of jubilation.
Fallen martyrs will return to life
while the marimba with its laments
will play the ancestral songs
so that the stars can dance. (39)

The described past becomes the future and announces a world resurrected by the Indigenous protagonist in search of lost sovereignty. These verses resemble some of the poems by González in providing an idyllic representation of the Maya past. The poem even refutes those who have interpreted pre-Columbian Maya rituals as bloody or asserted that the "Maya were cannibals" (44) to suggest their "barbarism" and lack of "civilization." To undermine those assumptions, Montejo employs strategic essentialism to celebrate the Maya's positive contributions. He imagines a world in the present where, similar to the Maya ancestors evoked, Maya temples like Tikal exhibit "the smoke of pom and copal for *Sat Kan*,[22] / the face of the powerful deity. / Games and smiles in the plaza, / recitations of sleeping *katuns*[23] / and stones that speak once more, / numbering the stars" (27).

The Problematic Contraction of Mayaness

The emancipatory project articulated by González and Montejo through their poetic works is characterized by a reconfiguration and dignification of Indigenous memories. Similar to the literary proposals of Ak'abal, Morales Santos, and Lión, these Maya authors constitute Indigeneity by associating it with the rural world. It is in this space that they imagine the expression of Maya cultural and linguistic specificities and a pre-Colombian past that survives through the ancestral temples, the hieroglyphic writing, the codices, and Maya dress. Furthermore, the fact that Ak'abal, González, and Montejo develop bilingual poetry books suggests a conscious desire to dignify Maya languages. According to critics like Santiago Bastos, these discursive Maya stances are established based on binary constructions in which modernity—ideas of "progress" and the urban realm—is interpreted as a threat to Indigenous survival. Mayaness, in this sense, is

> understood as "one's own," what is culturally "different" to what is
> non-Maya . . . a cultural condition with no oppressive class or
> political elements. And it is defined, not by complementarity or
> difference, but rather, by opposition to the West. It takes a category
> so (artificially) unified as "Mayaness": It is the image of "cultures"
> as billiard balls that invariably have to clash. The end result is a
> discourse that does not allow nuances; that unrecognizes concrete
> historical developments and that it can open gaps with other
> political actors from civil society defined by the supposedly
> "western culture." (Bastos and Cumes 2007, 67–68)

These positions are also manifested in these authors' essays, which more clearly associate ideas about Mayaness to Indigenous languages, the rural realm, millenarian spiritual values, and so on.

Although the efforts that these authors make to dignify and recognize a Maya identity, as well as to challenge hegemonic colonial power that denies our humanity and existence, should be recognized and celebrated, their discursive contraction of Mayaness becomes problematic once it is

contextualized in the complex and even contradictory dynamics of globalization. By celebrating linguistic and cultural specificities, these authors inadver-
tently construct a discourse of Indigeneity that reduces and obscures the
agency of Maya subjects who affirm their identities in urban social contexts
or who affirm nonconforming gender and queer identities. Moreover, such
constructions display similarities with a Guatemalan Indigenista discourse
that unconsciously affirms a colonial discursive order.

　　Through a careful examination of the construction of Mayaness in the
works of González, Montejo, and Ak'abal, as well as in the works of other
Maya intellectuals such as Kaqchikel Maya Demetrio Cojtí, a problematic
perspective emerges. Although these Maya authors frequently reference
how Mayas "are creating and re-creating our culture" (Montejo 2005, 33),
at other times they betray these perspectives by constructing an Indigenous cultural identity that is immutable and incapable of embracing modernization, much like early anthropologists who understood the Indigenous world and its subjectivity as a "closed corporate community."[24] This
perspective emerges in the representation and emphasis on the pre-
Colombian world in González's poems, but becomes more evident in his
narrative and essays. For instance, in *Kotz'ib' / Nuestra literatura Maya*
(Our Maya Literature, 1997), González talks about the Maya oral traditions, stating that stories have

　　been defended and preserved carefully in the minds of the mem-
　　bers of society, preserved against all danger, knowing that domi-
　　nant culture has tried to erase it. But for over twenty-five *katuns*, it
　　[oral Maya tradition] has survived in practice, within the intimacy
　　of the community, when surrounded by a bonfire, *there, in the*
　　far-away village with no electricity and with no mass media social
　　communication, the family or young people gather together to listen
　　to the guardians of the popular wisdom narrate their ancestral
　　stories, tales, myths, and fables that will soon be carried out to
　　other corners of the community by these skillful narrators who will
　　be responsible to perpetuate the literature of their elders. (103,
　　emphasis mine)

　　A similar perspective about how the Maya oral tradition has survived
"far away" from electricity and the mass media also appears in Montejo's
works. In the introduction to his epic poem, *El Q'anil, Man of Lightning*

([1982] 2001), Montejo argues that Western modernity threatens the existence not only of Maya oral traditions like the Q'anil but also of other cultural specificities: "It could be said that if this story [El Q'anil] disappears,
many aspects of our culture will also disappear, as has begun to happen with
the tragedies of the twentieth century, especially in the indigenous communities, where many of the languages, traditional dress, dances, music,
and other traditions are being lost" (xvi). The advancement of Western
modernity, Montejo suggests, subjects Maya cultures to extinction.[25]

It is worth pointing out, however, that Montejo's perspective is ambiguous and contradictory. Although he shows how Western modernity represents a "threat" to Indigenous cultures, on other occasions he expresses
a desire to embrace and promote it in Maya communities. In his book
Maya Intellectual Renaissance (2005), he once again demonstrates his concern for the negative effects that modernity has had on his native village of
Jacaltenango. According to him, modernity is erasing religious ceremonies
and the Maya calendar and has distanced young Indigenous people from
oral tradition (151). With a nostalgic tone, Montejo recalls how, in the
1950s, Maya communities maintained their traditions because they were
"undisturbed by major technological innovations; they lacked roads, electricity, radio, telephones, TV, and the like" (140). Yet at other times he wel-
comes these modern innovations. For instance, the author criticizes
governmental policies that have not favored "development" in Maya communities, "ultimately leaving them abandoned and without support" (188).
Talking about his own village, he explains that the streets of Jacaltenango
"have almost impassable potholes; the telephone system is still precarious; and a good access road is needed" (188).

Gonzalez's and Montejo's perspectives on "oral tradition" and Maya
culture display an uncontaminated or authentic idea of Mayaness that has
survived because it has remained distanced from Western modernity and
technology. These interpretations can be associated with their respective
representations of the Indigenous ancestral past in their poetry, in which
they represent a Maya world without social contradictions. For them, the
only force interrupting that Maya world is colonization. These Indigenous
writers are not the only ones to offer such romanticized interpretations of
the Indigenous world; other Maya intellectuals, such as Demetrio Cojtí,
share these attitudes. Cojtí, like González and Montejo, claims that a
model of authentic Mayaness exists in the rural areas of the country where
"electricity," "mass media," and "social media" are absent. It is in these

uncontaminated spheres that we can envision a model of Indigeneity. Referencing the "levels of ethnic consciousness" of Indigenous peoples, Cojtí writes,

> Illiterate Maya peasants have a lot more practice and *cultural authenticity*, and have a consciousness of the *pueblo* **as such;** that is, they recognize that they are members of the Maya People (that is now called in Spanish **natural, Indian, aborigine, or indigenous**), that is socially marginalized and ethnically discriminated against.... The educated indigenous middle and lower classes, for their part, *for having suffered under a ladinizing educative system, maintain fewer cultural practices and have less cultural authenticity.* (1997, 52, author's bold, emphasis mine)

Cojtí uses a similar logic of authenticity when he defines the "Maya people" through their languages, suggesting that their use is an essential, "authentic" marker to determine someone's Indigeneity: "By **Maya People** it is understood the ethnic collective members of the *Maya linguistic family,* a concept that not only wants to include Mayas that live in Guatemala, but also those who were ceded or remained under the jurisdiction of other states" (1997, 15, author's bold, emphasis mine).

A similar perspective to that of Cojtí characterizes the work of Ak'abal as well. His essay "Reflexiones de un poeta maya" (A Maya Poet's Reflections, 2012) begins with the following statement: "K'o jun kinrayij kinbij xa ne k'ut par i nutzijobalil / I ask permission to speak in my own language." Similar to Montejo's and González's views about the loss of traditions caused by the growing influence of globalization, Ak'abal expresses his worry that "there is less Indigenous knowledge, and even less use of our Maya languages." To the question, "Do Indigenous literatures have a future?" Ak'abal suggests that they do not because "today's generation," by being uprooted from the ancestral territories, not only lose their language but also their essential elements and cultural values that he delineates in his poetic works. González also echoes this concern about the growing role of cultural globalization when he states, "Progressively, people are less and less responsive to manifestations of spirituality. The media is a key factor in these invasions. The majority of Maya houses have a radio. That radio says nothing about the Maya. It plays no Mayan music, nor do we hear Mayan languages" ("In Our Own Words" 2006, 24).

These passages indicate several paradoxical stands I would like to examine closely. First, there is no doubt that one of the effects of colonization and the growing impact of neoliberal globalization is the gradual destruction of Indigenous languages and other cultural elements. This linguistic and cultural ethnocide has been ongoing since the Spanish invasion. As I mention in the introduction, the campaigns to impose Spanish—in tandem with colonial policies to impose Christianity, like the ones spearheaded by Pedro de Gante—were key to the colonization of our territories and our subjectivities. The processes of ladinoization, begun after independence, also contributed to alienating us from our cultural elements, in particular, our languages.[26] Furthermore, these Maya authors do not consider how certain social contexts make the loss of Indigenous languages an unconscious or unintentional process. Ruth Moya (1997, 152, n. 16) reminds us of Indigenous leaders in the Department of Sololá who, during the period of the armed conflict, sought to create bilingual educational programs to promote the use of Maya languages. For these efforts, they received death threats, and some were even murdered. The Guatemalan Army considered these Maya leaders to be "communists" who were exchanging subversive messages using their native languages. Such social contexts have further contributed, as Luiz Enrique López indicates, to diminished opportunities for Indigenous peoples, who "are the ones to have less opportunities to access the educational system. [Moreover], given the limitations and lack of relevance of the educational system, and the fact that it has been designed to transmit knowledge exclusively in Spanish, many Indigenous boys and girls end up leaving school earlier in their lives" (1997, 53). Owing to the lack of preparation of teachers, instruction in Indigenous languages is also very limited. Ak'abal himself indicated how learning to write in K'iche' Maya was entirely the result of his own efforts and intuition. In an interview, he stated, "We don't have bilingual schools in Guatemala; there is not yet a program that supports bilingual education or the learning of writing in K'iche' Maya. We are forced to use the Latin alphabet to give form to the writing in our Indigenous languages" (Ak'abal and Ollé 2004, 214). Even after the Peace Accords included a provision to establish and implement intercultural bilingual education, such programs do not provide adequate training for teachers in teaching Indigenous languages at the participating schools. Furthermore, there are not sufficient pedagogical materials like Maya grammars.[27]

Ak'abal, González, and Montejo maintain a contradictory position on linguistic revitalization. Although they seek to dignify Maya languages through their poetic works, paradoxically, they unconsciously end up attacking other Indigenous literary representatives such as Luis de Lión and Francisco Morales Santos for not speaking or producing books in their native languages. We must be aware that the use of Spanish and elements related to modernity on behalf of Indigenous writers does not automatically entail a submission to the hegemonic system; rather, it is an appropriation of the technologies of the colonizer to give agency to the knowledge and memories of Indigenous peoples. In addition, producing bi- or multilingual literary works should be understood from an intercultural perspective. That is, these writers not only aim to open a window to their worldview but also use and embrace Spanish or English as languages that help them express their aesthetic, ideological, and political ideals.

At another level, the ideas of Maya authenticity imagined by these Indigenous authors paradoxically bear some resemblance to the discursive tendencies they criticize. When we compare the Maya subject they construct to the neo-Indigenista tradition in Guatemala from the 1970s (as represented by Asturias, Cardoza y Aragón, and Monteforte Toledo), striking similarities emerge. Guatemalan Indigenismo favored ethnic policies that enabled Mayas to preserve their cultural and linguistic specificities to become citizens while at the same time distancing themselves from modernity. The essay "Panorama indígena del indigenismo en Guatemala" (An Indigenous Panoramic View of *Indigenismo* in Guatemala, 1972) by Alejandro D. Marroquín is representative of these discursive tendencies.

In his essay, Marroquín proposes—following Carlos Guzmán Böckler's and Jean Loup Herbert's *Guatemala: una interpretación histórico-social* (Guatemala: An Historical-Social Interpretation, 1971)—a critique of institutional Indigenismo, arguing that it was led by a hegemonic class that sought to maintain "Indians" at the margins of the nation-state. Challenging their policies, Marroquín argues in favor of Indigenous' integration by recognizing their cultural and linguistic rights. He praises ongoing projects that support the implementation of an educational system in Indigenous languages, the wearing of Maya *traje* in public spheres, and Maya spiritual practices. The project Marroquín directed, for instance, "organized an exhibition of traditional dress, cooperatives and sanitary assistance. Fellowships were awarded to young indigenous people to study"

(303–4). Referencing "social policies" embraced by some Indigenous communities, Marroquín celebrates the protection of the textile industry and laws that "recognized the validity of marriages that follow indigenous rituals" (303). In his view, these practices should be embodied in national laws that need to be "translated into native languages to be circulated in the communities" (303).

The project Marroquín directed also supported social vindication by promoting the efforts of some Indigenistas to defend the cultural and linguistic specificities of Indigenous communities. Thus, similar to the objectives of the Maya intelligentsia discussed earlier, Marroquín's perspective sees no contradiction between Indigenous peoples maintaining the essential aspects of their Maya "difference" and integrating into the nation-state. According to Marroquín, a nationalist agenda should be implemented to "elevate the economic, social and cultural levels [of Indigenous Peoples] without causing conflicts that may originate barriers of resistance to changes being proposed, making necessary adjustments in the personal and communal life by developing confidence, comprehension and coexistence" (1972, 308).[28]

As can be seen in these perspectives, the objectives of the Indigenista and the Maya intelligentsia discussed earlier share an understanding of the Maya subject as compatible with modernity, as long as their differences are respected. These accounts, however, suffer from serious conceptual inadequacies and end up affirming a colonialist logic. First, Marroquín, Ak'abal, González, Montejo, and Cojtí construct images of the Maya subject predicated on a series of binary oppositions that reduce the complexity of social and interethnic relations to Maya and non-Maya. In addition, they obscure and negate the specific sociopolitical and historical context of the Maya subject they construct by suggesting that, throughout history, Indigenous peoples have maintained intact and unchanged cultural aspects of their identity based on their distancing from modernity or their desire to not contaminate themselves with "modern," non-Indigenous cultures. In this sense, their discursive construction of Mayaness suggests that "traditional," "peasant," "illiterate," and so on create a fixed and essentialized construction of the Maya as real. This construction operates through an understanding of modernity as mechanisms (represented by the ladino education system, electricity, mass media, radio, and the like) that deform, displace, and annul Indigenous traditions, because they introduce a new sociocultural environment characterized by homogenization. From this

perspective, because urban Indigenous subjects left their natural environment or were touched by the hand of modernity, they became contaminated and their cultural specificities were erased; all contact that a Maya
subject has with Western modernity unavoidably cancels out his or her
"natural" world. The urban Maya are thus displaced to the margins of the
proposed model of Mayaness.

These analyses, however, do not consider the effects of the armed conflict in Iximulew, which required many to leave their communities and
establish themselves in other rural settings, cities, or the United States.
These are experiences that necessarily involved migration and interethnic
cultural exchanges for our survival. It is ironic that Cojtí, Ak'abal, Montejo,
and González do not reflect on these aspects, given that they themselves
were directly affected by the armed conflict and even suffered forced
displacement.

It is clear that Marroquín and the Maya intelligentsia occupy a position
of lettered cultural authorities that determine how Mayas are supposed to
think about and recognize themselves within modernity or the nation-
state. That is, they inscribe a "cultural authenticity" to rural subjects based
on what *they* consider to be the geographical and historical origins of the
Mayas—what in anthropology is known as the "etic" perspective (Arnedo
2001, 96). In addition, these authors apply what Santiago Castro Gómez
calls "the Hubris of zero degrees," an epistemic strategy of domination
that involves "a form of human knowledge that entails the pretense of
objectivity and scientificity, and takes for granted the fact that the observer
is not part of what is being observed" (2008, 282). The Maya rural subjects
these authors imagine are conceived of as passive entities who interpret
modernity/globalization indistinctly, lacking both control and an ethnic
consciousness; they insert themselves into its logic only to bury their own
traditions. These representations obscure and marginalize the situation of
Indigenous subjects whose experience does not relate to the rural realm,
but who instead live in metropolitan centers where other cultural, philosophical, religious, and technological changes occur. Likewise, the Maya
writers who express these views are able to navigate and develop intercultural and linguistic exchanges in the realm of modernity/globalization.
They have all traveled the world and lived in metropolitan centers like
Guatemala City, Mexico, or the United States; some earned university
degrees in Guatemala City (González), Belgium (Cojtí), or the United
States (Montejo). Furthermore, are not Ak'abal, González, and Montejo

using decolonial tactics similar to those employed by our lettered ancestors who appropriated colonial tools—like the Latin alphabet—to produce a literary register in Maya languages? And does not doing so enable
them to offer accounts of our historical memory and our survival?

In many ways, these Maya authors also have had to adapt to their urban
reality while still transmitting Indigenous memory and cultural identity,
forging imaginaries permeated not only by ancestral values and traditions
but also by new knowledge that affirms an epistemological continuity and
connection to our ancestral past. Indeed, poetry like that of Ak'abal,
González, and Montejo—similar to the *Popol Wuj, The Kaqchikel Chronicles,* and *The Books of the Chilam Balam*—function as powerful artifacts
that support our struggles for emancipation. Through them, these authors
not only communicate and share Indigenous worldviews but also leave a
material legacy that affirms our continuing decolonial struggles to the new
generations that aim to dignify, value, and activate their Maya identity. So,
why do they not see some of the subjects they invoke as capable of appropriating globalization to their own benefit?

In a related argument, Mexican critic Roger Bartra highlights Indigenous rearrangement, negotiation, and creativity in his anecdote about a
group of Indigenous Otomí youth from Mexico City. Bartra explains that
this group of young Otomíes play rock music "like this, with *guaraches*
[sandals]" (qtd. in Ferman 1993, 44) and are constantly confronted by officials from the National Indigenist Institute (INI) who tell them that they
are "losing" their traditions by using electric guitars and playing rock
music. "You will then see," Bartra adds, "the underdogs, screwed, defending themselves from nationalist outsiders. And what do they use to defend
themselves? Rock, as an affirmation of their Otomí being, before these
nationalists, who perhaps spoke about being Otomí and about Mexican
nationality in the abstract, but without them realizing it" (44). In this
anecdote, these Indigenous youth have appropriated this aspect of Western modernity not with the goal of hiding their traditions and their relationship with their community of origin, but to "affirm their being as Otomí."
Examples abound of the creativity of Indigenous peoples in appropriating
modernity to their own advantage.

In Iximulew, a similar expression to that of the young Otomí band in
México is represented in the Maya Mam rock group *Itz'x Qanq'ibil* (Survival); the work of Tzutuhil Maya hip-hop artist Tzutu B'aktun Kan; and
the artistic work of Kaqchikel Maya singer Sara Curruchich. These artists'

music, both in Maya languages and in Spanish, has been embraced by Indigenous and non-Indigenous peoples in Guatemala and disseminated widely via social media like YouTube and Facebook.[29] These experiences of Indigeneity are located, maintained, and rearticulated in a new geopolitical and sociocultural context through borrowing and appropriating the technologies offered by the West to initiate a new space of resistance and re-accommodation of their cultural identity.[30]

These Indigenous cultural manifestations show that Indigeneity does not necessarily reside exclusively in the rural realm; neither can Indigeneity be encapsulated in forms demarcated by specific cultural and linguistic markers. Indigenous decolonial and emancipatory struggles also develop in sociopolitical urban contexts with the purpose of creating spaces for Indigenous peoples. In this sense, the Maya diaspora in the metropolis—Guatemala City, Mexico, the United States, Canada, or Europe—operates through a selective adoption of values or cultural products offered by modernity to regenerate, reconceptualize, and expand our Indigenous knowledges.[31]

Yet I should also emphasize that, by developing a critique of some of Ak'abal, Montejo, and González's stances, by no means am I suggesting that their literary contributions should be marginalized or discarded. On the contrary, and to reiterate, I seek to highlight the need to go beyond just seeing Indigenous participation in globalization as a loss of our values and cultural specificities; in addition, we should consider new processes of accommodation and regeneration of Mayaness in the contemporary period. Although some critics interpret the discursive stance in these authors works as "essentialist," "fundamentalist," or "absolutist," it is extremely important to understand the decolonial dimensions in the immediate context under which such stances emerge.

Indeed, if we consider that Ak'abal, Montejo, and González were writing within the context of genocide, we can offer an alternative interpretation that does not critique these authors. I thus propose to read these literary works within the context of Gayatri Chakravorty Spivak's idea of "strategic essentialism"; that is, these Maya authors produce a discourse that particularizes "difference" and a nationalist narrative through "a strategic use of positivist essentialism in a scrupulously visible political interest" (1996, 214). In other words, the essentialized construction of Mayaness in Ak'abal, Montejo, and González represents a discursive strategy to see the world and challenge the status quo. Here, it is important to consider that

these authors wrote in a polarized context in which conflictive relationships between Maya and ladinos led to Indigenous subordination. Furthermore, as previously mentioned, between 1978 and 1984 the Guatemalan nation-state adopted terrorist counterinsurgent policies that sought to
eliminate Indigenous peoples. These efforts were nothing new. Since the
Spanish invasion, hegemonic institutions have been characterized by their
constant attacks on our cultural and linguistic specificities and on our
existence. To invoke Frantz Fanon's words, settlers orient their colonial
efforts toward the past of the oppressed people to distort it, disfigure it,
and annihilate it (1971, 168). As a response to this genocidal logic, Ak'abal,
Montejo, and González rewrite and reclaim their history by establishing
an affirmation of Maya difference, constructing a subjectivity that emphasizes an organic relationship with an ancestral past and presenting to their
readers—many times in idealized form—a continuation of our existence.
In my view, this is how Maya authors essentially say to the Guatemalan
nation-state, "You cannot eliminate us! Though you sought to 'kill even
the seeds,' our essential cultures continue germinating despite all the fratricidal attacks against our existence."
    In their respective representations of the Maya world, these Maya
authors aim to nourish the dignity and self-esteem of Indigenous peoples,
to lift our spirits to enable us to continue our struggles toward our decolonization and the restitution of Indigenous life. Thus Ak'abal, Montejo, and
González articulate a response to a feeling of being "degraded and despised,
hated and hunted, oppressed and exploited, and marginalized and dehumanized at the hands of powerful, xenophobic" imperial and colonial
powers (West 1993, 260). Their primary objective is the revitalization and
affirmation of the Indigenous world as a differentiated cultural entity, with
its own ancestral cultural and political history. Their literary constructions
of Mayaness thus allow us to reimagine Iximulew as an intercultural
nation-state that incorporates and recognizes Maya peoples on an equal
footing.
    In their representation of the Indigenous past and re-signification in
the present, these Maya authors recall the critical reading offered by Bain
Attwood and Fiona Magowan of aboriginal testimonies in Australia. By
invoking the millenarian past, these authors aim "to reform the present or
to change the future. By recounting histories of colonialism, indigenous
peoples have not only created an understanding but also a critique of it,
and in constructing stories of freedom they have been able to challenge

their oppression" (2001, xii). Along this line of thinking, the discursive proposal developed by Ak'abal, González, and Montejo—in their invocation of the millenarian Maya past, our ancestral values, and Indigenous languages—demonstrates that our condition in the present is very different from that of our ancestors in pre-Colombian times. In other words, we now live under colonialism, in a context in which non-Indians in power see us as a problem because we speak different languages, dress differently, look unlike them, and have spiritual values that differ from the religious values of hegemonic society. Hence, contemporary Maya authors perfectly understand that the promise of Western modernity / neoliberal globalization (economic prosperity, emancipation, progress, and the like) has failed them. Not only have these ideals been forcibly imposed on our material conditions of existence and our imaginaries but they have also brought about a slow moral, material, and spiritual decline in our lives as Indigenous peoples. Therefore, Maya authors employ the literary register as a political effort to imagine an Indigenous national emancipation. Indigenous memory becomes and constitutes conditions of possibility to restore our sovereignty.

Indeed, with the development of narratives that imagine journeys to our millenarian past, the idealization and representation of ancestral Maya values, and the vision of a socially and politically harmonious Maya pre-Colombian world, Ak'abal, Montejo, and González express a desire—and the conditions of possibility—to escape from the colonial tutelage and dependency under which we have lived for centuries. The poetic works of these Maya authors allow us to imagine an autonomous, self-regulated, and sovereign Indigenous world in which we can construct and materialize more inclusive and reciprocal social spaces. Furthermore, addressing and dignifying our millenarian past reflects a utopian vision that responds to our collective well-being. Along these lines Partha Chatterjee offers this thought: "it is our attachment to the past which gives birth to the feeling that the present needs to be changed, that it is our task to change it" (1997, 19–20). In this sense, the construction of Indigenous narratives that idealize or imagine journeys to our ancestral past and present it to the reader as full of beauty, prosperity, and a healthy sociability suggests, above all, a social creation of our own peoples, instead of something violently imposed. Hence, contemporary Maya literatures allow us the opportunity to create the conditions of possibility for a better present for those of us who have suffered the violence of colonialism in its various manifestations. Because of these experiences, Maya authors offer us transformed versions of the world where our values, our traditions, our languages, and customs contribute to rethinking and modifying dominant societies from our marginalized worldviews. Contrary to the assumptions that Maya narratives represent "victimization" or lack "political intentions," Maya poetics represented by Ak'abal, Montejo, and González—to follow James C. Scott's theoretical framework—can instead be thought of as daily acts of resistance. That is, these authors articulate "a struggle over the appropriation of symbols, a struggle over how the past and present shall be understood and labeled, a struggle to identify causes and assess blame, a contentious effort to give partisan meaning to local history" as well as "an effort by the poor to resist the economic and ritual marginalization they now suffer and to insist on the minimal cultural decencies of citizenship" (Scott 1985, xvii–xviii).

These assertions define much of modern Maya poetics by denouncing colonialism's efforts to eliminate Indigenous peoples through genocide or ladinoization/assimilation. In these works, we can see the constitutions of narratives of resurrection of our ancestral values that are based on celebrating the material culture, languages, spirituality, and ecological values that remain alive and constitute a powerful communicative force. What other evidence does the non-Indigenous Other need to corroborate our millenarian continuity? Are not the archaeological sites, the Maya languages, spirituality, and dress invoked by these authors evidence enough? That is why González, Ak'abal, and Montejo scream at those in power that we have the necessary basis to fight against colonialism, at the same time that such authors articulate our full right to demand our sovereignty and self-determination. In these proposals reside the decolonial potentialities of this Maya textual production—which allow us to continue feeding our cultural identity and dignity in a present conditioned by the operations of settler colonialism.

Nonetheless, while we understand the legitimacy of this political project in its challenge to the nation-state and colonialism, as previously discussed, its dangers cannot be ignored. On the one hand, we must recognize that the homogeneous discursive constructions of Mayaness may also be used to challenge other Indigenous subjectivities that do not fit the script of strategic essentialism with which we have been presented. It is important to recognize that the spaces of decolonial struggle are not limited to the rural sphere. On the other hand, we have to be conscious that these narratives, which substantially idealize Indigenous spirituality and our relationship with Mother Earth, can also be co-opted and employed against us by hegemonic sectors. Santiago Bastos explains, for example, that certain political spheres have appropriated some elements the Maya movement in Iximulew has sought to vindicate. Referencing a 2005 newspaper article published in *El Periódico,* Bastos states that, amid national debates about mining and extractivism in El Estor region in Izabal, a Maya ceremony was conducted to "solicit authorization from Mother Earth so its insides could be explored" (Bastos and Cumes 2007, 70). Government officials, including the minister of energy and mining, attended the ceremony. At the Maya event, the Maya priests started a fire that produced smoke and indicated that if the smoke from the bonfire turned black, then Mother Earth did not give her permission to be exploited by the mining company. However, if the smoke was white, then She did give her permission. Toward the end of the event, "the smoke that covered the area was the one that the miners awaited: white. The permit was granted" (70).

We must understand that Mayaness is heterogeneous, with diverse levels of complexity; it is a world characterized by differences at every level—socioeconomic, cultural, gender, generational, and geopolitical. Maya culture is also characterized by diverse political or spiritual conflicts and differences.[32] Our realities are neither alien nor do they exist at the margins of colonial processes. As Osage anthropologist Jean Dennison (2012) suggests, our experiences in contemporary hegemonic societies are characterized by "colonial entanglements"; that is, colonialism articulates diverse dynamics in various geopolitical and temporal spaces and its tentacles—as we see with the example offered by Bastos—also operate in our traditions. In other words, they sometimes can be co-opted by colonial power and used against us.

Comanche author Paul Chaat Smith argues, "Only when we recognize that our own individual, crazy personal histories, like those of every other Indian person of this century, are a tumble of extraordinary contradictions, can we begin making sense of lives" (2009, 27). This is to say that colonial tools can also be used for our struggles for self-determination. The experiences of those of us who have left our ancestral territories by force or choice can also offer creative solutions to Indigenous decolonization. Like the Otomí, Itz'x Qanq'ibil, Curruchich, and Tzutu B'aktun Kan, or the Zapatista Movement in Chiapas, we have learned to use the tools offered by the West to speak directly to the colonizer and to non-Indians in general—to express that in *every single* aspect of life, we as Indigenous peoples have been involved in continuous processes of self-modernization through unrecognized forms and strategies of resistance and liberation.

Conclusion

To conclude, the project of Maya vindication presented in the texts by Ak'abal, González, and Montejo, despite the shortcomings in their discussions of Maya cultural identity, contributes to inscribing the prominence of Maya views in the hegemonic Guatemalan register and to reflecting on a new intercultural national project. The literary works these authors produce activate "an awareness of the eminently violent, racist nature of interethnic relations. They highlight the need to redress these wrongs while also providing a continuous understanding of an alternative code of ethics provided by the *cosmovision* of the *Popol Vuh*" (Arias 2007, 78). Yet these literary works also "aspire to reterritorialize Mayas' displaced identities through a belated embrace of the 'lettered city,' one in which Maya languages are spoken and written before being translated to Spanish and English" (79). In this context, with their representations of Maya historical memory, Ak'abal, González, and Montejo compel us to rethink hegemonic history from a subaltern Maya perspective that denounces an unfinished colonial experience; they also challenge us to articulate an Indigenous epistemology that can help us reconfigure the world from the conditions of possibility offered by our ancestral values, our Indigenous languages, and the eminent millenarian material culture, all of which attest to our historical existence and continued emancipatory struggles. However, though we should consider the immense decolonial potentialities of this second Maya literary wave, we must also be alert to its shortcomings, which may lead to the negation of other spaces of struggle beyond the rural sphere.

That being said, how do Indigenous decolonial struggles for emancipation take shape in urban spaces? In chapters 3 and 4 of this book, I offer a response to this question through a discussion of Maya literature published after the Peace Accords were signed in 1996, a period now referred to as the "postwar period." Whereas some Maya writers may interpret globalization as a threat to our cultural existence, the new generation allows us to see some of its potentialities.

CHAPTER 3

Xib'alb'a and Globalism

Rosa Chávez, Pablo García, and Sabino Esteban Francisco

B ROADLY SPEAKING, A new phase in Maya literary insurgency began in the 1990s during which the Indigenous world of Abiayala acquired significant political prominence and political visibility. After the First Continental Gathering of Indigenous peoples in Quito, Ecuador, in July 1990, the continental Indigenous movement made its most significant effort to end the homogenizing discursive nature of modern nation-states. Indeed, with the fall of the Berlin Wall in 1989 and the Sandinista defeat in the 1990 presidential election in Nicaragua, much of the Left's foundational discourses were contested in Latin America. New debates and awareness about the rights of Indigenous peoples began to occur. In 1989, the International Labor Organization (ILO) approved Convention 169 about "Indigenous and Tribal Peoples" in independent countries: Article 2 calls for modern nation-states to assume the responsibility for developing— with the participation of Indigenous peoples—"coordinated and systematic action to protect the rights of these peoples and to guarantee respect for their integrity."[1] In 1992, there were debates and campaigns to resist the 500-year celebration of the so-called Discovery of the Americas along with global Indigenous demands for the rights and identity of Indigenous peoples. Such demands were symbolically affirmed that same year when K'iche' Maya activist, Rigoberta Menchú, was awarded the Nobel Peace Prize. This was followed by the proclamation of the United Nations General Assembly that the International Year of the World's Indigenous peoples would be celebrated in 1993. On January 1, 1994, the armed insurrection of the Zapatista Army of National Liberation (EZLN), a Maya movement struggling for land and Indigenous rights, began in Chiapas, Mexico. The movement also challenged Mexico's official homogenizing discourse of *mestizaje* or racial mixing in order to highlight the complex multiethnic, multilingual, and multicultural composition of the Mexican nation-state. The Zapatista discourse would serve as motivation for the resurgence and organization of other Indigenous movements that gradually strengthened the struggle against neoliberalism and its extractivist economic policies at the advent of the new millennium. By 2006, for example, with the presidential election of the Indigenous Aymara, Evo Morales, in Bolivia, Indigenous rights movements also realized conditions for political emancipation through democratic elections. Morales's victory set an important precedent and motivated others to follow similar paths. In Guatemala, Rigoberta Menchú ran for president in the elections of 2007 and 2011, albeit unsuccessfully. More recently, candidates in the 2019 Guatemalan general presidential election included Thelma Cabrera, a charismatic Maya Mam woman and peasant leader, who took fourth place, setting an important precedent for Maya political candidates in Iximulew. In Mexico, EZLN's representative, Maria de Jesus Patricio Martinez, or "Marichuy," ran for president; she is a Nahua activist who in the 2017 elections endorsed the Zapatista governmental ideals of challenging neoliberalism and defending Indigenous rights.

Events like these have certainly propelled significant political and discursive changes in how Latin American nation-states deal with Indigenous rights, especially in countries like Mexico, Bolivia, Peru, Ecuador, and Guatemala that have a strong Indigenous political presence. Guatemala, for example, approved and adopted the Agreement on Identity and Rights of Indigenous Peoples (AIRIP) in 1995, formally rejecting a homogeneous discourse of identity—only one national language, the criollo/ladino/mestizo or non-Indian as the "national subject," and one religion—and formally embracing an image of Guatemala as "multilingual, multicultural, and multiethnic." Indigenous movements and intellectuals used AIRIP to challenge the state's stereotypical ideas of Indigeneity and establish Mayaness as a political locus of enunciation.[2]

In 1996, Guatemala saw the formal end of the armed conflict with the signing of the "Accord for a Firm and Lasting Peace." Although many were optimistic that the peace would hold, the euphoria was quickly dampened. The Accord brought neoliberal globalization to Guatemala that was implemented through capitalist economic programs like the Central American and Dominican Republic Free Trade Agreement (CAFTA-DR), which promoted a predatory economic extractivism that affected both Indigenous and non-Indigenous sectors that experienced "globalization" from a position of subalterneity. Although the free trade agreement, CAFTA-DR,

was intended to offer opportunities for Guatemalans, it failed in its economic promise and instead resulted in the deepening of climate change
crisis and growth of crime and corruption that consequently led to unprec-
edented high levels of migration to the United States. In tandem with neoliberal economic policies, we saw the emergence and prominence of other
political actors: international criminal gangs like Mara Salvatrucha, or
MS-13, and drug cartels like the Zetas that challenged postwar social and
democratic governance.

The postwar period also marked the beginning of a new struggle
involving historical and political memory in which official hegemonic narratives emanating from the nation-state worked, once again, to bury the
past in order to restart the clock of history with a politics of forgetting.
A legion of intellectuals and journalists favoring these discursive tendencies began to produce works that hid the state's terrorism and negated
the genocide against Maya peoples in Guatemala. Despite these efforts
to cleanse the past, the return to democracy in the postwar period also
brought about significant victories for Mayas. Some Maya groups engaged
in legal action to indict military officers and dictators, such as the Sepur
Zarco case mentioned at the end of chapter 1. Similarly, Generals Romeo
Lucas García and Efraín Ríos Montt were accused of genocide and other
offenses. However, in 2013 Efraín Ríos Montt's eighty-year sentence for
crimes against humanity was overturned just ten days later when the high
Guatemalan court declared that there were "inconsistences" in the legal
arguments against the now-deceased general.

These political, economic, and social changes certainly influenced
Indigenous textual artistic production in what is now defined as postwar
Maya literature. The authors discussed in previous chapters (with the
exception of the late Luis de Lión, Luis Enrique Sam Colop, and Humberto Ak'abal) have continued to write and publish their work and have
been joined by a new generation of Maya writers who appropriate the
word to produce literary texts in both kaxlan tzij and Maya languages. The
writers of this new generation forge their own spaces of literary agency, in
many cases challenging and distancing themselves from their literary predecessors by developing new and refreshing images that make visible
other spaces of political struggle for Maya peoples. They explore themes
of migration and survival in various urban and rural settings, as well as
issues of gender and Indigenous sexual dissidence. Literature, in this sense,
becomes a weapon in the battle for Indigenous memory and for Indigenous

rights, allowing us to imagine our intellectual sovereignty (Warrior 2014) and self-determination. Indeed, postwar Maya literature continues the struggles to defend Indigenous territories and natural resources, as well as our right to affirm Maya identity. These authors, through their works, instead of turning the page of history, invite us to confront it. They suggest that the reconstruction of the Maya social body cannot occur without address-ing the trauma experienced in the past and that continues in the present.

Taking this context as a point of departure, I address in chapters 3 and 4 the third literary wave in Maya literary insurgency in Iximulew, demar-cated by the postwar period (1996–2012). In this chapter, I offer a critical analysis of Rosa Chávez's *Casa solitaria* (Solitary House, 2005), Pablo Gar-cía's *B'ixonik tzij kech juk'ulaj kaminaqib'* / *Canto palabra de una pareja de muertos* (2009) (Song from the Underworld, 2014), and Sabino Esteban Francisco's *Gemido de huellas* / *Sq'aqaw yechel aqanej* (Moan of the Foot-prints, 2007). I return to the metaphor of the journey that I use in chapter 1 in my discussion of Morales Santos's poetic work. However, my critical read-ings in this chapter highlight how these authors demystify and generate, on the one hand, a critique of the hegemonic narratives emanating from the nation-state about notions of citizenship and nationhood using *Xib'alb'a*, the K'iche' Maya underworld, in the *Popol Wuj* as an allegory of neoliberal globalization (Chávez and García) and, on the other hand, the reconstruc-tion of the Maya social body based on a confrontation with the fratricidal experience. As I show in the first section, Chávez develops Xib'alb'a as a literary trope associated with the city or the "solitary house" to explore the "infernal" modern condition we have inherited from the armed conflict and the introduction of neoliberal globalization through CAFTA-DR. In the second section, I expand the metaphor of Xib'alb'a by focusing on Pablo García's poetry. With the growing role of digital communication, especially in the massive diffusion of images that, for the most part, favors Western consumerist and capitalist ideologies, García—similar to Lión and González—explores the colonized condition of Maya subjectivity. With his poetry book, the K'iche' Maya poet develops a decolonial argu-ment to transcend the colonized infernal condition to which Maya peo-ples are subjected: ladinoization. I conclude the chapter with a critical analysis of Sabino Esteban Francisco's poetry. Through his poetry, Fran-cisco, a survivor of Guatemala's state terrorism during the armed conflict in Iximulew and a member of the Communities of Population in Resis-tance in the Ixcán region, addresses the trauma we inherited from the war, thereby drawing attention to the experience of Maya communities displaced in the mountains of Ixcan. In doing so, Francisco aims to dignify the courage of Maya war survivors and, in turn, feeds our optimism, which enables us to continue our struggle for survival and rebuild our historical memory.

The Journey through Xib'alb'a: Globalization and Its Postmodern Prison as Seen through Rosa Chávez's *Solitary House*

Rosa Chávez is a writer, actress, and artistic performer and one of the most prolific and celebrated Indigenous poets in Abiayala. Among contemporary Maya women writers, her literary work is perhaps the most widely disseminated beyond Iximulew, acquiring an international resonance. She also participated in international literary and academic events in Latin America, Europe, and North America, including the prestigious Poetry Festival in Medellin, Colombia, in 2006 and the Indigenous literary international festival, "Los cantos ocultos" (The Hidden Songs) organized by the Mapuche poet Jaime Huenun in Chile in 2007. Chávez was born in San Andrés Itzapa in Chimaltenango and is of Kaqchikel Maya origin on her mother's side and K'iche' Maya on her father's side. These two ancestral roots have marked and defined both her life and her literary and artistic production. Though she grew up in Chimaltenango and Santa Cruz del Quiche, because of the repressive political context in these Maya regions, her family feared that she, her sister, and young cousins would be considered "subversive" if they used their native language. Therefore, they were encouraged to speak only Spanish for their own protection. She initially complained to her parents and grandparents about their decision not to transmit Kaqchikel and K'iche' Maya to her, but she later "understood that the discrimination that her mother and her grandparents experienced was horrible; like living in a nightmare, things that she could never imagine" (Meza Márquez and Toledo Arévalo 2015, 170).

After her father died and she turned sixteen, Chávez decided to migrate to Guatemala City to continue her studies in higher education. She graduated as an elementary school teacher and then went on to pursue a bachelor's degree in law and literature at the University of San Carlos in Guatemala. In 2000 at the age of twenty, she began to participate in literary workshops at the university led by the poet Enrique Noriega. That same year, she offered poetry readings at the Blue October Festival, a public event in Guatemala City featuring urban dissident artists who sought to pay homage to Guatemala's October Revolution (1944–1954).[3] That festival gave rise to important artistic/cultural collectives, such as the theater group *Caja Lúdica* and *Folio 114*, a group of young artists who appropriated public spaces and abandoned buildings in Guatemala City's downtown to hold art discussions, literary recitals and workshops, and theater presentations. In 2004, Chávez joined *Folio 114*, which met at an old, abandoned office building that later became Guatemala City's Metropolitan Cultural Center; she participated in its literary workshops and performed her poetry. In 2005, the Guatemalan writer Marco Antonio Flores learned about her work and invited her to publish her first poetry collection, *Casa solitaria*, the book that I discuss in this section. To date, Chávez has also published *Ab'aj / Piedra* (Stone, 2009a), *Los dos corazones de Elena Kame* (Elena Kame's Two Hearts, 2009b), *Ri Uk'u'x Ri Ab'aj / El corazón de la piedra* (The Stone's Heart, 2010b), *Quitapenas* (Drown Your Sorrows, 2010a), and the play *AWAS* (with Camilla Camerlengo, a play on words that means both "be careful" and "watch out," 2014).

Chávez's *Solitary House* is an innovative poetry book that is notably different from the Maya literary production discussed in the previous chapters. Whereas earlier Maya authors created narratives that, for the most part, celebrate Maya identity, the rural world, and Indigenous cultural specificities such as language and spirituality, the poems in *Solitary House* are contextualized by urban settings in which the experiences of Indigenous characters coincide and coexist with those of other marginal subjects, such as prostitutes, homeless children, transvestites, drug addicts, and queer people. The book resists ethnic labeling. In contrast to Chávez's later poetry books, like *Ab'aj*/Stone or *Drown Your Sorrows*, *Solitary House* has very little to do with the political and cultural demands advocated by other Maya writers such as Luis de Lión, Francisco Morales Santos, Humberto Ak'abal, Gaspar Pedro González, or Calixta Gabriel Xiquin.[4] In its focus, Chávez's poetry book is similar to Manuel Tzoc's work, discussed in the next chapter. Only two poems in *Solitary House* may be characterized as Mayanist: "Hace un mes" (A Month Ago) and "Mujer solitaria / Ruyonil Ixöq" (Lonely Woman), a poem written in Spanish and Kaqchikel Maya. Chávez's book marks a generational distance from the first cohort of Indigenous writers, who, responding to a historical moment characterized by deep racism and political marginalization, wrote literature denouncing the human rights violations that many Indigenous peoples were suffering. That earlier group of writers wrote in defense of people directly affected by the internal armed conflict. They aimed to dignify Maya memory, as well as authorize and inscribe Maya linguistic, cultural, and religious specificities in the hegemonic narrative of the nation-state. In addition to exploring these issues, the new generation of Maya writers, which besides Chávez also includes Maya Cu Choc, Manuel Tzoc, Pedro Chavajay (Tzutuhil), Adela Delgado Pop (Q'eq'chi'), and Sabino Esteban Francisco (Q'anjob'al), among others, explores literary themes that go beyond the rural world, racism, and the class struggle to include valorization of the Indigenous feminine body and erotic and queer imagery that were not seriously considered by earlier prominent Maya writers in Iximulew.[5] The sounds inscribed in the poetry are not only those of birds, the wind, and trees but also those of the city: screams from the streets, cars, lights, or gunshots that interrupt the daily urban experience. From these surroundings, a transformed vision of Indigenous realities, rooted in a changed Maya worldview, emerges. In writing about the city, several of these urban Indigenous writers have not left their past or ancestral origin behind but have kept them and transported them to the urban sphere. The imagery depicts Indigenous realities rooted in repressive colonial urban contexts in which Maya spirituality and cosmogony can be freshly understood as also operating. Rather than seeing urban life as a threat to Indigenous cultural specificities, many urban Maya writers, through their work, suggest that the city needs to be appropriated and reclaimed in the name of Maya political, cultural, and human rights.

It is within this context that I read Chávez's *Solitary House,* which represents a profound meditation on the trauma we have inherited from the armed conflict, as well as a critique of neoliberal modernity or globalization, allegorized in the idea of Xib'alb'a. Indeed, *Solitary House* features an omniscient, first-person narrator: "it's true / I saw everything" (18). The poetic voice enters the underworld, or the "dark side of modernity" (Mignolo 1995), to focus her gaze on marginalized subjects and explore the concrete effects of the Civil War and globalization, which have resulted in the slow deterioration of humanity. The "solitary house" becomes a literary trope that acquires diverse metaphoric connotations associated with the personal interior and daily reality of those who survive modernity from the margins. The book demystifies and satirizes the urban setting— "an eternal circus" (9)—as representative of a modern world associated

with "progress," "development," "prosperity," "hope," "tolerance," "equality,"
"order," and "elegance." Yet, the images of the city offered by Chávez con-
vey grotesque, mundane, and nauseating surroundings where we witness
the survival of marginal subjects, despite their degrading experiences.

Page one of *Solitary House* features a black-and-white pencil-drawn
portrait of Chávez. She appears in what seems to be an empty room, sitting on what seems to be a bed placed against the wall. She is naked. Next
to her, there is only her shadow. She is in a curled-up position with her knees
drawn to her chest. Her long black hair falls loosely down her back. She
has a downcast look, with her eyes half-closed. The grayness of the portrait suggests a somber atmosphere, and Chávez's facial expression—the
focal point of the portrait—manifests anguish, isolation, and discourage-
ment. There is no doubt that the portrait foreshadows the themes
addressed in the book.

The poems in *Solitary House* are written in free verse and lack titles,
which creates an initial impersonal effect. The poems portray images
deprived of beauty, harmony, and order through the use of crude and grotesque language that creates a gloomy atmosphere of the city. Chávez
employs diverse rhetorical devices that include personification—"the
winter vomits" (18)—and irony. She concludes the description of the sinister routine of a transvestite who has been beaten with this line, "and
everything seems normal" (13). After the first poem, "A month ago" (I refer
to the untitled poems by their first line), the book is divided into two parts
that reveal a cyclical structure expressed in the line, "solitary house hidden
in a storeroom." This line appears in the poem that opens the first section,
"Pequeña dosis de placer autómata" (Small dose of automaton pleasure, 9),
and then again in the final poem of the book, "desenchufar" (To unplug, 36).
The phrase denotes alienation and even forgetfulness: the house *hidden* in
the storeroom is a forgotten object, and the loneliness is made explicit in
the adjective "solitary."

In the first part of the book, the protagonists move in an urban public
sphere, as the omniscient narrator describes her journey through the subterranean spaces of the city. The poems describe the actions of marginalized and despised subjects in the hegemonic social and discursive order.
The first part concludes with the poem, "It was her words," which describes
a conversation between the narrator and her mother. The mother offers a
prayer to the gods so that "the sadness I carry inside is removed" (19). The
poems in the second part provide more intimate and personal insights and

include those that speak of deceit ("Él, maquilló sus ojos" / He put makeup on her eyes), impatience ("El niño le habla" / The child speaks to her), abandonment ("Tú"/You), anguish ("Nacemos al dolor" / We are born to pain), and indifference ("Hoy somos los desencontrados" / Today we are the unknown). In most of the poems in this second part, the characters move in confined and private spaces, such as a bedroom or kitchen. It would seem as if they are inside the solitary house, with the exception of the last poem, "To unplug" (36), in which the poetic voice speaks in the first person, describing the action on the street, the public sphere.

The first poem of the book, "A month ago," is a preface to the themes of fear, confinement, and verbal and physical violence that Chávez explores through the experiences of her urban characters in the poems in the following two parts. I cite the entire poem to enable a more thorough analysis of it:

A month ago
I came to the city
my dad left us
and in the house hunger ached
I work in a house
(the lady says that I am a *domestic maid*
even though I don't understand what that means),
they gave me a uniform made of fabric,
that day I cried a lot, I cried a lot
I was ashamed of wearing it
of showing my legs,
the lady says that in my town
we are all filthy
so I take a shower every day
they cut my long hair
because of lice, she says,
I cannot speak Spanish well
and people laugh at me
my heart
becomes sad,
yesterday I went to see my cousin
the bus driver did not want to stop
and when I was stepping off, he sped off,

hurry up you stupid Indian—he said
I fell down and scraped my knee
the people laugh and laugh
my heart became sad
my cousin says
that I will get used to it
that Sunday we will go to the central park
that there are places to dance
with the music groups that arrive from the fairs
of my town,
I am in my little room
counting the money they paid me
minus the soap and two glasses I broke
the lady says that I am very stupid
I don't understand why they treat me so badly
aren't I a human being? (5)

Despite its apparent testimonial straightforwardness, the poem displays complexity through its various discursive layers. Through the metaphor of the house, the poem represents the dichotomy between the countryside (the house where hunger ached) and the city (both the house where she obtains a job as a "domestic maid" and the public sphere). The poem narrates the character's journey from the countryside to the city in a cyclical or spirally descending structure, which relates to the arrangement of the book as a whole. The character travels from the house where hunger aches (the countryside), to the house where she works (the city), and then to the little room within that house. The images of the room within the house and, in turn, of the house within the city are directly associated with the line "solitary house [small room within the house] hidden in the storeroom [house + city]." The poem also has a social dimension. With the father's abandonment and the protagonist's migration to the city, the poem suggests the rupture of the Indigenous social fabric. Although the poem does not mention the armed conflict in Guatemala, the experience of the "domestic maid" recalls the migration of thousands of Mayas who moved from the countryside to the city in search of better opportunities or merely survival. These migrations were the result of the poverty and social injustice endured during the armed conflict. However, as we can see, instead of finding the desired prosperity, the protagonist confronts a world that rejects and harasses her due to her Indigeneity.

In the city, the protagonist's Indigenous cultural specificities are attacked. The "lady" she works for as a maid prohibits her from wearing her Maya clothes, cuts her hair, and accuses her of being filthy and stupid. Her experience in the public sphere is no different. People make fun of her because she cannot speak Spanish well. The bus driver who takes her to her cousin's house refers to her as a "stupid Indian" and ridicules her in front of everyone when she gets off the bus. When she tells her cousin about these experiences, the response is that she "will get used to it," which indicates that the cousin has also experienced similar aggressions. The cousin's experiences suggest a historical precedent marked by a naturalized racism. When the protagonist returns to the house where she works, in her small room, she reflects on her own social condition as a dehumanized subject: "I don't understand why they treat me so badly." She asks a rhetorical question, "aren't I a human being?" that parodies the "civilizing" symbolism represented by the city.

Contrary to such symbolism and similar to Michel Foucault's idea of the prison as an institution of discipline and punishment ([1975] 1995),[6] the city emerges here as a place where violent mechanisms of control operate to regulate and domesticate the Indigenous body. In contrast to the progress, hope, and social well-being normally associated with the urban setting, the city turns into a hostile environment that at once segregates, excludes, and domesticates subjects in subaltern positions. In addition, the experience described in the poem illustrates modernity's modus operandi, built on coloniality (Mignolo 1995, 2000): it rejects Indigenous cultural specificities, but at the same time feeds on their human capacities to function.

The violence that characterizes the ambience of the city is not unique to Indigenous peoples. Other subaltern characters from *Solitary House* who have been pushed to the margins experience physical and verbal aggression similar to that experienced by the Maya "domestic maid." Using olfactory, tactile, and sensorial grotesque images, Chávez represents these characters in conditions so degraded that they acquire animalistic and monstrous dimensions. The prostitute in the poem "The little whore is mentally unbalanced," for instance, "is a dog on the sidewalk," "a big sad monster," "with lungs drowned in excrement" (17). She makes love amid "the flies that turn and circulate / tickling the genitals" (17). Similarly, the transvestite in "The lights are turned on" lives among "cockroaches" and "blows, whispers, asphyxiation" (13). Like the "little whore," he survives off of "poorly paid fucks" (13). The children from the streets in "City of little thieves" form a "small village of goblins" that wander around as "disguised street dogs adopting human orphanhood" (10). In addition to existing in repugnant conditions and spaces, these subjects live in loneliness and fear, like the children from "At this hour no one speaks," who, as soon as nighttime arrives, "hide themselves in loneliness while their parents intoxicate themselves" (14), or the child from "He is an anonymous son," who "fears the birds, the dogs, / butterflies." He is a "metaphor of scrambled letters" (15). Paradoxically, in this last poem, elements that traditionally symbolize freedom and beauty—birds and butterflies—acquire a new meaning to underscore the fear they provoke in the child. In turn, the child becomes a symbol of confusion and chaos, a "metaphor of scrambled letters." The images of animals in these poems contrast to Ak'abal's representation of animals in *The Animal Gathering* as complements of humans, as discussed in the previous chapter, since the child and the birds are disconnected and confused in the city.

The settings in which the characters from *Solitary House* operate are somber, marked not only by a gradual human degradation but also by a grotesque and hopeless ambience. As the poem "Hunger" expresses, society "stinks like a cadaver / we are the death" (18). The images depicting the inhumane living conditions of these characters is more explicit in "The sky is covered in gray," which describes the agony of a dying cat:

The sky is covered in gray
a dusty mist in the sky
it caresses the cat's loin
that bleeds through its mouth
blood clots in its nose
his last shit in the patio
it drizzles and the cat is stilled
it licks color and trembles
his childish eyes
are transparent marbles
he is gentle and repulsive
his last meows
in a plastic bag. (12)

This poem articulates a feeling of repulsion in a state of impotence. The somber atmosphere (the gray sky) is intoxicated by death, personified in the metaphor, "dusty mist in the sky," which caresses the cat in his last meows. The cat, in turn, allegorizes the mundane condition represented by the marginal characters previously described: they are marginal subjects in a banal society. The contradiction of "gentle and repulsive" underscores the degraded condition not only of the cat but also of the other characters Chávez invokes in the book. The "childish eyes" of the cat reflect feelings of dismay and impotence experienced by the characters in their precarious situations. Not even the "last meows" in the plastic bag hold meaning. It is indeed a hopeless reality that these characters experience in the city.

The representation of these characters and their inhumane animal-like condition is reminiscent of that of the beggars in "In the Cathedral Porch" in *El Señor Presidente* (The President) ([1946] 1969) by Miguel Ángel Asturias. Similar to the Guatemalan 1967 Nobel laureate, Chávez depicts a chilling ambience where characters' complaints or situations have no meaning. With the exception of the character in "A month ago," we do not even hear their voices, and we do not recognize their existence as human beings in the prison of the solitary house where they coexist. All the characters, the text suggests, are accustomed to experiences where "everything seems normal" (13). Reality is a "common daily cry" (12), a "daily routine, that's all" (14), and the characters move in confined spaces where they confront a naturalized physical and verbal violence in their everyday lives. Even the future seems to be marked by hopelessness as shown in "We are born into pain," which describes a "world that rids itself of bones" with an "invisible end" (31).

Far from the dictums associated with Western democracy and modernity—"liberty," "tolerance," "equality," and so on—what emerge from the metaphor of the city, associated with the solitary house, are surroundings filled with a "common quotidian cry" (12) and "songs from caged birds" (10). When the lights of the city are turned on at six in the evening in "Nacemos al dolor" (We are born into pain, 31), the streets become sad. The image of the city is related to a prison characterized by confinement and uncertainty in the poem "Ants run," where a "mysterious bird"

lost in the tree's branches observes
he is a friend of solitude and absence
a wise knower of universes

hypnotized
by the lights
that are never turned off
a lost small mammal. (28)

In the urban settings, the characters—allegorized here by the "mysterious bird"—are hypnotized and lost. They live in a world horrifically marked not by a military dictatorship, as in *The President*, but rather the experience of the Civil War and neoliberal globalization, both of which implicitly spread a violent democracy that dehumanizes certain subjects, pushing them to the most obscure corners of the city. In such "modern," globalized spaces, life becomes a metaphor for "blood" when Chávez writes,

Blood
it is not a mystery
it is sold, rented out,
it is stolen, given back,
it is spilled, drunk
it is urinated, discolored
it is worth nothing,
it neither unites nor stops
it does not clot, does not taste like iron
circles are formed to absorb it. (27)

The end of the armed conflict and the introduction of globalization were supposed to bring about material and spiritual prosperity and eradicate violence. However, the subjects who survived these conditions from the margins then confront the restoration of a new violent order, characterized by a gradual human degradation and dehumanization. The city, or modernity, emerges as a prison or hell for subjects made invisible by their profession (prostitutes), ethnic identity (the "domestic maid"), social status (the children from the streets), or sexual identity (queer subjects like the transvestite).

The representation of the city and the experience of subaltern characters may be associated with Xib'alb'a, the K'iche' Maya underworld in the *Popol Wuj.* Xib'alb'a is a world governed by the spirits of illness and death; it is a place characterized by pain, chaos, isolation, darkness, and hopelessness. In this space are the rivers of blood and rotten water and the houses of suffering (Sam Colop 2011, 68)—including the houses of darkness, cold, jaguars, bats, and cut glass—where the first set of divine twins, Hun Hunahpu (One Master of the Blowgun) and Wuqub' Hunahpu (Seven Master of the Blowgun), lose their battle against the Lords of Death: the twins are tortured and then decapitated.[7] Later, a new battle between the Lords of Death takes place in which the descendants of the first twin brother, Hunahpu (One Blowgun) and Xbalanque (Jaguar Sun) finally defeat the Lords of Xib'alb'a. According to Enrique Florescano, this victory "symbolizes the end of earlier contradictions that had emerged before"; it also "turns the cosmos into a harmonic order. From here on, the underworld, the earth's surface, and the heavens, instead of battling one another, join each other to infuse stability to the cosmos" (1999, 37). With the defeat of the Lords of Xib'alb'a, the Lord of Maize appears, which "symbolizes the beginning of abundance and stability, supported by the farmers that embrace the function of being providers of human nourishment and sustainers of civilized life" (51).

Solitary House may very well be read as a new journey through the underworld, represented by the contemporary globalized condition. Yet, in contrast to the sacred K'iche' Maya text, the trauma we inherited from the armed conflict and colonial oppression has not ended: we continue to live in Xib'alb'a, now ruled by neoliberal economic policies.[8] Moreover, *Solitary House* registers the story of Xib'alb'a to suggest that the incarcerated subjects in the underworld are not the first hero twins, but rather are marginalized subjects despised by the new hegemonic global order: abandoned children, homosexuals, transgender individuals, prostitutes, and Indigenous subjects in a subaltern position. These representations, one could argue, implicitly give shape to Chávez's political proposal: Is it possible to build a subaltern nationalist collective project that allows us to transcend the contemporary Xib'alb'a? In other words, is it possible to build an antineoliberal project, not merely an Indigenous one but a subaltern one that includes other marginalized subjects who struggle for political vindication within modernity and the settler colonial nation-state? In my view, Chávez develops a social proposal that is not as much interested in developing a politics of ethnic vindication as developing a social one that also addresses the needs of homeless children, prostitutes, gays, and the like.

Although *Solitary House* may express social situations that seem hopeless, we should not forget that narratives of creation-destruction-re-creation characterize the *Popol Wuj*. The conditions for the possibility of new life rest in teleological processes that suggest that death is necessary to re-create life. The creation of the men of maize is one iteration in a series of processes in which the gods, after creating the earth, the sky, and the animals, make humanity out of mud, then wood, and finally, corn.

In *Solitary House* the idea of death as a basic principle of resurrection can be associated with the Maya worldview, which provides sustenance in the poem, "It was her words." The words of the mother and the "prayers to the gods" in the name of the poetic voice serve as relief from the disillusionment and the "bittersweet mockery / that dances in the ashes" (19). In this environment reemerges "the death that has drowned," which has been "transformed / reborn in the center / of obliviousness" (19). This "obliviousness" allegorizes processes of social and epistemological erasure that characterize modernity; that is, Chávez understands the horrific social conditions of the characters she invokes to be the result of the violent legacy we inherited from the armed conflict and in which some subaltern sectors have been disenfranchised from "progress" and the "benefits" of modernity. Nonetheless, Chávez also suggests a future that necessarily entails "rebirth" and "transformation." This Maya worldview thus permeates the poetry book in the sense that it implicitly proposes the development of alternatives to counteract the impact of neoliberal economic policies on the subaltern sectors that Chávez evokes. It suggests that the degrading conditions of certain sectors will be transitory. Although they bring destruction these conditions will also bring about a new order characterized by the end of contradictions: a world of "abundance" and "stability" as suggested by Florescano earlier.

By proposing Xib'alb'a as a literary trope in *Solitary House,* Chávez develops—unconsciously perhaps—a connection to her own ancestral epistemological precedents as a means to understand her present condition. In doing so, she not only incorporates the Maya cosmogony embodied in the *Popol Wuj* but also rewrites it to adjust it to the new challenges faced under neoliberal globalization. The "solitary house" is added to the Xib'alb'a narrative to manifest a postmodern condition characterized by grotesque and gradual human degradation—a condition we first need to become aware of so we can develop alternative strategies to transcend it. Chávez places herself in that same solitary house, as suggested in the portrait that opens her book.

Some critics claim that Chávez's discursive strategy involves an epistemic violence in how she speaks for or about the subaltern subjects she observes. I argue instead that, far from speaking for or about transgender, prostitutes, or homeless children, Chávez aims to speak *of* the subjects she represents and invokes. In other words, the Kaqchikel-K'iche' poet— following Gayatri Spivak—highlights what has been hidden in order to make visible the unseen: "a change of level, addressing oneself to a layer of material which hitherto had no pertinence for history and which had not been recognized as having any moral, aesthetic or historical value" (1988, 285). It is the slippage from rendering visible the mechanism to rendering vocal the individual, both avoiding "any kind of analysis of [the subject] whether psychological, psychoanalytical or Linguistic" that is consistently troublesome (285). Yet, Chávez's discursive strategy relates the marginal experiences *of* these subaltern subjects to her own— suggesting that the story of isolation of these marginalized subjects resembles her own experience, given that Maya peoples have been historically relegated to the margins. In some of her poems, like "Hunger," Chávez articulates an inclusive collective perspective: "we are the dead / the books without owners / the eyes without letters" (18). In my view, then, to speak of these subaltern subjects is to articulate a collective demand emanating from subalterneity. It means conceptualizing not only an Indigenous "I" or "We" but also a subaltern "I" or "We" that can potentially develop alliances in the struggles for survival under neoliberal globalization.

Decolonizing Maya Subjectivity: Pablo García's *Song from the Underworld*

The idea of Xib'alb'a as a degraded condition is also developed by Pablo García in his K'iche' Maya / Spanish poetry book, *B'ixonik tzij kech juj'ulaj kaminaqib'* / *Canto palabra de una pareja de muertos* (2009). Instead of representing Xib'alb'a in the urban invocation of the city and the postwar neoliberal period, however, García explores the processes of ladinoization promoted by globalization. In this sense, he emphasizes the seductive mechanisms of modernity and some of their consequences for Indigenous peoples; in doing so, he confronts its cultural violence in order to reactivate Indigeneity. *B'ixonik tzij* is García's first and only book.

The K'iche' Maya author, born in Totonicapán, Guatemala, in 1965, is a teacher at the Western Regional School for Teachers (ENRO by its Spanish acronym) who writes poetry to reclaim and dignify the Maya cultural heritage. He received the B'atz' Literary Prize for Indigenous Literature

(*B'atz'* means monkey and the Mayan glyph dedicated to art), in 2007. García shared it with the Kaqchikel Maya writer, Miguel Ángel Oxlaj Cúmez, who received the award for his short story "Ru Taqikil Ri, Sarima' / La misión del Sarima" (Sarima's Mission). The creation of this literary prize and the subsequent publication of these two literary works have set a precedent that is important to share here.

The B'atz' Literary Prize was created by the non-Indigenous Guatemalan writer, Rodrigo Rey Rosa, in response to the actions of K'iche' Maya poet Humberto Ak'abal. As we discussed in the previous chapter, in 2003, Ak'abal was awarded the Miguel Ángel Asturias National Literary Award. It was named for the Nobel Prize–winning father of modern Guatemalan and Latin American literature whose works spearheaded the magical realism literary movement that gained global prominence with the writings of Gabriel García Marquez, Julio Cortázar, and others. In his honor, the Gua-temalan state created a national literary award in 1988. When Ak'abal was awarded the prize in 2003, he declined it, arguing that Guatemala should not have a national literary prize named after a racist writer.[9] The following year, the prize was awarded to Rey Rosa, who used the funds he received to create the B'atz' Literary Prize for Indigenous Literature to recognize the artistic creativity that emerges in texts like the *Popol Wuj*, with its twins Hun Chowen (One Howler) and Hun B'atz' (One Monkey), artists who are later turned into monkeys. Though there have been reservations about Ak'abal's and Rey Rosa's stands about the National Literary Prize, the debates enabled publication of the literary works of García and Oxlaj Cúmez.

Let me now turn to García's *B'ixonik tzij kech juj'ulaj kaminaqib'*, which was originally published in K'iche' Maya and kaxlan tzij (Spanish). The book was translated into English as *Song from the Underworld* by Victoria Livingstone and published in a trilingual K'iche', Spanish, and English edi-tion by Achiote Press in 2014. I use this edition in my references to García's work in this section. Although García explores themes of Maya cultural and linguistic rights that resonate with our discussions from earlier chap-ters, his work is highly original. It distances itself from testimonial and ver-nacular poetics to offer a literary aesthetic informed by the ancestral oral tradition in the *Popol Wuj*. García develops innovative avant-garde images with a truly transformative figurative language that references cultural knowledge about Maya society and spirituality. The Mexican writer Juan Villoro states that García's poetry book is "a poetic ensemble with an extraor-dinary force, full of unexpected metaphors, and a magnificent atmosphere where the reader feels that the poet's voice has been worked out by the dead characters invoked; that such voice comes from the other side of things" (qtd. in Villoro 2007).

In his book, García builds a discursive construction of Xib'alb'a that is associated with Indigenous subjectivity. Like Chávez, he uses the metaphor of the journey of a dead couple — a woman and a man (the collective poetic voice) — through the underworld. Through their journey, they slowly develop a process of mental and political decolonization in which they sing prayers and songs to the gods asking to be "resurrected." They also want to reconcile with their gods to avoid a "second hellish death" (16). The representation of the dead couple can be read in great measure as a rewriting of Adam and Eve's expulsion from paradise in the biblical book of Genesis and in John Milton's (1608–1674) epic poem *Paradise Lost* (1667), which illustrates Adam and Eve's journey in search of reconciliation with their creator, God. In contrast to *Paradise Lost,* however, *B'ixonik tzij* is not about Satan tempting the main characters to "eat the apple," but rather about how a world in which everything "is revelry and celebration" (28) for a man and woman becomes a punishment. Their condition has degraded because they adopted foreign values that distance them from their native ones. Where Milton uses the Bible as a point of departure for Adam and Eve's expulsion, García employs Maya oral tradition, which in many ways echoes the *Popol Wuj,* to reconceptualize "original sin." Moreover, unlike the Bible and Milton's epic poem, García universalizes his protagonists by not using proper names.

The book consists of an introduction and four songs. The introduction, comprising eight stanzas of forty lines, establishes the contrast between a "before" when everything "is revelry and celebration" (20) and an "after" when the couple fall to the underworld. Initially, the man and woman are the "seed of light" and "the flower of the star of the Creator / of the Creatress." They are then interrupted by a cataclysmic event that destroys the world and expels them to Xib'alb'a, where they become "the dead from both sides of the underworld" (20). Once they understand that "the great relative calm of silence" means they are now a "dead couple" (20), the man and woman begin a journey through the darkest roads of Xib'alb'a. They plead and pray that their "Father" and "Mother," creators of humanity and the universe, "pardon [their] sins."

The first song includes eleven hymns or prayers that describe the infernal situation and the characters' complaints about the punishments they suffer in the underworld. For instance, the man and woman have been emptied of "life essence." They are turned into "the underworld's rotten reeds" (38) and consumers of "dead animal" (44). They are "terrible sleepers" (76) and have been fried, toasted, and grinded by the Lords of Death, Hun Kame (First Death) and Wuqub' Kame (Seven Death; 30). The second song consists of one hymn, "Father—Mother Who Share Our Responsibility and Complete Us" (66). It evokes the creators so that the couple can carry out a process of liberation from the underworld through solar self-purification, self-correction, self-resurrection, and self-realization and then can be resurrected like the "flower of the star of the Creator / of the Creatress" (66). The third song, consisting of eleven prayers from "the underworld's school" (70), calls for the liberation from Xib'alb'a through a "shared solar education" (70). Here, the author describes the path toward resurrection as a desire for "the perennial life of our hearts" (66). The last song concludes with an expression of "Gratitude" to the Father and Mother for "having listened to us" (108).

For the most part, the poems are written in free verse. García uses language that is highly symbolic and creates complex discursive constructions to develop an ambience that recalls the dualist philosophic conception of the *Popol Wuj*. The sacred Maya K'iche' text emphasizes the paradox and reciprocity of binary opposites as an epistemological base for sociability and intersubjectivity. *B'ixonik tzij* displays this dual discursive tendency through the languages used (K'iche' and Spanish), the double temporality (before and after, yesterday and today), the dead couple, the Creator and Creatress or Father and Mother, and the binary oppositions that characterize the "hellish" ambience of the characters in Xib'alb'a: heaven/earth, life/death, light/darkness, and good/evil. In addition, the binary opposites serve to establish and "identify links between all forms of life as well as to express complementary aspects of a similar referent. Objects are not perceived as semantically isolated from one another, but rather they offer a natural contextualization of the reality being described" (Craveri Slaviero 2004, 35). García also emulates the K'iche' oral tradition and the sacred K'iche' text in the form of songs or prayers, which have continuous couplets and lines that feature contradictions: "once we were tender / then we were hard / once we were joyful / then we were angry" (28).

By using "songs" to structure the poetry book, García also legitimizes and performs orality as a vehicle of artistic transmission. Following Walter

Ong's (1989, 21, 36–37) approach, the orality in the book manifests itself in onomatopoeia—"iron heads hum through the air" (42); repetition—"our faces our bodies our tastes our words" (18); and the constant presence of epithets—"we're the sun clearing space in the clouds we're the white moon shining through" (10). Moreover, the poems are characterized by indents that represent long pauses, with intonations that alternate between nostalgic, aggressive, pretentious, and even burlesque. Indents are sometimes used to develop calligrams of the described referent, as in the first stanza of "Consumers of Dead Animal," one of the prayers from the first song. It draws the image of the fire at the entrance of Xib'alb'a:

> The fire's tongue flickers
>   casts light
>   and heat
> if we get the fire ready
>   its flames steady
>   we blow. (44)

That the fire is calm emerges from the sounds articulated in the onomatopoeia of the "flickers" of the fire, the acoustic pauses established through the indents in the stanza, and the phonemes at the end of each line: "light," "heat," "ready," and "steady." Onomatopoeia is once again used at the end of the song when García imitates the sounds a dog makes when it licks the liquids in the underworld: "riq' riq' riq' it sounds" (44).

The main figurative devices that García employs in his songs are metaphor and simile. He uses these to develop images that are paradoxical around the light/darkness dichotomy. As stated, in the beginning the man and woman are compared to luminous and radiant elements. They are "the seed of light," "the flower of the star of the Creator / of the Creatress," "the sun clearing space in the clouds," and "the white moon shining through this earth / to the underworld / the universe" (20). In Xib'alb'a, these images give way to an intensely somber ambience. For example, in the poem "Rotten Reeds" we find, "Our gaze reflects a smoky sky / and a naked heart without iridescence" (38). Similarly, García highlights how the pureness of a full life withers in the underworld, as in the poem "We Whisper," where the "tender faces become old and furrowed" (32). The man and woman are like "skinny sores / hunched over / and sickly," and they "look

like fat sores / oozing / stinking / and we howl" (38). Darkness becomes
the main protagonist in the "hellish" stage and is the place from which
"the voracious death" that consumes "the fire of life" (91) emerges. In the
underworld, the characters vanish along with the radiant imagery, leaving
us with a world marked by isolation and despair. The luminous images in
that ambience are evoked through prayers that display a tone of nostalgia
for a harmonious and full past that has been lost. With their prayers, the
dead couple petitions for a return to a world where everything is "revelry
and celebration," and harmony "with our fathers and mothers Star / Sirius /
Sun and White Moon" (32) is restored.

Nonetheless, harmony will not be reinstated until the "original sin" is
eliminated. The dead couple has assimilated ways of life that have distanced and alienated them from their original subjectivity, as is figuratively
expressed in the poem, "Lizard, Monkey." The poetic voice indicates, "We
drank a river of desires / and then vomited an earthquake of erudition" (41).
This metaphor—"we drank a river of desires"—is extended through rhetorical questions that allegorize the dead couple's alienation from ancestral values. For example, in "We Whisper," the poetic voice asks, "Why did
we shut ourselves up, asleep in the tomb?" (32). In "Consumers of Dead
Animal," the speakers wonder, "Why do we feed on dead animal?" (44),
and in "Disharmony," they ask, "Why do we fall out of harmony / with the
heart of the sky and the heart of the earth?" (50).

The experience of assimilation and alienation is more clearly represented in the figure of "Rational Animal," which is a metaphor for the violent imposition of modern values on the protagonists. The rational animal
is a "galloping" being (28) that rose "from the blackness of the Black Moon"
(28) to position itself "in the four columns and pillars of our hearts" (35).
The animal consumes "the fire of our essence," turning the dead couple
into decomposed and inactive bodies like "rotten reeds" from the underworld. Their heads become "desiccated pumice stones" and their organ-
isms "shriveled worms" (35). Instead of being "seeds of light," they are
"dry sap of rational animal / piled before Hun Kame Wuqub' Kame" (35);
they no longer see each other "in the heart of the sky and the heart of the
earth" (29). They have broken the "harmony / well-being / and the peace
of the living essence" (70) that connected them to their creators. As a
result of this disconnection from their values, they have been locked up
in the underworld:

With the bitterness and dryness of our pain
we say to you
      Father-Mother
our faces
our bodies
our tastes
our words and our work
are now the reflection of the rational animal, thinker. (28–29)

In another part of the poem, we read,

we no longer follow solar wisdom
we no longer plant our heart
we no longer plant our corn
we no longer plant our wheat
we no longer plant our rice
at dawn
at the dusk of the Sun and the White Moon. (47)

The solemn tone expressed through the anaphor "our" and "we no longer . . ."
underscores the imposition of alien values that mirror not an original
world, but rather the disfigured, alienated, and fractured subjectivity of
the poetic voice. The rational animal, in this sense, represents modernity's
march, destructively advancing to impose a logic characterized by alienation and fragmentation—"With the bitterness and dryness of our pain,"
"we no longer . . ."—of the ancestral values that enabled the dead couple
to enjoy revelry and celebration.

The images of light/darkness evoked by the poetic voice represent the
couple's efforts to overcome their alienation, which has been created by a
colonized condition associated with their degraded experience in Xib'alb'a.
Darkness represents the infernal condition, and light symbolizes the past, the
search to reconnect with and vindicate ancestral values, and the possibility of
overcoming their colonized condition. The nostalgia expressed in the tone of
the songs from Xib'alb'a suggests that a return to an original world, untouched
by the hand of modernity, is the only path to "resurrect" and escape from the
infernal death. This is clearly expressed in the hymn "Helping Each Other"
where the Creators, after listening to the couple's prayers, tell them,

in order to be free from the underworld
you must plant the flower of your star together
men as well as women,
to return to the everlasting harmony of Tulan Siwan. (94)

As indicated by the Creators, the liberation effort must be a collective and
mutual one—"together you must plant." The reference to Tulan Siwan—
the mythical place of the seven caves from where Mesoamerican peoples
emerged—suggests an exit from the degraded settings, which in turn would
allow for the resurrection of the dead couple as the Creators' seeds and
flowers of light. It would also permit them to live a harmonious and everlasting existence without the punishments experienced in the underworld.
    Although García proposes a return to origins, we should not interpret
his proposal literally. It is, in my view, an example of strategic essentialism
(Spivak 1996) similar to what we discussed in the previous chapter, which
he uses to defend and dignify Maya identity and counteract the hegemonic cultural and economic neoliberal model that promotes and imposes
capitalist values as strategies to alienate and separate Indigenous peoples
from their original cultures. A return to the origins, represented by Tulan
Siwan, aims to reimagine a world where Indigenous peoples maintained
their autonomy: it is another world, absent of a colonized experience that
began in 1492 and has been restructured until today by the descendants of
the first European settlers. This political project differs from other decolonial discussions proposed by Latinamericanism in that it affirms an ancestral memory free from a mercantilist economic model characterized by
alienation. This is not to suggest that, before the arrival of Europeans, the
Mayas did not have an economic model consisting of the division of labor
and social hierarchies. Nonetheless, García here argues for the need to rescue cultural elements that will help us claim, again, our sovereignty—a
sovereignty that we possessed before the European settlers invaded our
ancestral lands. In doing so, he dignifies our subjectivity as Indigenous
peoples in a world that has marginalized us for more than 500 years. To
"resurrect" as seeds reflects the desire to once again affirm ourselves as full
and autonomous subjects, owners of our own history and subjectivity.
The singing of the prayers to the Maya deities of life and death points
toward that direction through verses that invoke the desire to "see ourselves" (70), "still experience harmony / well-being / and peace of the living essence" (70), and "revive even now in the garden of living life" (76).

Hence, we must "pull the thorn of sin out of our breath" and "the rational animal from our bodies" (79) to open ourselves to the future. García's songs, in this context, recall Michela Elisa Craveri Slaviero's definition of the "word" for the Maya K'iche': it "represents a form of gratitude, a petition and a way to get close to the gods. Along with other offerings, it allows the collective voice in the poems to settle a debt with the creators and maintain a balance with the cosmos. Only the men of maize, after successive destructions, have been able to feed the gods through their prayers" (2004, 55).

As does Chávez, García interrogates the project of neoliberalism ("The Rational Animal"), associating it with colonialism. The adoption of its hegemonic values has slowly led us to alienation and social decomposition through the constitution of a subjectivity that has lost its ancestral Indigenous values. Implicitly, García references the armed conflict and the imposition of neoliberal economic policies that, instead of bringing social benefits, propel the constitution of a chaotic and violent social order that attacks Indigenous survival. Despite everything, García places his faith in "resurrecting" the values of our ancestors, because, by so doing we can find the conditions of possibility to decolonize our Indigenous subjectivity.

Sabino Esteban Francisco and the Poetics of Survival

As we have seen in the poetic works by Chávez and García, the metaphor of the journey through the postwar Guatemalan context is directly associated with the challenges created by the implementation of neoliberal economic policies and the growing role of a cultural globalization that promotes Western logics. The tensions that emanate from these processes, from a Maya subaltern perspective, result in an infernal condition that resembles that of the K'iche' Maya underworld: Xib'alb'a or the place of fear. These figurative representations of the journey as a literary trope acquire new dimensions when we consider how the survivors of Guatemala's state terrorism and the genocide reactivate their traumatic memories. In the last section of this chapter, I critically examine *Gemido de huellas / Sq'aqaw yechel aqanej* (Moan of the Footprints), the first poetry book written by Q'anjob'al poet Sabino Esteban Francisco. The book is an autobiographical account that offers an important register of the experiences of Maya peoples who were forcibly displaced from their ancestral communities during the armed conflict and who consequently joined the Communities of

Peoples in Resistance (CPR) during the first half of the 1980s. By narrating experiences of violence, pain, and chaos, Esteban Francisco not only reveals the operations of internal or settler colonialism but also *re-members* the Maya social body by confronting the traumatic past. In doing so, the Q'anjob'al Maya poet rewrites or *re-rights* history by inscribing and authorizing the memory of Maya peoples who were part of the CPR.

In 1982, in the Ixcan region in Iximulew—a territory where diverse Maya peoples from Huehuetenango, Quiché, Totonicapán, Quetzaltenango, and San Marcos coexisted under the most precarious and inhumane conditions—thousands of Indigenous families embarked on a long exodus, leaving behind their homelands, crops, and belongings: they were searching for a safe place where they could survive the Guatemalan Army's military incursions in the region. The forced displacement that Maya families in Ixcán experienced can be thought of as a contemporary Indigenous Maya "Trail of Tears,"[10] permeated with pain, chaos, and uncertainty. In their long walk, thousands of Maya peasants went to Mexico, hoping that as soon as they crossed the border they would find immunity from political persecution. Among those thousands of people who made this long journey was the Maya Q'anjob'al family of Esteban Francisco, who carried in their arms Sabino, a little boy of one year. Subsequently, this family and others found refuge in the CPR compounds that emerged during this time.

An unnamed war survivor who later told his experience to Jonathan Moller and Ricardo Falla (2004, 96) explains that those who went into exile in the region of Ixcán followed three paths. Some, like the Esteban Francisco family, found refuge in Mexico; others enrolled in the "model communities" compounds established by the Guatemalan Army and the Self-Defense Civil Patrols (PAC); and others, who joined the CPR, stayed in the Ixcán jungles, surviving and resisting the counterinsurgency campaigns. In *Buried Secrets*, Victoria Sanford (2003a) tells us that the CPR life in the mountains became "even more precarious, the realities of staying alive day to day were so harsh as to deny both humanity and dignity to massacre survivors. Civilians in the mountains suffered extreme hardship with no shelter, no clothing, no medicines, and no stable food or water sources" (131). Indeed, according to a survivor, members of the CPR "hid in the forests, in the folds of the ravines, on the high peaks, or wherever they could stay outside the military's reach. That was how a total of nearly twenty thousand people formed the Communities of Population in Resistance" (Moller and Falla 2004, 57) in Quiché and in the rainforest of the

Petén region, in the north of Guatemala. Given the great difficulties in obtaining food because of the military incursions, residents in the CPR compounds began to survive on a basic diet of beans, corn, and greens. As Ricardo Falla indicates, they "organized astonishing internal systems of production, defense, education, hygiene, health, pastoral care and even sports . . . they no longer believed that they would be in the Jungle for the short term; they now saw that they would be there for an undefined period that could last ten or fifteen years" (1993, 58).

In 1983, as an act of cooperation with the Guatemalan Army, the Mexican government ended its support of thousands of Guatemalan refugees on Mexican soil, obliging them either to migrate to the United States or to return to Guatemala. Among those who decided to return was the Esteban Francisco family, which in 1984 settled in "Los limones" (The Limes), one of the CPR compounds in Ixcán. From these surroundings and from those long walks infused with fear, anguish, and uncertainty, but also buoyed by the hope and landscapes of the Ixcán jungles, Sabino Esteban Francisco learned his first life lessons. There, he grew up, composing his first verses, writing them "at a little table / with remnants of carbon" (63). There, he survived on the very basic diet, quenching the silences of his throat (67) with corn grains, *pixtones* (101), *quiletes*, papaya roots, and *zapote* seeds (79)—struggling not only against the repressive forces that sought to eliminate the CPR but also against misery and curable deceases caused by the precarious conditions under which he and his family lived. These are the elements and the habitual contexts described in *Moan of the Footprints*, whose poetry has an extraordinarily expressive force. In addition to this book, Esteban Francisco also published *Yetoq' HunHun b'ijan aq'al / Con pedazo de Carbón* (With a Remnant of Carbon, 2011), *Xik'ej K'al Xe'ej / Alas y raíces* (Wings and Roots, 2013), and, more recently, the children's book, *La escalera de la luna* (The Moon's Ladder, 2017). Esteban Francisco continued to live in the CPR compounds, completing his education at the "Guillermo Woods" camp where he was trained to become an elementary school teacher, a job that he currently holds in the Ixcán region (Urizar Mazariegos 2004, 239).

In *Sq'aqaw yechel aqanej / Moan of the Footprints*, the poetic voice registers the experiences of persecution, survival, and tenacity of the CPR in the jungles of Ixcán. The poems were first written in the Q'anjob'al Maya language and later translated by Esteban Francisco into Spanish. In the following critical analysis, I focus on the Spanish translations of the poems.

The poetic voice describes not an experience of victimization or abandonment but rather acts of courage and survival that fuel the dignity, hope, and persistence of Maya peoples. Intense and devastating images that highlight institutional violence are contrasted with songs that celebrate the environment and the human courage needed to transcend the greatest obstacles. The "moan of the footprints" in this sense allegorizes a song of life that serves to disarticulate the failed attempt of those who sought to silence and kill Indigenous peoples. These moans or poems, characterized by their apparent simplicity, have the ability to awaken the most profound sentiments and move the reader with their intense communicative capacity. They simultaneously inscribe a traumatic experience and underscore the dignity and pride of the CPR. Additionally, they serve as songs to the jungle that sheltered members of the CPR and that witnessed members' harassment and ultimate survival.

Sq'aqaw yechel aqanej constitutes what Brian Swann calls "a poetry of the historical witness" (1988, xvii); that is, it is not just in the voice and from the perspective of someone who observes history but also from one who embodies it. It emphasizes the necessity of "remembering" and speaking out about the trauma experienced during the armed conflict in Guatemala. Francisco's objective is to inscribe and authorize the "small voices of history" (Guha 1996) in the hegemonic historical records. Five prominent themes emerge in the poetry book. First, testimonial poems like "*Ceiba Tree Base Camp*" (123), "Among the Trees" (115), and "Stage" (23) highlight the moments of uncertainty that the CPR experienced in the jungles of Ixcán. Second, poems like "Mending" (117), "Rebirth" (137), and "Resistance" (173) underscore the tenacity and perseverance of the people who survived in Ixcán. Third, poems like "Long Walk" (109), "Xalbal" (111), and "Wings and Roots" (121) seek to re-vindicate Maya cultural identity; specifically, they use the image of "footprints" to evoke re-signified millenarian images that organically tie together the past and the present of the Maya peoples of the CPR. Fourth, in poems like "Guatemala," "Diversity," and "Rainbow," the poetic voice reimagines the nation-state as intercultural, recognizing its multilingual and multiethnic character. Finally, there are several poems dedicated to Nature. As we see, these poems are organically related to the other themes, because remembering the history of genocide and re-vindicating Maya cultural history, identity, and the nation-state also entail the defense of Mother Earth.

Although some poems in the collection play with form, the majority are written in free verse. Significantly, they draw on a conversational language reminiscent of the poetics of the Committed Generation[11]; the poetic style of Maya poets like the Kaqchikels, Francisco Morales Santos and Luis de Lión; and the poetics of brevity of the K'iche' Humberto Ak'abal.[12] Esteban Francisco uses various literary devices including personification, alliteration, onomatopoeia ("Laugh River," "Weaves," and "Morning Song"), calligram ("Echo"), and *jitanjáfora* (a "nonsensical poem"). These literary elements evoke the context of the Ixcán jungle, although the Q'anjob'al poet most often uses personification to give life to the natural surroundings represented within the poems. Indeed, Esteban Francisco endorses the Law of Ecology—"Everything is connected to everything else" (Rueckert 1996, 108)—thereby developing a context where he argues that all things that inhabit the earth (people, plants, and animals) are organically linked. This idea is explicitly represented through the Maya *traje* or dress whose harmony is displayed with each of its strings and diverse colors: "The seas / the animals / the people / and everything that exists / we are strings and conjugated colors" (17), the narrator indicates. This is why all the plots in the poems occur within natural contexts—animals, plants, and people all move within the jungles of the Ixcán, the main literary referent in *Sq'aqaw yechel aqanej.*

Jungle elements like rivers, trees, and animals (which are mostly aquatic or have wings) are most frequently evoked, usually as allegorical representations of the subjects and experiences described in Ixcán. In addition, these natural elements often serve as metaphorical bridges that lead us through diverse temporal and spatial contexts that include the Civil War, the postwar period, or settings where the poetic voice simply takes the time to appreciate and contemplate his surroundings. In these poems, Esteban Francisco employs a patient poetic gaze that evokes Nature's elements in a mood of playful exaltation. In "Last Night," for instance, we find that the old trees catch a cold, "All of them [awake] / with a piece of mist / tied in their heads" (81). In "Dried Tree," a woodpecker is sad to see a tree dying. He decides to open a hole in the tree's chest to build a nest. The tree comes back to life, and forever after, the poem concludes, "Every morning from the tree / his heart goes out flying" (61). At times, these environmental elements acquire mythological dimensions. This is the case with the poem "A Day," which objectively explains the origins of the night. The poetic voice tells the story of a day who dares to touch the sun. In doing so, he burns himself to the point that he is darkened (*tiznado*). For his "daring," the sky gives him the moon as a present, and "in memory / of the event / nowadays this day still repeats itself as the night" (97).

Instead of tensions between the natural elements of daily life, what emerges from Esteban Francisco's poems is a vision of environmental bonding and mutuality in which natural elements complement one another within a persistent cycle of revitalization. For example, the tree comes back to life when the woodpecker pecks a hole in it, and in turn the tree serves as a home for the picidae bird. "Dried Tree," in this sense, endorses a biocentric perspective that aims to erase the opposition between humans and nature to suggest that they can depend on one another to exist. In addition, the poem could be interpreted allegorically: it is the story of the CPR, whose presence in the Ixcán jungle gives life to it and in turn receives sustenance from it, thus maintaining a mutually sustainable relationship. It represents, at the same time, an imagined world and an environmentalist political project that both emphasize the relationship between Mother Earth and the Indigenous peoples as constituted by reciprocal harmonic exchanges.

The environmental perspective endorsed by Francisco, as we can see, acquires an almost pastoral dimension that resembles natural elements that we discussed earlier with the works of Ak'abal, Montejo, and González. It is notable, however, that the invocation of Ixcán by Esteban Francisco is characterized significantly by what it does not mention. These are scenes where Nature and the people of the CPR operate in harmony, free from the influences of modernity. Nowhere in the poems do we find the presence of technological objects like radios or TVs or references to the city. Francisco's poems distance themselves from the urban contexts previously discussed with Chavéz (and later in the works of Maya Cu Choc and Manuel Tzoc). In contrast to affirming the city as a place where our struggles for survival evolve, Esteban Francisco does not even address it. Instead, for this Q'anjob'al poet, Nature acquires an authority that determines the experience of the CPR. Thus, with his representation of Nature, Esteban Francisco, like Ak'abal, aims to open the possibility of feeling to the wonders of Mother Earth, feelings that would bind us to it so we can interrogate the human/nonhuman binary that characterizes Western modernity and neoliberal globalization. It is only when pastoral peace and harmony give way to poetry that evokes memories of catastrophe that the reader is exposed to chilling snapshots of what the CPR confronted in the mountains. It is here where images of persecution, the struggle for survival, and death reveal the challenges that the CPR faced.

In the poem "Pleading," the people's pleas not to be killed are met with gunshots. The voices of the innocent "acquired the burnt stench of human flesh / in a clandestine / cemetery" (183). The people saw them die, the narrator tells us, listing an inventory of terrorist tactics carried out against them by the Guatemalan Army: "drowned, / hanged, / slashed by machetes, / bombed, / burned alive" (43). The eyes of the witnesses, the poem concludes, are today, "clandestine cemeteries / and their tears / the most transparent exhumation." As Michael Taussig indicates, perpetrators of twentieth-century counterinsurgency wars carried out public executions with the intent to instill fear and silence the victims. They hoped to reduce popular resistance not only through killing leaders and community organizers but also through controlling "massive populations, entire social classes, and even nations through the cultural elaboration of fear" (2002, 8).[13]

In this context, as a witness and mediator for his community, Esteban Francisco discloses the operations of settler colonialism by highlighting the efforts of the nation-state to "eliminate the native." The poem "Pleading" can be associated with the "storm" that Aimé Césaire describes in his seminal text, "Discourse of Colonialism"; that is, the counterinsurgency campaigns depicted by Esteban Francisco resemble colonialist strategies that rest on entire "societies drained of their essence, cultures trampled underfoot, institutions undermined, lands confiscated, religions smashed, magnificent artistic creations destroyed, extraordinary *possibilities* wiped out" (Césaire 1994, 178). This is indeed what the armed conflict represented for the CPR: it was an experience marked by memories of terror, fear, and political persecution. According to Victoria Sanford, the army, for instance, forced men, women, children, and elderly to retreat "to the mountains without shelter, food, or other protections" (2003a, 134); when they returned to their communities, "they would find their crops destroyed, which meant another season of certain hunger and death, struggling to survive on weeds and roots" (134).

Yet, amid these fratricidal experiences, in poems like "Caves" and "Among the Trees," Esteban Francisco describes how survivors escape, hide in the jungle, and manage to survive. Their stories of persecution and survival are then narrated and recorded as a way to underscore the courage of a people who in the most extreme conditions found ways to keep their existence, continuance, and hope alive. Memories of pain activate memories of resistance that aim to sustain and dignify the history of the CPR and, in turn, that of Indigenous peoples who have survived colonialism.

In the poem "Caves," the Q'anjob'al poet describes how Indigenous families hide from the Guatemalan Army in caves in the jungles of Ixcán: he depicts a morbid scene that features irony and sarcasm within a context marked by extremity. The poem describes a game of hide-and-seek played between adults and children inside a cave. The game is accompanied by a paraphrase of the children's song, "Sweet Orange," that adults and children sing and dance to (*Hambre-Despierto-Piñol Dormido*). The adults play this game to entertain the children and distract them from the violent noises of planes, gunshots, and bombs heard outside the cave. This is the "chorus of the earth," the narrator tells us, where people experience the night "inside" while there is a party of lights and fireworks "outside." Through its dichotomous structure, the poem marks the difference between inside and outside, between life and death. The survival of people takes place amidst a disturbing context of destruction and fear. Notice how the representation of the cave here acquires a different meaning from that of Luis de Lión in his poetry book, *Poems from Water Volcano* that we discussed in chapter 1. This cave, far from being a medium that leads to life—the birth of the child—becomes a collective shelter, a space of survival before the threats of colonialism.

Similarly, the poem "Among the Trees" draws on some of the strategies the CPR used to survive in the jungle:

In Emergency Plans
of the armed conflict
of hunger screamed
the children of the CPR:
    a rag
in their mouth was placed
to silence their scream
before the *pintos* [soldiers].

Instead of tortilla
they swallowed their scream.

Today the scream of many
still has an echo of hunger. (115)

The "silence" and the "screams" evoked in the poem are powerful. The effort to silence the screams of the children so the soldiers do not find the hiding places of the CPR acquires a significance associated not only with survival against premeditated death but also the misery inherited by many in the aftermath of the Civil War. The verse "Today the scream of many" evokes the Peace Accords that were signed in 1996 to end the armed conflict. It suggests that although there was a formal, diplomatic solution to end the Civil War, it did not eliminate poverty or the hunger of those who survived modernity or globalization in conditions of subalterneity. Such a proposal, as becomes evident, can be associated with what Chávez offers in *Solitary House* and the stands we discussed in the previous chapter in the works of Montejo and González. In turn, the poem depicts the silencing of screams as an act of narration and as the performance of memory to address a traumatic experience. By evoking the "silencing of the children" and "screams" (to suggest hunger), the poem establishes the authority of the CPR. Remembering experiences like this one not only means confronting the past, highlighting and denouncing the activities of the nation-state and its efforts to eliminate Maya peoples, but also re-*membering* the Maya social body. They invoke resistance against the "storm" that Césaire talks about, as well as the resilience of the CPR to survive the army's military operations.

Sq'aqaw yechel aqanej in this sense marks the limits of colonialism, its failure to entirely destroy a people. In addressing these experiences of survival, Esteban Francisco's poems tell us something about the nature of modernity itself. Its project has been constitutive of what it has violently aims to suppress and destroy; in other words, it has been established through genocide. However, for Esteban Francisco and the CPR, it is now time to re-*member* the Maya social body and the beginning of "national culture" as understood by Frantz Fanon. That is, *Sq'aqaw yechel aqanej* delves into the traumatic past "in order to find coherent elements that will counteract colonialism's attempts to falsify and harm": it describes the "whole body of efforts made by a people in the sphere of thought to describe, justify, and praise the action through which that people has created itself and keeps itself in existence" (Fanon 1971, 44). Indeed, Esteban Francisco's poetry book demonstrates how Maya peoples represent their own experiences and persistence despite more than 500 hundred years of systematic attempts of genocide and assimilation. By inviting his readers to consider the experiences of those who perished and survived the atrocities of one of the most shameful chapters in Guatemalan history, Esteban Francisco's poetry is an example of "witness literature." It is a "poetry that puts us in touch with raw facts of existence rather than effects produced by rhetorical technique" (Vogler 2003, 174); in doing so, he not only challenges the hegemonic versions of history endorsed by the Guatemalan state but also registers a courageous testimony that aims to restore our spirits and dignity as Indigenous peoples.

Xib'alb'a and the Maya Rebirth

The representations of the city and the Ixcán jungle and the experience of the subaltern characters through the metaphor of the journey that emerges from Chávez's, García's, and Esteban Francisco's books of poetry offer a fresh perspective on the themes of Maya cultural identity and rights. Through literature, these authors affirm and reactivate Maya ancestral memories in order to underscore the continuity of our political and discursive struggles and to strengthen self-esteem through our heritage. Both Chávez and García associate the postwar period and the arrival of economic neoliberalism and globalization with Xib'alb'a. As I showed, the Maya underworld represents the realm of illness and death, of pain, chaos, isolation, darkness, and hopelessness. Nonetheless, amid all of these uncertainties, Chávez and García still offer a glimpse of hope through rebirth. For his part, Esteban Francisco's poetics, in his representation of the CPR, offers a story of courage and survival as a testimony of the vitality of our existence; it is a story characterized by our constant efforts to keep going against colonialist incursions. The idea of rebirth to celebrate our survival through the invocation of Xib'alb'a or the CPR's experiences in the Ixcán jungle can in turn be linked to the critical reading developed by Frauke Sachse and Allen J. Christenson (2005) of the *Popol Wuj* and the journey of the divine twins, Hunahpu and Xbalanque, to Xib'alb'a to consequently defeat the Lords of Death as a metaphor for planting corn.

As is well known, in the *Popol Wuj* the first set of twins, Hun Hunahpu and Wuqub' Hunahpu (One Master of the Blowgun and Seven Master of the Blowgun, respectively), had traveled to Xib'alb'a after they were invited by the Lords of the Underworld. In Xib'alb'a they were tricked and punished for playing the ball game. They were tortured in the house of darkness by the Lords of Death and, consequently, sacrificed by decapitation. Hun Hunahpu's head was then hung in a calabash tree as a trophy. Pushed by curiosity, Ixquik' (Lady Blood), daughter of Kuchuma K'ik' (Gatherer of Blood), one of the lords in Xib'alb'a, went to see the head hanging from the tree. There, Hun Hunahpu told Ixquik' to extend her hand and he spit on it. She then became pregnant by Hun Hunahpu. The lords of the underworld then condemn Ixquik' to death. With the help of an owl, she managed to escape Xib'alb'a and find refuge in the house of Hun and Wuqub' Hunahpu's mother Xmucane (She Who Buries, She Who Plants). There, Ixquik' had her two sons, Hunahpu and Xbalanque, the hero twins who will also be invited to visit Xib'alb'a after the Lords of Death hear them play the ball game. Unlike their predecessors, however, they transcend all of the sinister challenges in the underworld and eventually defeat the Lords of Xib'alb'a. Afterward, the hero twins gather the remains of Hun and Wuqub' Hunahpu, and "the heart of their father was left behind [in Xib'alb'a] at Crushing Ballcourt" (Christenson 2007, 191). The hero twins then "arose as the central lights. They arose straight into the sky. One of them arose as the sun, and the other as the moon. Thus the womb of the sky was illuminated over the face of the earth, for they came to dwell in the sky" (191). As this occurs, maize begins to emanate from the earth. "The yellow ears of maize and the white ears of maize were then ground fine with nine grindings by Xmucane (She Who Buries, She Who Plants). Food entered their flesh, along with water to give them strength. Thus was created the fatness of their arms. The yellowness of humanity came to be when they were made by they who are called She Who Has Borne Children and He Who Has Begotten Sons, by Sovereign and Quetzal serpent" (195). Hence, humanity is created out of corn, framed by Xmucane.

Sachse and Christenson read the mythic narratives of creation from an agronomic critical perspective. For them, the stories of the Maya twins and their journeys to the underworld "clearly define Xib'alb'a as a place of creation as well as of human defeat and death" (2005, 24). The rebirth or human resurrection, they state, requires a necessary escape from the underworld, just as it occurs with Ixquik', who finds refuge with Xmucane. From this line of thinking, Sachse and Christenson see Hunahpu and Xbalanque's journey to the underworld, and their consequent defeat of the Lords of Death, as allegorical of maize's life cycle. Indeed, the process of planting corn requires digging into the land where the seed of corn is placed and then covered with dirt. The planted seed receives water—from irrigation or rain—and sun and moonlight so it can properly germinate. Hence, the first journey to the underworld by Hun Hunahpu and Wuqub' Hunahpu may be interpreted as a failed attempt to plant corn or a bad harvest. Nevertheless, with the defeat of the Lords of Death, we finally obtain a successful harvest of corn and its birth on earth. Sachse and Christenson state, "We may thus interpret the story as a modern account of death and resurrection—a concept that in Maya belief always involves a passage through the underworld. The central analogy is clearly that of the life cycle of maize as embodied by the death, rebirth and resurrection of the Maize God in Classic Maya iconography. The life cycle of maize is the archetypical religious-ideological underpinning of Maya worldview—it explains the origin and creation of human life and the purpose of human death" (2005, 16–17).

From this critical perspective and taking the *Popol Wuj* as a central literary reference in the poetic works of Chávez, García, and Esteban Francisco, we can better interpret their respective representations of the journeys the characters take. The experiences they invoke under a neoliberal condition (Xib'alb'a) or the jungles of Ixcán allegorize maize's life cycle. The protagonists in these poetic works personify seeds of corn that navigate the underworld; in other words, the marginal conditions we have inherited from the armed conflict and neoliberal globalization. In the respective contexts invoked, Chávez, García, and Esteban Francisco highlight circumstances marked by human degradation, death, and resurrection that suggest that our emancipation from colonialism resides in developing the conditions of possibility for a decolonial project that emanates from the underworld. What does this mean in our contemporary experience? It is about highlighting processes of marginalization and oppression established in the postwar period while at the same time developing a politics of alliance and solidarity to struggle against neoliberal globalization. It is, in this sense, a necessary death (acquiring a political consciousness of colonialist mechanisms in the present) that will lead us to awaken a political consciousness to prepare us to fight against its repressive mechanisms.

In sum, these narratives make a lot of sense when we also consider the closing of the *Oxlajuj* (Thirteen) *B'aktun* in the long count sacred Maya calendar, corresponding to December 21, 2012, in the Gregorian calendar. On this date, we closed a long chapter and, at the same time, began a new one in our long ancestral walk on this planet. We can conclude then that contemporary Maya authors like Chávez, García, and Esteban Francisco propose not only to vindicate Maya values but also to extend them to

other subjects who under neoliberal globalization suffer oppression, violence, and marginalization similar to that experienced by Indigenous
peoples. The Maya worldview becomes the cornerstone for a subaltern
collective emancipation, since it offers important lessons about how we
can recover the balance lost because of settler colonialism. As a first step to
materialize it, these authors develop a rigorous critique of modernity and
the alienating effects that it endorses to highlight its concrete consequences. In doing so, these poetic works offer the conditions of possibility
to think about some of the historical events that have marked our collective continuity and, certainly, the pride we need to continue this journey
and face the challenges of an uncertain future where we imagine ourselves
free of the exploitative chains of colonialism.

CHAPTER 4

Maya Feminism and Queer Poetics

Maya Cu Choc and Manuel Tzoc

THE POETIC WORKS I have analyzed up to this point operate within social contexts marked by rural (Lión, Ak'abal, Montejo, González, Morales Santos, and Francisco) and urban settings (García and Chávez). These texts represent the city as a symbol of Western modernity and the repressive colonial forces of the modern nation-state against Maya peoples. Understanding the city as a symbol of colonial power, these writers contrast urban settings with ideas of a return to the rural community and/ or activation of their ancestral origins; that is, the rural area is where they can make a deep connection to their Indigenous and spiritual traditions and where Indigenous authenticity is located, as exemplified in the works of Morales Santos, Ak'abal, González, Francisco, and Montejo. Moreover, the rural world is where these authors reactivate the essential elements of Maya cultures that modernity has suppressed and denied to Indigenous peoples. However, these literary assumptions, as we have also seen, are not free of ambiguity and contradiction. Even though these authors see the urban setting—or the transnational one in the case of Montejo—as the space defined by the physical and imaginary boundaries of settler colonialism, it is also the space that makes possible the development of a social and political Indigenous consciousness that resists colonial policies. Indeed, all the writers discussed so far earned academic degrees from national and international schools and universities located in cities in Guatemala or in other countries. It is in this context that they became "Indigenous cosmopolitans," or subjects with the political capacity to navigate in more complex urban and transnational settings, which enabled them to intervene in both rural and urban environments, challenging cultural and political representations of the Maya world (Forte 2002, 2–3).

As such, although it is important to recognize the city as an ambiguous space that embodies the repressive policies of colonialism, we must not overlook its emancipatory potential. Indeed, the city, like rural spaces, must also be accepted and embraced as a place where we are able to develop literary practices and the conditions of possibility for our political emancipation. As I argue in chapter 2, we must abandon Indigenista and Indigenous ideas that suggest that an "authentic" Maya identity "must be racially unmixed, culturally undiluted, geographically remote, and materially impoverished" (Forte 2002, 1), as has been the discursive tendency of some of the Maya authors. With this in mind, in this chapter I focus on the poetic works of Q'eq'chi writer and activist Maya Cu Choc and K'iche' Maya writer and artist Manuel Tzoc, both of whom envision the city as a space where we can develop ways not only to dignify a cultural Maya identity[1] but also to generate Maya feminist and queer loci of expression that challenge the heteronormative and patriarchal hegemonic structures permeating Guatemalan society. The works of these authors, moreover, help demystify ideas that "there is a false dichotomy dividing Indigeneity and cosmopolitanism by demonstrating that this binary construct does not adequately describe the realities of indigenous peoples" (20).

Maya Cu Choc's Decolonial Feminist Poetry

After Jacobo Árbenz Guzmán was removed from office in 1954, Maya Cu Choc's parents moved to the capital city from Alta Verapaz in search of a better life. There, they lived in poverty and experienced racism and discrimination for being Indigenous. As a survival strategy, they adopted ladino ways of life, which they later transmitted to their four daughters. Maya Cu Choc was born in Guatemala City in 1968 and remembers how her parents told them not to wear the Maya Q'eq'chi *traje* or dress in public and to speak Spanish instead of Q'eq'chi. They hoped this would help their daughters to better adapt to the city and avoid the racism and discrimination they themselves had experienced (Alba Skar 2008, 55). As she grew older, Cu Choc experienced firsthand what her parents had warned her about. While attending university, Cu Choc tried wearing her Maya dress, but after a few days she stopped because she felt "disqualification from my university classmates" (55). In literature, however, she found a place to confront some of these traumatic memories and to dignify her Maya identity. Her literary explorations began at the age of thirteen when she would meet with her school friends to talk about literature. At home, her father, who had leftist political leanings, had a library that included the works of the Guatemalan poet Otto René Castillo. She later discovered the writings of Kaqchikel Maya writers Francisco Morales Santos and Luis de Lión, who had a profound literary influence on her. Cu Choc's experiences of racism, poverty, and gender inequality are some of the constitutive thematic elements of her poetry (Avendaño 2001, 12).

Under the pseudonym of Nicté del Valle, the Q'eq'chi poet published some of her first poems in *Revista Folklórica Latinoamericana* (Latin American Folklore Magazine) in 1986 and, later, in *Noticias de Guatemala* (Guatemalan News; Meza Márquez and Toledo Arévalo 2015, 51). In 1993, she began to participate in the poetry workshops organized by the Guatemalan-ladino writer Marco Antonio Flores at the San Carlos de Guatemala University. It was there, Cu Choc tells us, that "I found that poetry could be a paid profession" (Alba Skar 2008, 54). Her first book of poetry, *Poemaya*, came out of that workshop and was included in the literary anthology *Novisimos* (The Newest Ones), which, published in 1997, also included the poetry of several participants from Flores' workshops. After *Poemaya*, Cu Choc published *La rueda* (The Wheel, 2002) and *Recorrido: Poemas* (Paths, 2005).[2] Her work has also been published in various national and international journals and literary anthologies, including *Messengers of Rain* (2002) and *Antología de conmemoración: Quinto centenario de la llegada de los portugueses al Brasil* (Anthology of Remembrance: Fifth Centenary of the Arrival of the Portuguese in Brazil, 1999).

Cu Choc's literary expression is characterized by experimentation, differing from the testimonial and conversational poetics that we discussed in chapters 1 and 2. The Q'eq'chi' poet uses a variety of literary devices to develop complex and suggestive metaphors, as well as poetic structures that include calligrams (e.g., in her poem "The Wheel") that are reminiscent of the avant-garde Cubist literary movement. In various texts, such as "Distances" (*Poemaya*) or "I'm at the Top" (*La rueda*), she uses free verse, with most lines having no more than five syllables alternating with shorter lines of a single word. This strategy gives her poem "Ix Tzib' / Woman Scribe" a fluid rhythm interrupted by frequent enjambments and brief pauses, after which the dynamic rhythm resumes. In her poetics, Cu Choc explores themes of isolation, the loss of a lover, vindication of a Maya cultural identity, and gender politics related to the rights of Indigenous women. The Q'eq'chi poet aims to transgress hegemonic artistic-literary spaces that have been "negated" to Maya women.

In this section, I explore how Cu Choc establishes these literary trans-
gressions in her work. In particular, I am interested in how her poetics
inscribe the historic role and prominence of Maya women in the hegemonic textual register. In earlier chapters I discussed the decolonizing literary tendencies in the works of Maya authors, which explore themes of
Maya spirituality, self-determination, land recovery, and intellectual sovereignty (Warrior 2014). Yet the Maya decolonizing narrative is incomplete
if we do not consider the artistic perspectives of Maya women. As I show
in this section, Cu Choc's poetry lends itself to an inquiry of this narrative,
precisely because her intention is to question both the dominant and the
Maya heterosexual patriarchy that permeates our societies, particularly in
the colonized postwar Guatemalan context.

In one of her most beautiful poems, "Ix Tzib'" (Woman Scribe, 2011),
Cu Choc sketches her inescapable fate as a "woman scribe." Her artistic
labor and "her love of the word," the poem suggests, have an ancestral lineage. I include this poem in its totality:

> *since always*
> *I drank words*
> *submerged in dreams*
> I come
> from a lineage
> that inherited
> magic
> my tiny
> grandmother
> was immortalized in clay
> she used to carry the power
> between her hand
> and a stone
> after centuries
> the stone
> was transformed into a spindle
> and the colors came
> with the threads
> my mother, a weaver
> transformed in canvases
> the words

that endure today
an heiress
of multiple languages
I lost the stone
and the spindles
pushed by the necessity
to put together words
images
a bat, my animal spirit
looked up in the cave of light
and brought me a pen
my daughter
reached for the ink
and my hand started
to name things:
and I write
because this is my nature
because
I need to thwart silence
to give form to sounds,
sounds that represent my steps,
your steps
your frame
your moans
the ancestral screams
and the laughter of knowing that I am a part of you
of your blood
of your breath
of your winds
of your heartbeat
because the word moves me
it invites me
it explains me
it names me
it renames me
it sculpts me
it draws me
I am

a wild
thorny
bittersweet
blackberry
that multiplies itself
vivacious
I look for
new symbols
to reinvent words
and I hold a *pitaya* color
poet
I nourished myself from
the sweetness
of her name
to share this love
for the word.

"Ix Tzib'" was commissioned by the conference for the Second Feminist
and Gender Mesoamerican Symposium organized by the Latin American
Social Sciences Faculty (FLACSO, its Spanish acronym) in Guatemala in
May 2011. The event organizers asked Cu Choc to contribute a poem connected to some of the themes to be discussed in the symposium; it was
subsequently included as a prologue to the event's program. In many ways,
"Ix Tzib'" can be considered Cu Choc's manifesto or personal hymn in that
it constitutes her aesthetic-political mission: to make visible the prominence of Maya women in the production of a historical register through
hieroglyphic and alphabetic writing and textile weaving.

With its sixty-nine lines written in free verse, Cu Choc's poem invokes
an artistic-literary matrilineal genealogy. The composition begins with a
three-verse epigraph that comes from the poem "Poesía de lo propio"
(Poetry of One's Own), which is part of Cu Choc's first book of poetry
Poemaya. This book includes five poems and, as mentioned, is part of the
anthology *Novísimos*. I discuss *Poemaya* in more detail later, but for now, it
is important to underscore how the epigraph—in particular, the verse
"since always"—appeals to a millenarian temporal memory that suggests
continuity in the practices of maintaining historical memory through
writing. The verses that make up the first section of "Ix Tzib'"—the first
nineteen lines, from "I come from" to "endure today"—emphasize that the

artistic creativity of the poetic voice is a result of the artistic inheritance from women scribes. First, we see the artistic work of the "tiny grandmother," who has the power of the word between a "stone" and "her hand." Such an assertion allegorizes her capacity to inscribe history through hieroglyphic writing. The poem invokes the Maya textualities inscribed in stelae or on the walls in the capital's sacred sites that may include Tikal, Tak'alik Ab'aj, or Chichén Itzá. Cu Choc holds that the writings in these temples or stelae were also inscribed by women. From this critical position, the Maya author challenges not only the assumption that Maya hieroglyphic writing was entirely reserved for men but also the conscious erasure of Maya women from the historical register.[3] Gabrielle Vail and Andrea Stone, for example, confirm Cu Choc's assumptions in their critical reading of Maya hieroglyphic writing that represents Maya women in the pre-Colombian period. These authors conclude that Maya codices were constituted through androcentric perspectives that suggest that "females were the structural equivalent of males (in terms of a series of paired oppositions) but were not their equals in the social or religious sphere" (2002, 204).

Then we have the "mother, weaver" who adopts "spindles" to craft colorful textiles, sprouting colors and transforming "words into canvasses." In their diverse, colorful designs, the production of textiles and *huipils*, the poem suggests, embodies the cultural inscription of our ancestral memories and histories. With the verses in the sixth stanza ("an heiress of multiple languages"), the poetic voice suggests that the devices used by her ancestors have been lost: "I lost the stone and the spindles." The "loss" implicitly references the European conquest and its violent interruption of the creative continuance of Indigenous historical memory, brought about by the destruction of hieroglyphic writing systems, ceramics, and textiles and the imposition of European patriarchal and Christian values.[4] Indigenous peoples have lost the capacity to express themselves using hieroglyphic and pictographic writing. Nonetheless, amid adversity, the narrator appeals to her "nahual" or animal spirit ("the bat") to search for writing tools that are similar to the stones and spindles that may enable her to continue the writing traditions of her ancestors. In the "cave of light," she finds the "pen" and the "ink" that her daughter hands to her—her daughter, we assume, will also continue the tradition of communicating the word after she finds her own tools of artistic expression—and the poetic voice then begins to "put together words" and "images" to "name things"

using alphabetic writing. The task of writing does not merely aim to produce words but also to articulate them in a creative form by giving "aesthetic form to sounds."

With this task, the author displays a desire to distance herself from the
testimonial poetics we discussed in chapter 2. The task of writing is associated, on the one hand, with the need to "thwart silence," which indicates a
context marked by adversity, specifically certain forms of censorship that
have been imposed on women.[5] On the other hand, by "giving form to
sound," the poetic voice—which moves from the first to the second person, "your step, your frame, your moan"—underscores the written word
in alphabetic writing as an imperative tool to reactivate and restore Maya
ancestral memory. In doing so, the poetic voice dignifies and renews herself because "the word moves me / it invites me / it explains me / it names
me / it renames me / it sculpts me." Such dignity is strengthened by the
pride of having a daughter—embraced by "poetry *pitaya* color"—who
feeds the force of her spirit. The ability to resist occurs not only by recognizing her ancestral history (the grandmother and the mother) and holding her present/future (her daughter) but also by developing a rebellious
social consciousness ("a wild / thorny / bittersweet / blackberry"), an
attitude that will help her confront the challenges that, like her predecessors, she will find on her path.

As we can see, "Ix Tzib'" maintains an organizing principle based on
metonymic sensory images that involve all the senses: "bittersweet blackberry" (taste); "tiny grandmother," "cave of light" (visual); "ancestral
screams" (auditory); the "hand that names things" (tactile); and being
part of "your breath" (olfactory). These metaphors reveal a full process of
feeling and thinking associated with the marginal experiences of Indigenous women, which have been made invisible in the hegemonic historical
register. This becomes more evident in the stanza where the poetic voice
goes from the first to the second person—"I come / from a lineage" . . .
"your steps / your frame." Here, she displays a discursive strategy associated with the idea of "relationality" proposed by the Goenpul scholar
Aileen Moreton-Robinson: "that one experiences the self as part of others
and that others are part of the self; this is learnt through reciprocity, obligation, shared experiences, coexistence, cooperation and social memory"
(2000, 16). Cu Choc offers an artistic-creative genealogy that illustrates
Indigenous women's political obligation to continue and share the activity
of producing Indigenous historical and social memory. In addition, by

invoking the "love for the word" and underscoring the role of hieroglyphic, weaving, and alphabetic writings, Cu Choc's poem alludes to specific female historical figures. In many ways, the poem allegorizes the Maya goddess of writing and textile weaving, Ix Chebel Yax.[6] This goddess's iconic representation was found and later destroyed by Spanish invaders in what is today "Isla de Mujeres" (Women's Island) in the Caribbean, near Cancún, Mexico. Ix Chebel Yax is referenced in Maya historical texts like the *Ritual of the Bacabs*, sometimes with different names.[7] According to Timothy Knowlton (2015), the goddess is responsible for various functions, including giving green colors to the trees; in particular, the Ceiba tree or *Yaxche'* (The Green Tree), the sacred tree of the Maya. Ix Chebel Yax also made certain plants and trees sacred, capable of producing sap from which dyes were made to give colors to threads used in the production of textiles.

Through its emphasis on the written and visual word (hieroglyphic, textile weaving, and alphabetic), "Ix Tzib'" distances itself from theoretical and critical assumptions that interpret and reduce Maya and Indigenous cultures as a whole as being highly dependent on "orality." I refer, in particular, to views held by Francesc Ligorred Peramon and Kenneth Lincoln who, respectively, indicate that "Maya literature is rooted in the great colonial works and in the old Maya culture, whose origin continues to be, in great measure, the oral tradition" (1997, 75), and that "tribal peoples evolved without written languages, as oral cultures living mouth to mouth, age to age, passing on a daily culture. Their literatures survived as remembered myths and rituals, songs, poems, narrative, tales, legends, and parables" (1982, 88).[8] Challenging these assumptions, Cu Choc underscores the role of the millenarian "written word" in Maya and Indigenous cultures by alluding to different semiotic systems of representation that made possible the transmission of our historical and social memory through registers recorded in paper, ceramics, stelae, temples, textiles, and so on. Certainly, oral traditions existed among Indigenous cultures, but orality, as Roland Barthes indicates, is not something exclusive to Indigenous peoples. Instead, it has been present in "infinite variety of forms, it is present at all times, in all places, in all societies; indeed [oral] narrative starts with the very history of mankind; there is not, there has never been anywhere, any people without narrative; all classes, all human groups, have their stories, and very often those stories are enjoyed by men of different and even opposite cultural backgrounds" (1974, 237). In this context, it would be much more fruitful to talk about how, as a result of colonization and the consequent destruction of native documents, Indigenous peoples after 1492 became more dependent on orality than written records. At the same time, we have still managed to produce written records using alphabetic writing since the colonial invasion.

"Ix Tzib'" also challenges hegemonic narratives that give authority to Indigenous and non-Indigenous heteropatriarchal historical figures. As is known, colonial patriarchy has operated from White-criollo/mestizo/ladino ethnic/racial supremacist ideas disseminated through colonial institutions planted on our ancestral territories. These institutions include the Roman Catholic Church, town halls, the educational system, state laws, and print media that promote political and ideological paradigms that subjugate women, especially Indigenous women, by sustaining a heterosexist patriarchal system that favors masculine authority in their spaces. It began with European colonization carried out by White men and has been sustained by the imposition of White-criollo/mestizo/ladino male authorities in positions of power since the rule of colonial viceroyalties and afterward, with the establishment of independent modern nation-states. In addition, with the emergence and dissemination of ideas of the nuclear family, the "man" has been placed at the "head" of the family, making the decisions at home, thereby displacing women from prominent roles and locating them at the margins; she is the one who is supposed to take care of the "husband" and the "children," to cook and take care of the home. Such marginalization is also sustained through Christian-Western notions of marriage and monogamy, and even by ideas of "complementarity" or the equilibrium between women and men and the natural environment, assumed as part of Indigenous communities that demarcate positions of power favoring masculine subjects; for example, Indigenous *cofradias* or brotherhoods.[9]

These ideological, repressive processes revoke the prominent role of women and queer subjectivities by creating significant societal organizing principles that specifically affect Indigenous women the most. Despite the growing role of social movements like feminism, Guatemalan women continue to be considered the property of men—whether the father, husband, father-in-law, or even the son or the community. Women's dignity and personal autonomy are not recognized. For example, Margarita, a K'iche' Maya activist who was interviewed by Norma Stoltz Chinchilla about her role at home, said, "In the family, the man is the owner and the one who brings the money home. Because of that we (women) must serve him and take care of him" (1998, 30). Situations like Margarita's limit the ability of women to express or decide and act for themselves regarding their own bodies, their material possessions, and their lives in general. In many cases, their social and individual conduct, as Margarita's words demonstrate, are governed and determined by men's decisions, men who, by right or in fact, feel capable of imposing their command over women as they see fit, even if that means imposing such commands through violence. Because of their ethnic/racial condition, in which their labor in public and private spaces is considered inferior, Indigenous women are the most affected by such patriarchal politics. K'iche'-Xinka activist Lorena Cabnal confirms Margarita's comments as well and in her discussion about Indigenous women oppression in their communities in Guatemala states that it "is shameful for a man that a woman occupies positions as Stewards or Mayors in the local Indigenous Xinka government because that has never been the case. According to the customs of the elders those positions are supposed to be occupied by men because women cannot lead the men of the town" (2010, 18). In this line of thinking, Kaqchikel sociologist Aura Cumes states that "Indigenous women are never seen as subjects that think and have feelings, but rather as women destined, by nature, to do unrecognized manual labor. In other words, Indigenous women's place in society is that of maids" (2012, 2). Thus, "Ix Tzib' " responds to the colonial patriarchy still in place in Guatemalan society.

The poem is characterized by the absence of masculine figures and of ideas of marriage and relationships between men and women, including sexual ones. Here Cu Choc does not feature Indigenous women in rural settings, carrying out agricultural tasks or traditional activities in the home, like the women represented in the works of Morales Santos and Luis de Lión. These themes are explored in her other poems, such as "Hablar de mi fantasia" (To Speak of My Fantasies) in *Poemaya* and "Pobrecita yo" (Poor Me) in *Recorrido*, which use a satiric tone to problematize and challenge male chauvinism. To challenge patriarchal dominant ideals in "Ix Tzib'," the Q'eq'chi poet imagines a world that locates Maya women in spaces of agency, highlighting their active role as women scribes with a capacity to produce historical registers. In this sense, the authority that Cu Choc grants Indigenous women invoked in the poem allegorizes the various and continuous processes of liberation and emancipation in which Indigenous women—our grandmothers, mothers, and daughters—have historically been involved. To highlight this prominence not only suggests

an ancestral continuity of our survival in general but also a constant process of de-patriarchization.

Cu Choc's poetic labor is intrinsically connected to her own feminist
praxis, as seen in her political activism and articulation of feminist stances
in interviews and scholarly essays. She has asked, "Why are women, and
Indigenous women in particular, eclipsed from the historical register?"
Regarding Western epistemological literary references, she has raised the
question "Will we continue employing [European literary references] or
do we want to use our own Indigenous epistemologies in the construction
of thought" (qtd. in Gargallo 2014, 215). In one of her essays, Cu Choc
advocates that "we as Indigenous women must take a quantitative step and
insert ourselves in artistic creative spaces that have been denied to us. We
must leave the patio where we weave textiles and take care of the chicken
to assume artistic expression and creation as our own, because we must
exercise a right that belongs to us" (2011, 299). Cu Choc's own feminist
praxis is thus based on the significant role that the written word plays in
materializing Indigenous women's rights.

The feminism expressed in Cu Choc's work can also be tied to the political struggles of other Maya women in Iximulew. For example, the structure
of the poem "Ix Tzib'" begins by invoking the role of the grandmother, then
moves to the mother and the weaver, and ends with the poetic voice's daughter; this generational transmission reflects the work of the Maya collectives,
The Maya Women of Kaqla and *Uk'ux B'e Maya Association.*[10] The goals of
these collectives, which developed in the 1990s, are to train, strengthen,
and support Maya women in Iximulew in political participation and leadership roles. They have presented numerous workshops to dignify Maya
identity, cultivate a sociopolitical feminist consciousness, and offer training
for leadership roles in their communities. In addition, their members discuss strategies for combating domestic violence, sexual abuse, ethnic/racial
oppression, political exclusion, economic exploitation, and gender inequality. The collectives also have published important texts that include *La
palabra y el sentir de las mujeres mayas de kaqla* (The Word and Feeling of
the Maya Women of Kaqla, 2004) and *Fortalecimiento de la participación
política de las mujeres mayas* (Strengthening the Political Participation of
Maya Women, 2005), which offer a written record of their workshops.[11]
The second book was the result of research carried out by Kaqchikel/
Poq'oman sociologist María Estela Jocón González, and it is interesting
that its structure is very similar to that of Cu Choc's poem "Ix Tzib.'"

Jocón González's book is composed of five chapters. The first, "Opening the Eagle's eyes," discusses Maya peoples' cosmology from the perspective of our ancestral grandmothers: Xchel, Xmucane, Xquic, and Xbalanque.[12] The author underscores the importance of feeding our strength and "deepening the material and immaterial cultural legacy we have inherited from our grandmothers and grandfathers" (9). The second chapter of the book is titled "To Pinch our Ears," and it discusses the role that Maya women played during the colonial period. History is narrated from the perspective of our mothers, making visible "the survival strategies employed by our grandmothers and mothers to overcome the holocaust" we experienced in the colonial period (9). Here we find the stories of Maya heroes like the eighteenth-century Kaqchikel activist María del Carmen Contán from Jocotenango, Sacatepéquez. Contán worked for a Spanish family as a maid and wet nurse. In October 1797, she denounced the family she worked for to a Spanish court because of economic exploitation and domestic violence. She also denounced the local Spanish governor for the political abuse he carried out against Indigenous peoples in Jocotenango (56).

The third chapter of Jocón González's book, titled "And We Continue Pinching Our Ears," is written from the perspective of our "Maya daughters," who narrate experiences of pain and dignity in our contemporary epoch; in particular, the author underscores the challenges we face as a result of the state terrorism and genocide we experienced between 1978 and 1985. For Jocón González, it is important for women

to rescue from the fratricidal history all those elements that Maya women contributed in the struggle for life. The physical weight of the genocide left in every pathway a feeling, a family member or an anonymous grave where no one will ever place flowers. But in every obstacle we encounter, we build hope for a new life . . . the fact of being alive means a rebirth. (93)

The rest of the book, chapters 4 and 5, narrates specific strategies to strengthen Maya women's struggles for their rights and political vindication. Among other actions, there is a call to rebuild our history and to weave "our individual and collective self-esteem" (115) by revaluing "our self, strengthening our capacities and potentialities with regard to making political decisions, developing dialogues, elaborating strategies and participating in the consensus about the control of the situations that block our integral development" (121–22). Cu Choc's poem connects with these principles and efforts to reconstruct the history of Maya peoples and feed Indigenous women's self-esteem through an invitation to explore the role of Indigenous women in the pre- and postcolonial history from the perspective of our grandmothers, mothers, and daughters. Indeed, Cu Choc allegorizes our desire to "rescue our history," in particular the contributions Maya women have made in the struggle for life; theirs is a constant rebirth that can potentially lead us to imagine the conditions of possibility for collective emancipation.

Why is it important for Cu Choc and the Maya women's collectives, Uk'ux B'e Association and the Maya Women of Kaqla, to reference and give agency to our millenarian history by highlighting the perspectives of our grandmothers, mothers, and daughters? In my view, Maya feminist assumptions aim to challenge theorists who have traced the origins of feminist ideas back only to the 1960s and 1970s. Toril Moi, for example, states that in the 1960s, "for the first time since the women's vote was won, feminism again surfaced as an important political force in the Western world" (2001, 21). Similarly, with regard to the particular context of Iximulew, Morna MacLeod relegates feminist Indigenous agency to the 1970s:

In the last few decades, there have been different factors that have made possible Indigenous women's social agency in public spaces in Guatemala. A first factor was the inclusion of Indigenous women in the organization and consciousness raising that the Catholic Church carried out through Catholic Action and Liberation Theology in the 1970s. Many Indigenous women became catechists and delegates of the word; that is, they would leave their communities, learn about other women's experiences, and propel diverse organizing experiences at the local level. Many of them later joined the Committee of Peasant Unity (CUC) and, subsequently, revolutionary organizations. This incipient and growing experience that began in the 1970s, not only through the revolutionary movement, but also the emerging Indianist expressions, *constitute the roots of the actual political participation of Indigenous women.*[13] (2011, 36, emphasis mine)

As we can see, although these discussions emphasize the role of Indigenous women in the struggle to materialize their political demands after the second half of the twentieth century, they also draw our attention to their obvious silence about the prominent role of Indigenous women in the struggles against colonialism and heterosexual patriarchy long before that time. Contrary to these perspectives, Cu Choc's and the Maya women's collectives, Uk'ux B'e and the Maya Women of Kaqla, propose a different temporal genealogy in which Indigenous women's activism and political agency started in precolonial times. In this sense, they suggest that Indigenous women were never at the margins, but rather represent an invisible presence at the center of discussions about women's rights hidden underneath the Eurocentric and non-Indigenous gender logic of settler colonialism for more than five hundred years (Arvin, Tuck, and Morrill 2013, 14). The work of the Q'eq'chi Maya poet and of the Indigenous collectives leads us down a critical path that suggests that no discussion about feminism and decolonization can occur without recognizing the fundamental role Indigenous women have historically played, long before the twentieth century, in the articulation of a feminist register that contributes to the dignification of our histories and the prominence of Indigenous women in the creation of that history. Taking this alternative feminist genealogy into consideration, we come to understand that the struggles for the rights of Indigenous and non-Indigenous women extend back earlier than the twentieth century or even 1492.

Indeed, Cu Choc's perspective is not limited to a vision that condemns European colonial patriarchy or settler colonialism. Quite the contrary, the Q'eq'chi poet suggests that repressive policies against women also characterize pre-European colonial contexts. In her poem, "And Another Zaz!" (qtd. in Valle Escalante 2010, 303–4) she develops some of the aforementioned critiques alluding to feminicide politics that have characterized both the precolonial and Guatemala's postwar context. The poem reads:

Zaz
a machete blow
zaz, another one
zaz, another one
zaz, another one
zaz, another one
zaz, another one
zaz, another one
zaz, another one

zaz, another one
zaz, another one
zaz, another one
and I am alive
incredibly, I am still alive
and I see the faces of those who hit me
I see the faces of the others
my mouth covered
my absent eyes
not wanting to see
and I am alive
wanting to see
now my body weakens
and it does not feel pain
my mouth covered
ears open
the final zaz
and my head falls
it rolls to my feet and their feet
there is blood boiling
but I was gone with my rolling head
one of them took it
taking it to the center of the plaza
me, who had a savage ancestor
that offered the body of my great grandmother
to his eternal gods
today, I am sacrificed again,
without reason
and my head remains there
open eyes
open ears
covered mouth
but it still feels like screaming
my mouth
it will scream . . .

In this composition, Cu Choc once again explores the need to "interrupt the silence" that we saw in her poem "Ix Tzib." In this poem, however, this theme is developed through the idea of censorship as a principal element of patriarchal ideology. Written from a first-person perspective, the poem narrates the capture and consequent decapitation of a rebel woman by a group of men ("I see the faces of those who hit me"). It is suggested that this woman has been imprisoned and punished for denouncing social and patriarchal injustice ("covered mouth"). After several "machete blows," her head finally falls to her feet and then to their feet. Her executioners pick it up and take it to the center of the plaza, showing it to the crowd. Despite the punishment and her decapitation, she "incredibly" is still alive. Even though her executioners have covered her mouth to silence her efforts to freely express herself, she still feels like screaming, and she "will scream."

This poem, written in 2008, invokes the poetic voice's mutilated body and decapitated head, which are metaphors of the Maya female social body. Her dismemberment and subsequent decapitation highlight the genocide perpetrated by the Guatemalan state against Indigenous peoples in the highlands. The head, separated from the body, once shown to the crowd, represents a trophy for the executioners; it is a political act to silence and punish dissidence. But the head also represents knowledge, history, and ancestral memory (the death of the great-grandmother). Most importantly, however, the head symbolizes resilience and resistance against repression, a continuation of the struggle against censorship and physical attacks against the Maya female social body, which have been historically punished. The decapitated woman does not express pain or agony; there are no screams when the machete blows are dealt and the decapitation takes place. On the contrary, the poem underscores the courage and bravery of the narrator and the desire to continue "screaming," despite the fact that her body has been mutilated.

The invocation of the "machete blows," the mutilation of the body, and her consequent decapitation in the poem are not merely figurative images. Unfortunately, they represent literal realities. "And Another Zaz!" can be read from the context of the armed conflict and postwar period in Guatemala and, in particular, as a denunciation of the femicide that many women have suffered in the country since the beginning of the war. Let me mention here just two of the newspaper headlines that reported these murders of women in Guatemala in recent decades, one from the national news outlet, *Guatevisión*, on December 12, 2016—"Crimes Continue: Two Mutilated Women Have Appeared"[14]—and another from July 29, 2015, in the newspaper *Prensa Libre* (Free Press), "The Body of a Decapitated Woman

Has Been Found in Zone 6."[15] As noted several times earlier, the 1996 Peace Accords did not end the violence in the country. In recent decades, in a contradictory and complex fashion, several political, economic, and social processes converged, including the emergence of the Pan-Maya movement, the struggles to materialize human rights, the implementation of an extractivist neoliberal economy via free trade agreements (e.g., CAFTA), the increasingly large migratory waves to the United States, the growth of corruption within high positions of governmental power, and the consolidation of gangs, organized crime, and drug trafficking cartels like the Zetas.[16] These criminal sectors, in particular, have heightened a social crisis that has created a climate of impunity in the country, given the increase in crimes of violence—kidnappings for ransom, bribery of officials and corporations, money laundering, and daily lynching and murders. The most vulnerable sectors in society—the poor, Indigenous peoples, children, and youth—have been most affected. Indigenous women in particular, who find themselves in disadvantaged economic, ethnic/racial, and social conditions, have become vulnerable to sexual, domestic, and homicidal violence. According to Guatemala's National Statistics Institute (INE), the incidence of the murder of women increased 112.25 percent in the country between 2000 and 2004: during those four years, 1,501 women were murdered (*Investigación sobre feminicidio en Guatemala* [Research on Femicide in Guatemala] 2005, 33).

This 2005 report stated that these murders

> have been characterized by elements of fury and savagery that are different from other kinds of violent murders. The femicides are distinguished, among other things, by the frequency with which the murdered women are victims of sexual violence that includes sexual harassment, rape, mutilation of genital organs, etc. The mutilation of the body is also frequent; body parts are abandoned in different places in order to "leave messages" of intimidation. This *modus operandi* highlights the interest of the victimizer in showing how the cruelty of the crime was carried out. (37)

That study determined that the origins of these crimes against women could be traced back to the internal armed conflict, in particular when the Guatemalan government implemented its "scorched earth" and "beans and bullets" military campaigns orchestrated by General Efraín Ríos Montt:

Thousands of women, primarily Indigenous Maya, were raped
during torture or before being murdered. This was a common
practice among the State agents, directed to destroy the dignity
of the person in one of its most intimate and vulnerable aspects.
The humiliation and bullying of women (like demanding that
they dance before the soldiers), not only aimed to make their pain
invisible, but to transmit a sense of passivity and conformism that
would not allow them to act; for them to accept their suffering as
natural.[17] (25)

Despite the existence of laws against these kinds of offenses, as seen in
news reports, femicides continue to this day.

The conclusions exposed in *Investigación sobre feminicidio en Guatemala*
and news reports are directly associated with what Cu Choc denounces in
her poem "And Another Zaz!" The "machete blows"—the mutilation of
the speaker's body and her consequent decapitation—not only allude to
this particular social context but also to a precolonial one. Cu Choc's
poem associates femicide violence with Maya human sacrifice: "me, who
had a savage ancestor / that offered the body of my great grandmother / to
his eternal gods / today, I'm sacrificed again, / without reason." Human
sacrifices, particularly those based on decapitation, were in fact common
ritual practices among Maya peoples in pre-Columbian times. Some of
these practices are described in existing Maya registers, including, for example, Hunahpu's decapitation by the Lords of Xib'alb'a in the *Popol Wuj*. His
head is later replaced by a calabash. Stephen Houston and Andrew Scherer
(2010), focusing on the Maya classic period (c. 250–900 AD), discuss
some of the strategies Maya peoples used to execute war captives and
other people selected for these kinds of rituals. They indicate that various
existing texts, like ceramics or Maya stelae in temples, display rituals involving not only decapitation and heart extraction but also slow and painful
forms of extinguishing life that include stoning victims and acts of extirpa-
tion of other internal organs (167–68). According to these authors, human
sacrifices, contrary to assumptions that they were nonsensical rituals without a "specific reason," as Cu Choc's poem suggests, were instead types of
special offerings to Maya deities and gods. The suffering of war captives
and their agonized screams were not only a form of imposing dishonor on
the warrior but also a test of their honorable resistance (167–68). In fact, in
2013 in the old city of Uxul in what is today southern Mexico, archaeologists

from the University of Bonn discovered a massive 1,400-year-old tomb that included twenty-four dismembered and decapitated bodies. Two of the bodies were female. The victims, according to the study, could have been war captives or noble figures from Uxul city.[18]

It is important to emphasize that Cu Choc's poem, by alluding to the Maya classic period—"savage ancestor," "my great grandmother," "eternal gods"—implicitly suggests that patriarchy characterized Maya societies. Thus, Cu Choc's perspective organically aligns itself to that of Aymara activist/intellectual Julieta Paredes (2010), who proposes the idea of "*entronque patriarcal*" (patriarchal interlocking), which suggests the existence of patriarchy among Indigenous peoples in Abiayala before the arrival of Europeans. Focusing on Bolivia, Paredes states that we have to "recognize that the unjust relations between men and women here in our country also occurred before the colonial period; patriarchy is not the result of colonization. There is also patriarchy and chauvinism that is Bolivian, Indigenous and popular. To decolonize gender, in this sense, means to recover the memory of the struggle of our great-grandmothers against the patriarchal system that was established before the colonial invasion" (24).[19] As we can see, in her reference to the sacrifice of her great-grandmother, Cu Choc affirms the idea of patriarchal interlocking proposed by Paredes in order to "recover the memory of the struggle" of her Maya great-grandmothers.

These Aymara and Maya Q'eq'chi activists are not the only ones to articulate a critique of patriarchy as a pre- or postcolonial oppressive system within Indigenous communities. The perspective of patriarchal interlocking also emerges from the discourse of Mapuche leader Isolde Reuque Paillalef, who states that "European chauvinism combined itself with the Mapuche one. . . . This chauvinism displays itself in the feelings of jealousy and male authority; that superiority that the male feels it has over women" (Reuque Paillalef and Mallon 2002, 227). These critiques of an Indigenous patriarchy also characterize the work of the aforementioned Maya Women of Kaqla collective. Many of the Maya women who have participated in the workshops offered by the group seek to boost their dignity and self-esteem. To achieve these goals, many have offered important testimonies about how patriarchal ideologies operate in their towns. A book published by the collective, *La palabra y el sentir de las mujeres mayas de kaqla* (The Word and Feeling of the Maya Women of Kaqla; Grupo de Mujeres Mayas Kaqla 2004), includes stories that denounce domestic violence and sexual abuse. One of the participants, for example, narrates how in her own K'iche' Maya culture she felt discriminated against, particularly after she earned a higher degree in education. Her long-time partner decided not to marry her because she "does not eat the same food I eat. You eat like a ladina [non-Indigenous person]. You don't speak the language, and you dress and think differently now" (74). Another participant took the opportunity offered by the workshop to denounce how certain Maya *ajq'ij* (spiritual guides) from her community "abused the women who worked with them. Some have been victims of sexual assault given that the ajq'ij feel they have authority over them" (99). These examples illustrate that, as subjects who live under and in colonial societies, we are not exempt from reproducing and internalizing oppressive attitudes, in this case heterosexual patriarchal ideologies. Indigenous communities are not immune from these power dynamics. As Kaqchikel Maya sociologist Aura Cumes points out,

> Both sexism and racism, fed by excessive hegemonic imagery channeled through diverse social mediums, exercise social and influential pressure in conducts that lead to the exclusion of Indigenous women by some men . . . so that Indigenous women are not only exposed to the racism coming from "non-Indigenous" sectors, but also the ethnic shaming imposed on them by some Indigenous men. (Bastos and Cumes 2007, 175–76)

Thus, Cu Choc's position aligns with the work of other Indigenous feminists who aim to disclose the operations of a patriarchal system that is not merely the result of European colonialism and modern nation-states but also of precolonial Indigenous societies characterized by similar systems of domination. The oppressive heterosexual patriarchal ideology, as we can see, continues today, manifesting in tragic forms as exemplified in the femicide occurring in Guatemala.

Let me conclude this section with a discussion of the poem "Poesía de lo propio" (Poetry of One's Own) that begins *Poemaya,* and its relationship to Cu Choc's emancipated feminist collective ideals. In this poem, as well as in the rest of the book, the Maya Q'eq'chi poet explores some of the themes already discussed in this section: the vindication of Ingenuous women's rights through a rigorous questioning of a pre- and postcolonial heterosexual patriarchal system, isolation, and lack of love. "Poetry of One's Own," in particular, displays Cu Choc's intention to challenge widely disseminated stereotypes that describe women's bodies and minds as fragile and weak. Contrary to these prejudices, the Maya Q'eq'chi poet suggests that our social and political emancipation and vindication rest in the dignification and restitution of Indigenous women's rights.

The poem is divided into three parts structured into twenty-five stanzas. Similar to "And Another Zaz!" and "Ix Tzib'," "Poetry of One's Own" consists of short verses without conventional punctuation and with a series of line breaks and ruptures that many times read like a form of syntactic diction. The composition starts with the following verses: "I was born a woman / destined / to cry" (71). The narrator then goes on to describe her survival as a woman who faced challenges on her own: "I was born a woman / born alone / grew up alone / I continue / alone" (71). In the following section, the poem personifies women's tears. Far from symbolizing weakness, tears represent the female courage to overcome the "conflict born at the arrival / of the foreigner / five centuries ago" (74). Since then, Indigenous women have lived under "the shadow of the other gender / of the monster / the almighty / over our land" (75). Tears are a metaphor that serves to denounce the abuses caused by the heterosexual colonial patriarchal system against women:

They [the tears] are the rage for the pain
of my sisters
with them
I wash the abuse
from the streets, cinemas and chiaroscuro rooms . . .
with them
I condemn the chains
in my house, my city
my country. (72)

The process of consciousness raising with regard to a history of abuse and dispossession illuminates the rebirth of the poetic voice as a collective subject. In the last section of the poem, the "I" becomes a collective "we" ready to fight to change the exploitative conditions under which women live in a heteropatriarchal society. The section has a hopeful tone, emphasizing that women "are the white force / that conquers little by little," the hand, the path, the force, stone, and life; women are "flowers / seeds / trees," the "new germination" (76). Women, the poem concludes,

Are the human
tomorrow
soon to be discovered

we are the woman
that tries
to build. (76)

Cu Choc's poems illustrate the tenacity of Indigenous women who have
been defining and constituting our collective survival as Indigenous nations
by suggesting that their millenarian struggles transcend European and
criollo-ladino / mestizo colonial expansion. For Cu Choc, there is no doubt
that our collective emancipation resides in the vindication of Indigenous
women and the eradication of heteropatriarchal and racist colonial logic.
Decolonization, in this sense, will never be possible without organically
tying our struggles for land or linguistic and identity rights to the vindication of Indigenous women's rights. As Cu Choc's feminist poetics shows,
Indigenous women represent the "new germination," a "human tomorrow /
soon to be discovered." It is important, then, to highlight the valuable emancipatory contribution that Cu Choc's work makes to Maya decolonization
in Iximulew. In addition, the Q'eq'chi poet's literary contribution emphasizes that such emancipation has become possible because of the struggle
of our great-grandmothers, grandmothers, mothers, and daughters.

The Mayas Come out of the Closet: Queer Poetics
in Manuel Tzoc's *Gay(o)*

Let me state at the outset that the title of this section is not meant to suggest
that Mayas only recently came out of the closet.[20] As Pete Sigal's (2000)
research on sexual desire in Maya colonial societies in the Yucatán suggests,
homosexual practices (or sodomy, as the Spanish characterized it) were
common within Maya societies.[21] Similarly, Stephen Houston and Karl
Taube emphasize that in Mesoamerica "sexual identity was more fluid and
representations of such fluidity are sometimes forthright and open and at
other times are more discrete: they obscure much more than what it is
shown" (2010, 39). However, Maya peoples did not view sexual desire with
the same types of taxonomies as early modern European peoples did or as
Western societies tend to now; that is, they did not categorize individuals

as either homosexual or heterosexual or classify certain sexual acts as sinful or not sinful. An example of this is the Yucatec Maya category "antzil xincb'ok," which literally means "feminine-masculine."[22] Nor did the Maya at the time of the Spanish conquest understand sexual behaviors and ideas in the same ways as their European conquerors, who developed the notion of sexuality as a discrete category of experience. The title of this section therefore suggests that, with the arrival and consequent colonization of Indigenous territories, Indigenous homosexual practices in Mesoamerica were banned and punished, and sexual differences were incarcerated in the closets of settler colonial societies and Western modernity.

Manuel Tzoc's poetry book, *Gay(o)*, as I demonstrate, aims precisely to challenge the imposition of heteronormative and heterosexual politics by the colonial nation-state and so to assert—following Mark Rifkin's work—an erotics of sovereignty that allows us to reimagine "peoplehood and placemaking in ways that register the complex entwinement of unacknowledged survivals, unofficial aspirations, and the persistence of pain" (2012, 31). In addition, Tzoc's *Gay(o)* articulates an Indigenous erotics that "expresses past, present, and future possibilities that can provide principles for defining, envisioning, and living Indigeneity less predicated on codes of authenticity and modes of sovereign selfhood privileged in and realized through settler discourses and institutions" (39). Indeed, Tzoc's aim is to articulate and delineate a queer urban cartography permeated by homoeroticism to counteract the hegemonic order that seeks to impose heterosexuality and heteronormativity.

Manuel Tzoc is one of the most prolific contemporary Maya K'iche' literary voices and visual artists from Iximulew. Tzoc migrated with his family to Guatemala City from San Andrés Xecul, Totonicapán, when he was twelve years old. In the urban public sphere and at school, he soon experienced the consequences of racism and discrimination resulting from his ethnic and sexual differences. At school, kids made fun of his last name and the way he looked. Tzoc recalls a particularly painful memory that occurred during a Mother's Day celebration at his middle school. His mother, Micaela Lucía Bucup Elías, arrived at the school wearing her Maya *traje* from her hometown of San Andrés Xecul (Tzoc 2013). When the students saw him with his mother, they made fun of him. The bullying got worse when his behavior at school displayed "effeminate" characteristics. At the time, he did not know how to deal with his homosexuality.[23] Nonetheless, the traumatic experiences—along with his sexual attraction to Bruce Lee in the 1972 film *Way of the Dragon*—made him realize that he liked men. In trying to come to terms with the intolerant racist and homophobic context within which he lived, Tzoc developed feelings of insecurity that for a long time made him reject his own Maya and homosexual self. He experienced rejection not only at school but also at home: his parents were very traditional and very Christian when it came to sexuality. These experiences made Tzoc repress his queerness and remain closeted until he was eighteen years old. It was then that he finally found the courage to confront his parents and tell them he was gay. After a long conversation about his sexual identity, to his surprise, Tzoc's parents accepted him and offered him their unconditional love and support.

In Guatemala City, after he came out, Tzoc began to meet and interact with other writers and artists who encouraged him to express himself artistically. They shared with him the literary works of Indigenous writers like Luis de Lión and gay writers like Pedro Lemebel, Reinaldo Arenas, and Allen Ginsberg, which influenced and motivated him to develop his own artistic voice. Furthermore, his friends supported him in his artistic efforts to dignify his Indigenous and homosexual identities. In poetry, Tzoc found a platform to explore and exploit his artistic creativity, enabling him to articulate his own cultural and artistic liberation as well as develop his multiple axes of identity: his Indigeneity, his homosexuality, his urban self, and his artistic identity. He indicates that these are the pillars that sustain "my desire, my own self-recognition and dignification; what names me before a political system that rejects me and excludes me."[24] In 2006 he published his first book of poetry, *Esco-p(o)etas para una muerte en ver(sos) b-a...l...a* (Poetic Shotguns for a Death in Verse-Bullets). In addition, he has also published *De textos insanos* (On Insane Texts, 2009), *Gay(o)* (2011), *El ebrio mar y yo* (The Drunk Sea and I, 2011), and *Constante huida: Crimen de un corazón que no recuerdo y/o pronunicamientos del habla tartamuda* (Constant Escape, 2016) as well as the poetic play, *El Jardín de los infantes locos y la escafandra de oro* (The Garden of the Crazy Children, and the Golden Scuba Diving Suit, in collaboration with Cecilia Porras, 2013) and his handmade books *Polen* (Pollen, 2014) and *Cuerpo de niño triste* (The Body of the Sad Child, 2015).[25]

Tzoc's literary works offer a unique and original Indigenous queer perspective on the Maya literary movement. He arguably represents the first Maya gay literary voice in Iximulew whose artistic work challenges the heteronormative policies of the modern nation-state and its hegemonic institutions, as well as Indigenous homophobic attitudes, by centralizing Maya queer poetics. Indeed, despite the fact that homosexuality has been technically legal in Guatemala since the Liberal Reform of 1871, the Two Spirit, Lesbian, Gay, Bisexual, Transgender, Queer, and More (2sLGBTQ+) community continues to suffer various forms of discrimination, verbal abuse, physical violence, and persecution.[26] Nor does the Guatemalan state offer a guarantee to legally protect gay people, transgender subjects, or same-sex couples from those abuses. In the 2015 Guatemalan presidential elections, for example, Jimmy Morales won on a platform characterized by homophobia and conservatism. In an interview several months before his election, he was asked what he thought about abortion, gay marriage, and legalizing marijuana. He responded, "I don't accept any of the three. In the case of marriage between people of the same sex, I reject it because I don't believe in that and because in Guatemala, 97% of the population value Christian morals. To approve a law like that [gay marriage] would generate social disorder" (see Ahrens and Elías 2015). That such beliefs have become public policy is demonstrated by Law 5272, approved by Congress in 2017, which reads, "It is forbidden for public and private educational entities to teach and promote politics and programs to children and young adults related to sexual diversity or to teach as normal distinct sexual behaviors that are not heterosexual" ("La comunidad LGBTI de Guatemala" 2017).

Unfortunately, most Guatemalans, including some Indigenous communities and organizations, share those sentiments.[27] In *Ru rayb'al ri qach'akul / Los deseos de nuestro cuerpo* (Our Body's Desires, 2010), Kaqchikel Maya sociologist Emma Chirix, for example, discusses a memo circulated by the organization *Wajxaqi'b Noj*—a Maya NGO that, ironically, fights for Indigenous rights in Guatemala—that enforces "the moralist grounds of the Catholic church" (77) with regard to heteronormative ideology. In the document cited by Chirix, this organization expresses concern about the demands to legalize gay marriage: "What do we say about gay people? What is strange for our [Maya] people is that two persons of the same sex united in marriage don't contribute to our social fabric, especially if they have the intention of adopting children. What future awaits these children when their parents are neither man nor woman?" (77).

Similarly, in the literary realm, moralist and homophobic attitudes emanate from canonical texts. In *Time Commences in Xibalbá* (2012), Kaqchikel Maya writer Luis de Lión represents the character of Juan Caca as a homosexual man who displays a physical attraction toward his counterpart Pascual Baeza. Employing nahualism, or the invocation and association of people with animal spirits (Juan = Hen and Pascual = Coyote), Lion describes the first encounter of these characters after years of not seeing each other. The narrator states that Juan/Hen "Saw him [Pascual] as a single God; his heart trembled wishing to become a female coyote" (49). Juan's sexual identity becomes more evident when the narrator recounts, "Who knows what happens inside his body, inside Hen's soul. What we know is that he sees Coyote as if he was his own creation. And he wants him to eat him because he feels that his Hen being is breaking, ripping" (53). Juan's repressed homosexuality, however, is associated with ideas of cowardice, invoked through the pejorative epithet of *hueco* (fag).[28] In the novel, the character of Concha—who married Juan to silence the gossip in the community about his homosexuality—thinks "He is not a man" (25) when Juan decides not to have sexual relations with her. Later, she labels him a "hueco" for not supporting Pascual after he incites the destruction of ladino or White religious symbols such as the wooden image of the Virgin from the church, "the only ladina in the town." Concha decides to leave Juan because he does not like getting in trouble and he "is a fag" (81). For his part, Gaspar Pedro González, in his novel *A Mayan Life* (1995), portrays a Maya world that adopts and adheres to the heteronormative and heterosexual dominant society through the idea of the nuclear family. In the novel, the idea of the family represents an allegory of the Maya Nation. Through the figures of Mekel (the father) and Lwin (the son who continues the idea of the family when he marries the character of Malin), the novel presents heterosexual masculine figures that, through marriage, affirm a putative organic unity of heteronormative interests. The idea of Maya nationalism displayed through Mekel and Lwin suggests the preservation of patriarchal relations that marginalize queer, transgender, and feminist decolonial perspectives.

In this context, Tzoc's literary works can be read as a response to the homophobia and heteronormative politics that characterize dominant society. The K'iche' Maya author articulates a queer geography, permeated with homoeroticism that radically interrupts and counteracts the heteronormative dominant order. His work invites us to explore spaces where Maya decolonial struggles take place; this time, in favor of the rights of Indigenous 2sLGBTQ+ subjects in Iximulew/Guatemala.[29] His writing is organically tied to the specific struggles of the 2sLGBTQ+ community, which has become more vocal in the last few decades. Indeed, its prominence has been growing, especially since the beginning of the twenty-first century. The first public gay parade in Guatemala was held in June 2000, in which more than two hundred transvestites, transgender, and gay activists marched down the public plaza, holding signs that read, "Don't be afraid, tell them with pride you are gay."

I now turn to Tzoc's third book of poetry, *Gay(o)*, which was published in 2011. Emerging from Guatemala's postwar period amid the implementation of neoliberal reforms, the book delineates a politics of queer difference that aims to bring visibility to the 2sLGBTQ+ community. The book includes twenty-nine poems written in free verse in which the poetic voice, in first, second, and third person, uses his "Gaydar" to travel throughout a city, interacting with and displaying the activities of queer subjects in public and private urban spaces. Seven poems have titles, but the rest are designated by cardinal numbers. Moreover, the poems display a variety of narrative structures. Some, like "Versa-TIL" and poems "1" and "19," consist of one stanza of four or six lines; other poems, like "11" and "15. GAYDAR," are written in poetic prose. The book, through various epigraphs and literary and cultural references that appear throughout, shows the profound influence of queer writers such as the French Arthur Rimbaud, the North American Allen Ginsberg, the Argentinian Alejandra Pizarnik, and the Chilean Pedro Lemebel. My discussion of "GAYDAR (Queer Eye is Always Right)" shows that Tzoc pays special homage to Lemebel, particularly his queer manifesto, "I Speak for My Difference" (2001). Two of the poems in *Gay(o)* include epigraphs from Lemebel's work. In addition, there are similarities and intertextualities between the queer emancipation proposed by Tzoc and the international movement Queer Nation, founded in New York in 1990.

My discussion of Tzoc's book of poetry explores his critical stance toward the nation-state's political and discriminatory marginalization of its queer subjects. Although I show and celebrate the potential of this critique, I also disclose some of its limitations regarding collective Indigenous and non-Indigenous rights. My concern is that Tzoc does not extend his perspective to other spaces where struggles for Indigenous queer rights are being fought, nor does he develop a critique of some of the complexity and class contradictions that characterize the 2sLGBTQ+ community in a context like Iximulew. Such oversights, I argue, may risk the development of a critique for recognition that may not materialize in intense politics of territorial and intellectual Indigenous autonomy and sovereignty like the ones proposed by other Maya writers in this and earlier chapters. I complement my critical reading of Tzoc's work with K'iche' Maya sociologist Dorotea Gómez Grijalva's (2014) ethnographic account of racist and discriminatory attitudes toward Indigenous peoples held by some segments of the gay and lesbian community in Guatemala City.

Gay(o) begins with the following satirical warning: "Danger! The reading of these texts may cause serious harm to your 'sane' heterosexuality." This suggests that the author is primarily addressing heterosexual readers and intends to challenge their homophobia and heteronormativity.[30] In addition to the warning, we find a drawing of a "Gallito inglés" (little English rooster, or cock) that looks like an erect phallus/penis, and below it, the slang: "This is the Little English cock / watch him with pretense / take away his beak and claws / and stick him up your ass."[31] Through slang and drawing, Tzoc invokes the satirical graffiti that usually appears in bathrooms or other public spaces of the city poking fun at homosexuality. Both the language and the drawing are associated with the title of the book: *Gay(o)*. The Spanish pronunciation of the title is similar to that of the noun "gallo" (rooster), a word that not only refers to the domesticated bird but also figuratively is used in Spanish to refer to ideas of masculinity, courage, and bravery, connoting cockfights. As in the English "cock," "gallo" is also used to refer to the phallus. The letter "*o*" in parentheses in the title of the book suggests the anus, a recurring literary trope in the book, emphasizing the role of masculine, "pillow-biters" and "passive" gay men.[32] The image of the "*o*" in parentheses could also suggest the idea of imprisonment or a closet. The title and image of the little English cock, then, create a linguistic game that playfully evokes the figure and prominence of—mostly male—queer subjects and their homoerotic activities in the city.

After the epigraph and the image of the little English rooster, the book includes the following epigraph from Arthur Rimbaud's poem "A Dream for Winter": "In the winter, we shall travel in a little pink railway carriage / With blue cushions. / We shall be comfortable. A nest of mad kisses lies in wait / In each soft corner . . . Then you'll feel your cheek scratched . . . / A little kiss, like a crazy spider, / Will run round your neck." The epigraph challenges homophobia in the sense that the journey of the poetic voice will take us through "each soft corner" that may lead the heterosexual reader to feel the tickle, "like a crazy spider," that goes up and down our neck and can provoke feelings of pleasure-repulsion. Moreover, the poems are combined with a series of early twentieth-century black-and-white photographs from the Young Men's Christian Association (YMCA). These images are of men's basketball and boxing teams training and a men's volleyball game at a lakefront. There is also a satirical image about the cure for excessive "Cell Phone Face-Itis": "Any outdoor physical activities that will require using both hands." As is well known, in the late nineteenth and early twentieth centuries, the YMCA taught that homosexuality was an illness or disorder, but later the YMCA became a space for homoerotic hookups for many gay men who were members of this institution. The Village People were inspired by this history to write their famous song "YMCA," which has become an anthem for gay pride in the 2sLGBTQ+ community.

Along with the photographs, warnings, and epigraphs, there is a short prologue written by Ioshua—pen name of the late Argentine poet, painter, and performer Josué Marcos Belmonte—who describes *Gay(o)* as "perverse and clear," "carnal and cynic," "a vicious retelling of faggy acts; a close-up to the intense fleeting of love that is taken only because it is offered to us." Also included are the "missing words," or a sort of epilogue written in poetic form by the Chilean writer Jeremias Maggi. It is titled "Ioshua-Tzoc, Two Faces of the Same Cuteness." The epilogue describes Tzoc's and Ioshua's friendship, locating their respective poetic-artistic projects in the "geography of homosexual desire" amid the "territories of the struggle against sexism"; they are cultural projects that aim to restrict "*machismo* and the Western grammar." This characterization of *Gay(o)* by Ioshua and Maggi is accurate and, indeed, is aligned with Tzoc's literary mission: to highlight and dignify the experiences of the 2sLGBTQ+ community. Tzoc invokes and makes visible diverse sexual identities to humanize the queer experience within various urban settings. He challenges the nation-state whose purpose—as we saw earlier with the anti-gay laws proposed by the Jimmy Morales government—is to incarcerate sexual diversity within the closet of Western modernity and support criollo-mestizo / ladino supremacy, heterosexism, and Christian heteropatriarchy.

In its journey through the city, Tzoc's work articulates a literary neo-baroque as described by the Italian critic Omar Calabrese: *Gay(o)*, in its evocation of the diverse queer experiences, explores "limit and excess; detail and fragment; instability and metamorphosis; disorder and chaos; node and labyrinth; complexity and dissolution; 'more or less' and 'I don't know what'; distortion and perversion" (1999, 35). The neo-baroque in Tzoc's poems displays crude language saturated with explicit sensual images that illustrate queer experiences in the private and public urban settings. From such representations emerge metaphors about homoerotic "hidden pleasures" that expose readers to "blow jobs in porno cinemas," "voyeurism in public bathrooms," penetrations of "eyes and cocks" in "dimensional anuses" (1), "phallic hallucinogen mushrooms" (1), "lipstick and semen on the lips" (3), and "wet fingers" (19) navigating naked bodies. Interpellated for the heterosexual reader, these images may provoke the discomfort of the unknown or taboo.

The poems in *Gay(o)* have three themes. First, poems such as "3. Shemale," 4–6, 16, and 24–28 deal with isolation: the poetic voice's and the invoked characters' "perfect murderer."[33] In other words, the lives of *Gay(o)*'s protagonists unfold in urban settings and, despite the innumerable parties and fleeting sexual encounters, they remain in a constant state of isolation. The sadness that this situation creates after failed monogamous relationships is ameliorated through one-night stands, masturbation, or alcohol and drug excess. Amid hopelessness, the characters search for profound human connections; however, it is suggested that they inevitably end up alone, waiting for something that will fulfill their lives. This is the case for Shemale in poem "3," a transgender woman with "boobs and cock" who sells "hidden pleasures" to "hidden people / in a hidden city." She walks with a knife in her purse to defend herself against physical aggression, which implicitly suggests her constant struggle against homophobia in the city. Her only words are "oral anal," and in the "dark" corner, Shemale risks her life for money—"a quickie" or "sex" in exchange for "powder." Shemale, it is suggested, is emotionally broken inside and outside—"torn stocking and soul"—with "lipstick and semen on her lips." Amid adversity, however, she does not stop hoping that one day, "something that looks like love" will arrive to rescue her from the "corner of death." Similarly, in poem "4," the poetic voice narrates his strong feelings for a man who does not love him. This provokes in him "anger anger anger." Isolation and lack of love lead to one-night stands, to swallowing "alcohol by sips (or a whole load)," watching "gay porn" in cybercafés, masturbating without "knowing where to go," and feeling "alone and lonely." The same theme of heartbreak and isolation appears in the poems dedicated to "H" or "Hugo." Without "H," the narrator turns to anguish and feels emotionally "empty." "Without you—'H'—/ when in the hell / will I feel anything?" (poem "5"). Such feelings lead the narrator to a constant search for human connection that he pretends to find through "pure sex," "jacking off," voyeurism, and "giving blow jobs in porno cinemas." Similarly, poem "16" narrates the story of an "old, sad, and solitary gay man" whose urban travels lead him to places where he can "pay for sex" with young boys who usually reject and despise him. After fulfilling his sexual needs, his being fills up with the "empty silence that extends over the city." Just like Shemale, he waits for a "beautiful young boy" who loves him in return; however, that love "will never arrive."

In tandem with the theme of isolation, Tzoc also explores romantic gay relations and contempt in homoerotic fleeting encounters. Poems "2," "7," "17," and "19" narrate the experiences of gay men and their sexual hookups in diverse urban contexts in both the private and public spheres. For example, poem "2. Versa-TIL," talks about a gay man who, when asked whether he is a "neck blower or pillowbiter?" responds: "I go with everything!!!!" Poem "7" narrates the casual hookup between the poetic voice and "Evanescent Cocksucker." They are sitting on a bench in the park, and evanescent cocksucker begins to touch himself. The narrator notices, becomes excited, and gets "an accelerated erection." Evanescent cocksucker then says that his own "cock" grows to nineteen centimeters. The narrator, interested, responds by saying that "this must be proven." After accepting the invitation to "fuck for money," they both end up in a "shitty motel," "with condom and lubricant" until they get to feel the "double orgasm with the warm milk spreading in the back and the mattress." In poem "19," a passive "cunning fag" opens "his butthole" so he can be penetrated. In this way, he shows "the truth about his hidden desires" and activates the pleasure that at least, in a "27-second orgasm," can fulfill and satisfy his existential anguish.

Lastly, Tzoc addresses the theme of queer pride and affirmation. Poems like "8. Gay Disco," "15. GAYDAR," 18, 20–23, and 29 highlight queer diversity and prominence within the urban settings invoked. Both "Gay Disco" and "GAYDAR" illustrate Tzoc's project to imagine how the nation-state can become queer, an initiative inspired by the late Chilean writer Pedro Lemebel in his manifesto "I Speak for My Difference." The first of these poems takes place at an "antro" or gay disco where people in dark rooms dance to Gloria Trevi's[34] music—in particular her song "Todos me miran" (Everyone Watches Me)— and there are dark kisses and "porno scenes." One says, "I'll touch it," and the other responds, "OK. You touch it!" Dark spaces within the disco are associated with the dark city, where queer subjects like Shemale and Old Gay Man appear. Nevertheless in these poems there is celebration in which the characters engage in playful and ephemeral homoerotic affective exchanges. The metaphor of darkness in this disco setting, in contrast to that in the city's corners, does not evoke the feelings of isolation and marginality we see in the other poems. Instead, we are presented with a sense of community; the characters are closely connected through their desires and the satisfaction of homoerotic pleasure. It is a space where, in addition to drinking, singing, dancing, and shining, gay people behave freely. "Gay Disco" is a place where "Gay parties / are the greatest of all."

From the semi-private and obscure space represented in "Gay Disco," we move into the public sphere in the poem "GAYDAR (Queer Eye Is Always Right)." This poem in poetic prose describes the itinerary of the narrator through the public spaces of a city. He "detects" the activities of "queensfairieshomossissiesfaggotsbutterfliespoofiescocksuckersgays-andmore . . ." The poem's words in parentheses—"queer eye is always right"—and the epigraph that accompanies it, "Are you afraid of life becoming homosexual?" come from Pedro Lemebel, who wrote a weekly column titled "Adiós mariquita linda" (Farewell, Sweet Ladybird).[35] In his columns, Lemebel offered an alternative queer perspective of contemporary Chilean society in which he denounced, among other things, the homophobia of the Chilean state and hegemonic society in general, as well as the violence and political marginalization of the 2sLGBTQ+ community. Lemebel discussed and highlighted the struggles for 2sLGBTQ+ rights in Chile and other parts of the Americas; he also included literary translations of major gay writers from other countries, such as Ginsberg, Rimbaud, Oscar Wilde, Walt Whitman, and Virginia Wolff. This is how Tzoc became familiar with their writings and learned about gay rights movements in other parts of the world, such as the movement Queer Nation. To pay homage to the work of Lemebel, especially his political manifesto "I Speak for My Difference," Tzoc writes and structures this particular poem as a chronicle that aims to make visible the public and private activities of the gay community within an urban setting.[36]

"GAYDAR" is divided into three parts. The first talks about gay men who have openly embraced their homosexuality. They walk publicly on the streets and avenues, or hang out in parks or at the mall, speaking of their partners or buying the "latest in fashion and Madonna CDs." The second part focuses on the "gay(o)s" who have not yet come out of the closet. In public, "they boast of their manhood, but are the first to fall into the trap of gay activities." That is, they publicly assume a heterosexist masculine demeanor that conforms to what is demanded in a heteronormative dominant society—they are married, have kids, "act like a man," and so on; however, once nighttime arrives, they stop by gay bars after work, and following a few drinks, their "queen side comes out, sing gloria trevi songs, and, once they are drunk, leave in their big cars to search for sex (travesties or pimps) on the streets." Afterward, they "return to their wives as if nothing happened." Cowboys, lawyers, businessmen, Indigenous men, and others are in this group. Lastly, there are gay men who "wear masks," like priests, evangelical pastors, the Pope, military men, and politicians who "display double standards, and a double life." On the one hand, in their public discourses, they "negate, forbid, demonize same sex love," but on the other hand, in private, they suck "very erect, huge, juicy, and poisonous cocks with big bull testicles." After observing what happens in the city, "GAYDAR," who came from another galaxy, leaves a message on a public outdoor big screen: "SAME SEX LOVE IS NO DIFFERENT."

"GAYDAR" exemplifies a politics of gay liberation and tactics of queer power. Tzoc plays with ideas of sociability in the private and public spheres. On the one hand, the K'iche' Maya author imagines a world where queer subjects who embrace their homosexuality operate in public freely, without being assaulted or penalized for being gay. On the other hand, the poem's satirical tone exposes the hypocrisy of those who suppress their homoerotic desires; in doing so, they embrace the heteronormative and heterosexist ideologies imposed by the nation-state. In public they not only express sexist attitudes but also demonize and punish homosexuality. Nonetheless, they turn to the private sphere—the dark streets in the city where they find "transvestites" or "pimps," or people of the priesthood or from military barracks—to satisfy their suppressed sexual desires. In this way, Tzoc aims to vindicate marginalized 2sLGBTQ+ subjectivities. Both "GAYDAR" and "Gay Disco" underscore a politics of sexual difference that aims to make visible the prominence of the 2sLGBTQ+ community. For Tzoc, despite the efforts by the modern nation-state and its institutions to impose a heteronormative order and ideology, the queer community saturates and gives life to the urban context, queering all the "underground" and "public" dark spaces of the nation. Tzoc imagines characters that, through erotism, reclaim the nation for homoerotic pleasure. We become exposed to a world that for many, particularly the heterosexual readers that the K'iche' Maya author apostrophizes, had until now, been invisible.

Tzoc's stance, which turns the nation-state into a queer one, articulates a utopian vision that in many ways is reminiscent of some of the central ideas of the gay-lesbian liberation movements in the 1970s. These movements, according to John D'Emilio, proposed that if we all recognized our homoerotic nature, we would all come out of the closet and put an end to homophobia once and for all (2006, 59). Moreover, Tzoc's perspective can be organically associated with Queer Nation's political stand as represented in "History Is a Weapon: The Queer Nation Manifesto" (1990). This slogan underscores that queer people "are everywhere." This movement, which became very prominent by the 1990s, advocates for the rights of the 2sLGBTQ+ community. Its manifesto develops an indictment against the criminalization of queer subjects and denounces the dissemination of heteronormative politics by the modern nation-state through mass media and the institutionalization of marriage and heterosexual relations. "Straight people," the manifesto states, "have a privilege that allows them to do whatever they please and without fear. But not only do they live a life free of fear; they flaunt their freedom in my face" ("Queer Nation Manifesto"). It calls for a fight for the rights of 2sLGBTQ+ people to publicly express their sexual difference, given that "no one will give us what we deserve. Rights are not given. They are taken, by force if necessary." Moreover, it states,

It is about the freedom to be public, to just be who we are. It means everyday fighting oppression; homophobia, racism, misogyny, the bigotry of religious hypocrites and our own self-hatred . . .

Being queer means leading a different sort of life. It's not about the mainstream, profit-margins, patriotism, patriarchy or being assimilated. It's not about executive directors, privilege and elitism. It's about being on the margins, defining ourselves; it's about gender-f—and secrets, what's beneath the belt and deep inside the heart; it's about the night. Being queer is "grass roots" because we know that everyone of us, everybody, every c—, every heart and a—and d—is a world of pleasure waiting to be explored. Everyone of us is a world of infinite possibility.

As we can see, the Queer Nation Manifesto advocates dignifying a differentiated sexual identity within an intolerant, racist, and homophobic social context; its stance is strikingly similar to Tzoc's queer endeavor. Indeed, the K'iche' Maya author's work seeks to make visible the experiences of queer subjects who operate at the margins of an intolerant and homophobic nation-state as well. The references to "defining oneself" at the "secret" and "obscure" margins are similar to what Tzoc depicts in his work with figures like Shemale, Old Gay, and even *Gay(o)* subjects who operate within the closet of settler colonial modernity. Both the Queer Manifesto and *Gay(o)* make visible "living a different life" and the fact that "same sex love is no different."

When we consider the Queer Manifesto in relation to Tzoc's queer dignifying stand, it becomes clear that *Gay(o)*, more than articulating a collective Maya identity as we have seen represented in the works of Maya authors in previous chapters, projects an affirmation of queer social consciousness within an urban context. Tzoc's literary perspective does not consider Indigenous and non-Indigenous queer subjectivities that operate in the rural areas. For example, in the Maya Mam region of Huehuetenango, a beauty contest in September 2017 crowned Quetzalí the first Indigenous Maya Mam transgender queen in Iximulew. In her acceptance speech, twenty-two-year-old Quetzalí stated, "It does not matter how we dress or what our sexual identity is; we are 'all human beings'" (2017). Hence, we can read Tzoc's intention to focus only on the queer experience in the city as having particular political objectives that may be related to Mark Rifkin's reading in *When Did Indians Become Straight?* (2011) of Leslie Feinberg's novel, *Stone Butch Blues*. Tzoc articulates a queer urban geography, permeated with homoeroticism in contrast to the hegemonic order that aims to impose heteronormativity and heterosexuality. This is why Rifkin claims it is important for Tzoc to highlight "the city as the space that matters— where queer subjectivities can flourish and a range of intersecting communities can come to realize the value of solidarity" (258):

Despite not being permanent occupants of legally recognized native lands, Indigenous persons in the city still participate in peoplehood, emphasizing their "strong rooted connection to tribe and homeland" and "extending the sense of territory" to encompass both urban and reservation sites as part of the more capacious vision of "Indian country." Such a remapping of urbanity and Indigeneity works against both the reification of the reservation/ reserve as the only "authentic" place for native life, a perspective that elides the dislocating effects of structural underdevelopment,

and the narration of migration to the city as freedom from reserves
for individual families. (259)

As Rifkin underscores here, *Gay(o)* suggests that the rural world may not
be interpreted as the "only" and "authentic" space of Indigenous life. The
sense of belonging to a community, the urban sphere in this particular
context, is articulated through a queer invasion of the city in which we are
offered different views of it from the perspective of 2sLGBTQ+ subjectivities. From these perspectives are found cosmopolitan experiences that
express the conditions of possibility to imagine and live an Indigeneity
under terms that may be reduced not to an ethnic adscription, but to queer
ones. Indeed, Tzoc is interested in developing a discourse of solidarity
through a queer remapping of the urban sphere; his is a conscious appropriation of the most intimate spaces of the city in order to re-create a broader
and comprehensive vision that embraces dissident sexual identities.

However, while Tzoc develops this re-signification of the city through
the alienation and superficial relations of the characters invoked, we are
exposed to the alienating and traumatizing effects of neoliberal globalization and the fratricidal experience in Guatemala during the armed conflict. Through his characters, Tzoc evokes sentiments of isolation, anguish,
neglect, nihilism, indulgence, and hedonism that display social dislocation
as manifested in his characters. In addition, by portraying homoerotic
ephemeral relations, Tzoc interrupts hegemonic ideals and narratives of
romance and harmonic love imposed by the West. These narratives speak
of love and happiness on the basis of heteronormative ideologies; for
example, "love" between two heterosexual people ("my other half"), having a family with a comfortable economic status, and experiencing feelings
of "love" that last "until death do us apart." In contrast to these ideals, the
K'iche' Maya poet offers us a perspective of love in its various contradictions; love represents a destructive force that leads to isolation, alcoholism,
nihilism, suicide, and lack of self-esteem. In this sense, *Gay(o)* interrogates
capitalist and colonialist intentions based on ideas of progress and happy
endings. As we can see in characters such as Old Gay Man or Shemale, the
idea of love leads to profound anguish, despair, and uncertainty. Despite
their alienated condition, these subjects still aspire to human connection.

The representations of these alienating elements are understandable if
we consider what it means to be a queer Indigenous person within a colonial setting like Guatemala. As I have discussed in previous chapters, Maya

authors use the word to denounce and expose the operations of colonialism by the colonial nation-state. Our experience as Indigenous peoples is marked by our marginalization caused by our differentiated linguistic, cultural, or national specificities. From the perspective of the nation-state, we are considered a problem because we speak different languages, dress differently, and have specific spiritual and cultural practices. Such conditions, as previously discussed, led the Guatemalan state to put into practice a state terrorism that sought literally to eliminate us. If, as Indigenous peoples, we are born into contempt and marginalization for being Indigenous, can we imagine the even more incredible isolation and pain of being publicly queer? The contempt for our existence then does not come only from the hegemonic society but also from our own Indigenous communities that have internalized dominant heterosexual and heteronormative attitudes and see homosexuality as a "problem" (for example, with Wajxaqi'b Noj or the homophobia that emanates from some Maya literary works). For these reasons, Tzoc's poetry expresses anguish and isolation as definitive experiences for 2sLGBTQ+ communities, while also expressing a sensibility and solidarity toward queerness, emphasizing the need to advance an acceptance and understanding of nonconforming sexual identities.

Tzoc's *Gay(o)* suggests that the 2sLGBTQ+ community has the potential to offer us ways to imagine "existing alternatives to hegemonic systems" (Halberstam 2011, 89). With these ideas, he also echoes what Mario Muñoz calls "a moral alternative whose vision of reality is opposed to the accepted one" (1996, 18). *Gay(o)* represents

> the idealization of "sexual immorality," the cult of the body, the attraction to the sordid, a constant search for long lasting relationships, the production of erotic fantasies that focus on the adoration of the masculine, the personal affirmation through a specific life-style that conjugates pleasure, frivolity with inclinations toward culture and art. The almost total omission of the feminine presence and the demand for a self-affirmation. (18)

Therefore, Tzoc's work stresses the need to recognize sexual diversity as central to any possibility of social or national vindication.

By developing images that may be viewed as perverse or cynical, Tzoc articulates what Chilean writer Jeremias Maggi calls a "geography of homosexual desire" within the "disputed territories of sexism" and colonialism in the epilogue of *Gay(o)*; in doing so, Tzoc aims to invalidate the "Western grammar of heteronormativity." He invokes the homoerotic activities of figures like the pope, priests, military soldiers, and politicians—the officials upholding colonialism—and infuses them with the juices of "unofficial" desire and enjoyment: embarrassment, pleasure, spectacle, longing, and accusation inter-articulate to produce a public scandal (Queer Nation). In short, Tzoc argues that despite the efforts of the "modern" nation-state and its hegemonic institutions to impose a heteronormative order, queerness and homoeroticism nonetheless give life to the public and subterranean spaces of the nation.

This does not mean that Tzoc does not address his Mayaness in his work. On the contrary, his ideas about queerness as a condition of possibility connect to the Maya worldview in the representation of the phallus in *Gay(o)*. In the book, there is a continuing recurrence of somatic images that aim to expropriate the phallus from its traditional heteronormative significance. The phallus has symbolized fertility; it is an emblem of generative power and a means of human continuity, a symbol of virility and patriarchy. Within the ancient Maya and Mesoamerican world in general, the phallus was a symbol of power. As mentioned in the first chapter, according to Mexica mythology, we owe the creation of humanity to Quetzalcoatl or the Feathered Serpent, who, in his journey to Mictlán (the place of the dead), found jade bones, made his penis bleed, and spread his blood over the bones to give life to the humans who would populate the earth. Our Maya ancestors worshipped the phallus during the classic period (c. 250–900 AD). In archaeological Maya sites such as Chichén Itzá, Uxmal, and Yaxhom there are ceremonial areas like the "House of the Phalli" with sculptures dedicated to erect, uncircumcised, and flaccid penises. According to Laura Amrhein, these sculptures commemorate ceremonies related to Maya creation stories and symbolize the strength, legitimacy, and lineage of certain rulers (2006, 121). It is well known, for instance, that some Maya rituals recognized governmental legitimacy and authority through public ceremonies in which a ruler made incisions to his penis to shed blood. In contrast to these symbolic tendencies, however, Tzoc resignifies the figure of the phallus not as a sexual organ with fertile reproductive force or as a symbol of governmental legitimacy, but rather as an instrument or organ that carries or brings homoerotic pleasure. The phallus opens the masculine body to erotic games that offer sexual gratification. Let us turn, for instance, to poem "10," which reads,

15 ½—16 ½—18 ½ centimeters
I want to see-touch-suck the center of your body
your package/ bulk/ ding-dong
your sweet phallic erection
your huge well erect cock
THE EROTIC TOOL
ENTERING
IN MY ALL MACHINE BEING

Through the representation and personification of the phallus, Tzoc sepa-
rates sexual pleasure from reproduction to offer images of homoerotic desire,
associated here with phallic erogenous excitement. Here, the phallus ("your
package / bulk / ding-dong") is imagined as a voluptuous, erect, and vigor-
ous organ—a "very erect cock" measuring 15–18 centimeters—on which
erection-pleasure depends. Without such an erection, there can be no
penetration to satisfy homoerotic desire. These ideas, in fact, become
recurring themes in *Gay(o)*. For example, in a similar fashion, poem "1"
associates the idea of love with the phallus. Love is a "phallic hallucino-
genic mushroom" with "testicles of blue rain" that produce "semen of light."
As we saw with "GAYDAR," Tzoc also imagines authoritative figures suck-
ing a "very erected, huge and juicy, venomous cock." The penis's size—"19
centimeters"—in poem "7" is what motivates the narrator to engage in a
sexual encounter with the "Evanescent Cocksucker." Hence, the phallus,
in a sort of ritual display, is offered not only to the mouth but also the
"multidimensional anus." Homoerotic sexual enjoyment depends on the
very erect phallus.

Tzoc's major contributions with *Gay(o)* should be understood as an
assertive critique of assumptions that Mayaness is merely associated with
dominant heteronormative ideologies that promote ideas about the nuclear
family, specific gender roles (the father as the head of the home, the
mother as the caretaker of the children), and traditional religious ideas. By
addressing these hegemonic ideas, *Gay(o)* intends a radical rupture with
the status quo. Nonetheless, in its constitutions of a queer subjectivity,
Tzoc's book also marginalizes certain collective strategies to combat the
growing economic and imperialist threats brought about by neoliberal
economic models. In this sense, *Gay(o)* and its articulation of queer politics
as a condition of collective political possibility have limitations, especially
their emancipatory proposal. Similar to our discussion in the second chapter,

queer politics, through the use of strategic essentialism, may become a struggle for the recognition of sexual queer difference that does not substantially explore class and the ethnic/racial dynamics of exclusion created by colonialism. Despite its critique of the modern nation-state, queer politics, because of this oversight, may become co-opted by the same nation-state to benefit a neoliberal economic agenda. Tzoc, for example, does not address certain challenges that must be resolved for the achievement of the collective rights of the queer community, such as the AIDS epidemic, social inequality, or ethnic/racial discrimination within the 2sLGBTQ+ community. Despite displaying the alienation and isolation of queer subjects as a result of capitalism, Tzoc often portrays the queer sphere as a romantic space characterized by collective solidarity. Though this can be understood within a politics of recognition, how does the 2sLGBTQ+ community perceive the specific land struggles that many Maya sectors are fighting for now? Or the struggles for Indigenous rights more generally? As a way to complement Tzoc's stance in *Gay(o)*, let me bring into the conversation the perspective of K'iche' Maya lesbian feminist, Dorotea Gómez Grijalva.

In her autobiographical and ethnographic essay "Mi cuerpo es un territorio político" (My Body is Political Territory, 2014), Gómez Grijalva examines existing power relations within the gay and lesbian communities in Guatemala City. The essay generates a critique of Maya and non-Maya feminist essentialism that, on the one hand, challenges the patriarchal stance that universalizes the category of "woman" to champion diverse and heterogeneous feminist subjectivities. On the other hand, however, these "decolonial feminists" censure certain Maya subjects who do not adhere to their proposals or to the imagined decolonial feminist models being articulated by academic centers. Gómez Grijalva shares, for example, how certain feminists accused her of becoming a "ladina" or White for cutting her hair in a certain way or for assuming her lesbian identity. She also talks about how she felt discriminated against in gay/lesbian bars in Guatemala City for wearing her Maya *traje*. "Gay men and lesbians stared at me with bewilderment" (272), she indicates. Moreover, when Gómez Grijalva "came out of the closet," she did not experience the same positive responses that Tzoc did. Whereas the K'iche' Maya artist found support from his family and friends, Gómez Grijalva recounts that embracing and becoming open about her lesbian self "had negative repercussions in my social life because I lost close friendships" (273). These experiences of marginalization led her to ask, How do we assume a lesbian identity in a conservative Maya social context and in a profoundly racist, classist, and patriarchal society like Guatemala?

Gómez Grijalva initially imagined that these questions could be answered through an understanding that her marginalization was the result of policies implemented by a heteronormative nation-state that recycled colonial logics. She soon realized, however, that her experiences in gay bars and her exchanges with other feminist scholars suggested that "the majority of gay couples that attended gay bars reproduced heterosexual imageries and attitudes. There were women who had adopted male chauvinistic attitudes toward their partners; they were behaving like rude aggressive men. . . . Those who assumed a male 'macho' identity would impose their power over their partners by paying the bill at the gay bar" (273). In addition, she noticed that, in contrast to lesbians, "many gay men had more freedoms and better socio-economic conditions to live more freely their dissident sexuality. On various occasions, after leaving the bars, I observed that male gay couples, once on the streets, tended to hold hands, kiss, and caress each other, while I barely saw lesbian couples do these things" (274). These experiences led the K'iche' Maya sociologist not to "mystify nor much less idealize the lesbian or lesbian-feminist spheres" and to conclude that "the lesbian and lesbian-feminist world, unfortunately, is not alien to racism, misogyny and ethnocentric abuses of power by those who feel they are 'white'" (273).

Gómez Grijalva's critique of the queer urban context highlights how colonialism and its power dynamics have the capacity to seduce sectors of the 2sLGBTQ+ community. That is, some queer people have internalized and reproduced hegemonic patriarchal attitudes manifested through sexism and inferiority complexes. We therefore need to develop critical approaches that do not marginalize Indigenous and non-Indigenous community members because of their nonconforming gender identities. We must recognize the complexity of the social and power dynamics to address their potentialities and shortcomings in the struggles for emancipation. I do not intend to diminish Tzoc's work; as I indicated earlier, *Gay(o)*'s significant contribution lies in making visible queer experiences, thereby demystifying the settler colonial nation-states and their heteronormative and heterosexual policies. In addition, both Tzoc and Gómez Grijalva call on the Indigenous movement to take seriously the demands of sexually dissident Indigenous subjects in our decolonial struggles.

Cu Choc's and Tzoc's Transnational Connections

In the postwar period there are fresh and new poetic artistic expressions that make visible alternatives that complement the Maya movement's struggles for emancipation in Iximulew. With Maya Cu Choc's and Tzoc's poetry, as well as Gómez Grijalva's ethnographic account, we move beyond discussions of Maya identity politics, usually associated with the rural world, and beyond heteronormative ideas, as described in earlier chapters. Maya Cu Choc's work illustrates the efforts and prominence of Indigenous women in the struggle for Indigenous rights. She draws inspiration from her ancestral history, represented by our great-grandmothers like Ix Tzib'. For Cu Choc, women's rights today must be understood as a long struggle that began before the European invasion. In this, she offers a transnational perspective informed by communitarian feminism and the idea of patriarchal interlocking proposed by Julieta Paredes and Lorena Cabnal as an effort to de-patriarchalize modern societies. In doing so, the Q'eq'chi' poet suggests that patriarchy is not merely the result of European colonization but is something that has also existed in Indigenous societies for centuries. Its contemporary manifestations are represented through the femicides in Guatemala's postwar period. In this context, it is necessary to feed Indigenous women's dignity and learn from our ancestors on our path to the materialization of social justice.

For his part, Tzoc expands ideas of Mayaness by inserting queer rights into our discussions, creating a poetics that aims to make visible the experiences of the 2sLGBTQ+ community in urban settings. In contrast to his predecessors and as portrayed in *Gay(o)*, his literary perspective problematizes heteronormative and heterosexual ideologies represented in the works of other Maya writers like Lión, Morales Santos, Montejo, and González. Gómez Grijalva adds to the discussion by demystifying queer politics, suggesting that these political spheres are not immune from reproducing power dynamics and racist ideologies. Further, informed by literary and theoretical frameworks beyond Iximulew, these authors organically tie their works to discussions of Indigenous women and queer rights in other parts of the world. In their dialogues with Julieta Paredes's communitarian feminism or Pedro Lemebel's dissident poetics, both Cu Choc and Tzoc develop important transnational connections.

Conclusion

The Maya Word Will Never Die

The flower of the word will not die. The masked face that today has a name may die, but the word which came from the depth of history and the earth can no longer be cut by the ears with its cannons.

—Zapatista Army of National Liberation,
"Fourth Declaration of the Lacandon Jungle" (1996)

I N 2012, after his immunity as a political leader was removed, the now-deceased General Efraín Ríos Montt was brought to court and accused of genocide and crimes against humanity. In May 2013, the eighty-seven-year-old general was found guilty of these charges and condemned to eighty years in prison. He was the first dictator on the continent condemned for crimes against humanity. Ten days after the sentence, however, the Constitutional Court (CC) revoked the charges, arguing that two of the judges who had voted for the conviction had "unresolved conflicts" in the genocide case. Without specifying what the "conflicts" were, the CC annulled the sentence, removing from the case the testimonies that had been recorded since April 19, 2013. It indicated that the case had to be retried. The High Risk Tribunal "B" in Guatemala decided to restart the legal actions against Ríos Montt on July 23, 2015. Even though the general's legal counsel argued that he was mentally incapacitated, the trial continued. Ríos Montt passed away on April 1, 2018—never seeing the walls of prison where he deserved to die.[1]

Despite the results, the legal case and the sentence set an important precedent for Maya genocide survivors in Iximulew. It was followed by another case against the Guatemalan Army, the Sepur Zarco case, in which an army officer, Steelmer Reyes Girón, and an ex-military commissioner, Heriberto Valdez Asij, received long prison sentences for crimes against humanity, murder, and sexual slavery. Guatemalans are awaiting the trial of ex-military and ex-Guatemalan president, Otto Pérez Molina, and his vice president, Roxana Baldetti. In a context like Guatemala, where impunity deals a slap in the face every day, these legal actions offer small glimmers of hope. Let us recall the words of Andrew Beckett (played by Tom Hanks in the film *Philadelphia*, 1993) when asked, "What do you love about the law, Andrew?" He replies, "Every once in a while—not always, but occasionally—one gets to see how justice can be achieved. When that happens, it is really something."

In addition to the advances and retreats in achieving justice, these legal cases underscore the value of the word; the need to use it not only to combat injustices we have inherited from colonialism but also to reconstruct our dignity and offer hope for our emancipation. As the Maya poets discussed in this book manifest, these are the lessons of Indigenous peoples who have resisted colonization since the invasion of Europeans. We need to understand, as Francisco Morales Santos writes, that every word we say "is a delivery / against the order of silence" (2008, 127), or as Humberto Ak'abal reminds us, "I speak / to cover / the mouth / of silence" (2006, 204). Those in power have tried to keep us silent and oblivious. Linda Tuhiwai Smith asserts that

> there are numerous oral stories which tell what it means, what it feels like, to be present while your history is erased before your eyes, dismissed as irrelevant, ignored or rendered as the lunatic ravings of drunken old people. The negation of indigenous views of history was a critical part of asserting colonial ideology, partly because such views were regarded as clearly "primitive" and "incorrect" and mostly because they challenged and resisted the mission of colonization. (1999, 30–31)

Hence, the Maya word, whether oral or written, is essential in reestablishing all those aspects of our humanity that colonialism has sought to negate and destroy.

In this study, I emphasized both the major role that literature— particularly poetry—has played in our struggles to vindicate Indigenous rights in Iximulew and how literature is the result of a historical legacy to decolonize our current condition. The poetic works analyzed here remind us that the past is not simply a box where you place things, but rather the scene where intense discursive and conceptual struggles take place—

struggles to reinterpret and rewrite or re-*right* what at every moment has involved our constant creativity to regenerate the Maya world in *all* aspects of social and daily life at the local and (trans)national levels. Through poetry we express our demands, our desire to recover our territories and sovereignty. The book proves Craig Womack's assertion that "Native literature, and Native literary criticism, written by Native authors, is part of sovereignty: Indian people exercising the right to present images of themselves and to discuss those images. Tribes recognizing their own extant literatures, writing new ones, and asserting the right to explicate them constitute a move toward nationhood" (1999, 14).

I have highlighted three historical moments of Maya literary insurgency in our contemporary history in Iximulew. First, Maya writers like Francisco Morales Santos and Luis de Lión respond to the interpretation of the Indigenous world as a problem from the perspective of the nation-state and the Guatemalan Left. Far from conceiving themselves as a "problem," these Kaqchikel Maya writers appropriate the word to challenge these hegemonic sectors and to develop a discourse of Indigenous cultural and political vindication through ideas of national liberation. A second moment of Maya literary insurgency is represented in the poetic works of writers like Humberto Ak'abal, Victor Montejo, and Gaspar Pedro González within the context of 1978–1984. In those years, the nation-state developed new military strategies to defeat the opposition that turned into state terrorism through indiscriminate attacks against Maya peoples in the highlands, culminating in genocide. As a response to the fratricidal experience, Ak'abal, González, and Montejo develop poetic works that affirm Maya languages and cultural and spiritual specificities. They draw their creativity from our millenarian legacy to dignify our culture in a present where the nation-state seeks to eliminate Indigenous peoples. Using strategic essentialism, these authors suggest that colonialism has failed in its fratricidal efforts. But although their literary contributions are essential, I also point out some of the dangers such an approach may bring in constituting a Maya identity exclusive of other identities (e.g., queerness and gender identity) that may not fit within the model being proposed. Thus, I argue that we must understand the Maya experience as heterogeneous.

Finally, after the Peace Accords were signed in 1996, we entered what I consider to be the third phase of Maya literary insurgency. In this period, a new generation of Maya writers is emerging who, taking advantage of the opening brought about by globalization, develop a diverse Maya literary register. Rosa Chávez, Pablo García, and Sabino Esteban Francisco address Mayaness in the postwar period amid the implementation of neoliberal economic reforms. From the spaces of the city and the rural world, they rescue and re-signify their ancestral traditions as a way to face the new challenges from marginalized perspectives. In chapter 4, Maya Cu Choc's and Manuel Tzoc's poetry further challenges the heteronormative and heterosexual policies not only of the Guatemalan nation-state but also of the Maya movement. From their feminist and queer perspectives, these Maya authors show other dissident and nonconforming struggles for Indigenous rights.

In their demands for sovereignty, their call to defend or recover our ancestral territories, and their advocacy for the restitution of Indigenous life in its totality (Maya spirituality, Indigenous languages, cultural specificities, and sexual and gender difference), Maya literary productions are organically tied to the demands of the Indigenous rights movement in Iximulew. My critical discussions can be related to two documents that demand Maya political rights. The first, written by the Council of Maya Peoples, is titled *Proyecto Político: Un nuevo estado para Guatemala* (Political Project: A New State for Guatemala, Consejo del Pueblo Maya 2014); the second, by Coordinación y convergencia Nacional Maya Waqib' Kej (Maya Coordination and Convergence Waqib' Kej 2015), is titled *Demandas y propuestas políticas de los pueblos Indígenas de Iximulew* (Demands and Political Proposals by Indigenous Peoples from Iximulew).

Both documents develop a rigorous critique of the modern Guatemalan nation-state for recycling colonial policies that have maintained and "imposed on us the highest indexes of social exclusion" (Consejo 2014, 1). Hence, entities like the Council of Maya Peoples assert that our decolonial point of departure can begin "through an Indigenous Peoples uprising and in unity with the *mestizo* population," developing a new political constitution that establishes "a regime of autonomies for Indigenous Peoples" (4). Such autonomy can be achieved through mutual respect for our differences and through a rejection of individual, mercantilist, and destructive capitalist values that have been endorsed by the nation-state to destroy Mother Nature. The document exhorts,

> Let's defend our territory! Let's fight for our demands! Let's develop collective agreements where there are none yet to stop the imposition of colonial economic policies! Let's reject the oil,

mining, and hydro-electric contracts from companies! Let's create assemblies to form and strengthen Territorial Counsels in Defense of Natural Goods and let's think about how we can apply economic alternatives that help us live well and respect Nature and Guatemalan sovereignty. Let's fight for the unity of all Maya Peoples so our collective rights are reflected, at last, in the official laws and the Nation-State. (20)

Similarly, the Waquib' Kej document departs from Maya and "Utz Kaslemal" (Good Living or Living Well)[2] philosophical principles to fortify an Indigenous praxis that enables us to "rebuild the balance between Mother Nature and human beings through human relations based on decolonial, anti-mercantilist, and antipatriarchal principles in the foundation of the Plurinational State" (Coordinación y Convergencia 2015, 7). By defining alternatives that can help us address the challenges we face in light of neoliberal capitalism, these documents have become the cornerstone of our contemporary struggle to vindicate our lives.

We concluded the *Oxlajuj B'aktun* on the date the Gregorian calendar represented as December 21, 2012, and entered a "New Era" that brings new challenges. Although these times may be viewed—justly so—with cynicism and exceptionalism, the Council of Maya Peoples, Maya Coordination and Convergence, Waquib' Kej, and the Maya authors discussed in this book share with us their experiences of renovation and restoration in our struggles for sovereignty and rights, and present us with new opportunities. *Le Maya tzij*, or the Maya word, continues guiding us on the road of our survival and offers hope for the emancipation of Indigenous peoples.

Acknowledgments

The writing of this book has been the result of many years of research that would have not been possible without the support of my family, friends, and colleagues with whom I was lucky to share my ideas and receive valuable comments and feedback. My deepest gratitude goes to the Maya writers I discuss in this book. Their wonderful poetic works motivated me not only to write about them but also to value our Indigenous cultural and creative richness and history. I hope that my critical readings—even in disagreement—display my profound respect for and admiration of their creative work.

At the University of North Carolina at Chapel Hill, and in the Research Triangle more broadly, I had the good fortune to meet many colleagues with whom I engaged in stimulating intellectual discussions and conversations that helped me better define many of my ideas for this book. I thank Sam Amago, Kia Caldwell, Teresa Chapa, Greg Dawes, Jean Dennison, Arturo Escobar, Diana Gómez-Correal, Natalie Hartman, Jennifer Ho, Sharon Holland, Joseph Jordan, Mark Katz, Anca Koczkas, Valerie Lambert, Federico Luisetti, Walter Mignolo, Claudia Milian, Diane Nelson, Hannah Palmer, Beatriz Riefkohl-Muñiz, Mark Rifkin, Miguel Rocha, Greg Severyn, and Miguel Rojas Sotelo. I also thank Sarah Booker, Gail Naron Chalew, and Lara Aase for their wonderful suggestions and comments and for their help with copyediting this book.

I would also like to express my gratitude and appreciation to the following people who encouraged me many times, lending an ear and enthusiastically or critically commenting on my ideas: Silvia Castillo, Aura Cumes, Junyoung Verónica Kim, Victoria Livingstone, Juanita Cabrera López, Mark Maranto, José Cal Montoya, Irma Alicia Velásquez Nimatuj, José Yac Noj, Louis A. Pérez, Therese Tardio, Jaime Gómez Triana, Anja Ulanowicz, and Yanira Yaxon. My conversations with Luis Cárcamo Huechante offered me much-appreciated support, guidance, critical insights, and ideas that illuminated my own thinking. Thank you, *Peñi*. Arturo Arias has also been a great friend and mentor to me. His support and encourage-ment have been invaluable in this long journey.

At the University of Minnesota Press, I express my gratitude to Robert Warrior, who has been an inspiration. I am grateful for his acknowledg-ment of this project's importance and for the honor of publishing it in his series, Indigenous Americas. I thank Jason Weidemann and Zen Miller for their patience, flexibility, and support during the process of completing this book. I also thank Melody Negron at Westchester Publishing Services for her guidance in the final steps of the process.

At the University of North Carolina at Chapel Hill, I am grateful for the support and financial assistance provided by the Institute for the Arts and Humanities Wilmer Kuck Borden Fellowship; in addition, the Romance Studies and Provost's Senior Faculty Research and Scholarly Leaves offered me much-needed time to write this book. I am also grateful for the funding I received to travel to conferences to present my work and to enable the copyediting and translations of some chapters. I received travel and research stipends from the Institute for the Arts and Humanities Kenan Endow-ment and Faculty of Color / Indigenous Faculty Fund, the Institute for the Study of the Americas, and the UNC-CH / Duke's Consortium on Latin American and Caribbean Studies. Please note that all translations from Spanish to English in this book are my own, unless otherwise noted.

During this long writing process, my family and friends helped fuel my motivation and enthusiasm. I particularly thank my mother Dora Escalante for her unconditional love and support. I hope that amid her daily hard work and health challenges she recognizes that this book owes much to her immense sacrifices. I also hope that it awakens a feeling of pride and joy in her heart. I want to thank my brothers Edwin and Jeff, whose cour-age has been an immense inspiration to me. My aunt Gloria, who lost her battle to cancer in 2015, always encouraged me to be the best person I could be; she also served as an inspiration to complete this book. In 2016, I had the immense fortune to meet my partner Rhea, who has offered me love, encouragement, and support. I thank her for listening and for her invaluable comments that sharpened my ideas.

My son Dakota has been my rock. I apologize for the many moments I was absent and distant because of researching and writing this book. I only hope that in the near future, when you get to read it, you will find a little bit of light that illuminates the resilience and courage of our people and that such resilience and courage feed your spirit.

Notes

Introduction

1. Geopolitically speaking, the Mayab' region represents what is today Southern Mexico (the Yucatan Peninsula and Chiapas), Belize, Guatemala, Honduras, and northern El Salvador. This region represents the heart of Maya civilization and is the home of important Maya ancestral confederations that include the K'iche', the Kaqchikel, the Tzutuhil, Mam, and Itza Nations. At present, these territories are inhabited by diverse Maya nations, speakers of thirty-one Maya languages derived from four different linguistic branches: Huastecan, Yucatecan, Western, and Eastern. Maya peoples also inhabit other parts of the continent. The majority of them have settled in various parts of what is today called the United States and Canada.

2. As part of colonial expansion, one of the strategies employed by the Spanish was to impose Christian names, or the names of Spanish soldiers or political leaders who had been loyal to the Spanish crown, on Indigenous peoples. The tendency was to start with high-profile political leaders, which would later facilitate the domination of other peoples. It is probable that the last name "Rojas" come from the Captain Diego de Rojas, who had arrived in the K'iche' region in 1524 with fifty soldiers to support Alvarado. The last name Cortés possibly comes from the recognition of Hernán Cortés, the Spanish general who conquered the Mexica empire.

3. Regarding the names of the authors of the *Popol Wuj*, see Sam Colop (2011, xvii–xx), Christenson (2007, 35–37), Tedlock (2010, 298–300), and Falla (2013, 7–9).

4. The Spanish Inquisition was established by the Catholic kings in 1478 to recognize Roman Christianity as the "true" religion of the Spanish Crown. Its objectives included locating, processing, and sentencing (even with death) people guilty of "heresy" and idolatry against the Church and the Crown.

5. The quotes in K'iche' from the *Popol Wuj* are taken from Luis Enrique Sam Colop's edition of the text (2001), and those in English come from Allen Christenson's 2012 translation.

6. For a complete description and summary of the *Popol Wuj*, see Arias (2017, 51–53).

7. For a history of the Guatemalan military coup, see Schlesinger and Kinzer (1982).

8. See *Comisión para el Esclarecimiento Histórico* (2006) and Rothenberg (2012).

9. The initial recording of the Maya calendar—translated to the Gregorian calendar—dates back to August 11, 3114 B.C.E. On December 21, 2012 C.E., 5,200 *tunes* were completed. A *tun* represents 360 days. 5,200 *tunes* represent a period of 1,872,000 days that close the so-called *Oxlajuj* or Thirteen B'aktun. A b'aktun is a measure of time that comprises 144,000 days. December 22, 2012, was not the "end of the world" but the beginning of the *Kanlajun* or Fourteen B'aktun. For detailed information about the Maya calendar, see Stuart (2011).

10. According to Mario Roberto Morales, "*ladino* refers to those who, accepting or not an evident biological and cultural miscegenation, identify with the values of the so-called 'Western culture', follow their models and accommodate them to the reality of their countries, usually scorning what they perceive as autochthonous, indigenous, and different from those models, unless the differences are viewed as an archeological trace of a mythic, splendorous past" (2003, 1).

11. In addition to the writers I study in this book, it is also worth mentioning the Maya tzutuhil artists, Tzutu B'aktun Kan, Benvenuto Chavajay, Pedro Chavajay, Lorenzo González Chavajay; the Kaqchikel Maya, Paula Nicho Cumes, Marilyn Boror Bor, Edgar Calel, Ángel and Fernando Poyón, and Sarah Curruchich; the Q'anjob'al Daniel Caño; the Q'eq'chi' Adela Delgado Pop; the Tuujal poet Kaypa' Tziken; the Mam writer Wilson Loayes; the K'iche' Maya writer and journalist Irma Alicia Velasquez Nimatuj, among many others.

12. In Yucatec Maya, Kukulkan, and in Nahuatl, Quetzalcóatl.

13. Criollos in Guatemala refer to people born in Latin America but of European, usually Spanish, ancestry. Mestizo people claim to be half-Spanish and Indigenous, but for the most part they deny their Indigenous and embrace their European ancestry.

14. The Mexican anthropologist Gonzalo Aguirre Beltrán provides a relevant definition of Indigenismo: "The organic base of such an ideology [Indigenismo] is represented, not certainly by the Indian, but rather by the mestizo. Indigenismo and mestizaje are polar processes that complement each other to a point where it is impossible to think of their existence as separate. Indigenismo requires as a condition sine qua non of its existence, the human substratum that mestizaje supplies" (1992, 113). For studies about Indigenismo in Latin America, see, among others, Cornejo Polar (2003), Moraña (1998), Favre (1998), and Tarica (2008). Literary representatives of Indigenismo in Guatemala include José Milla y Vidaurre, Miguel Ángel Asturias, Luis Cardoza y Aragón, and Mario Monteforte Toledo.

15. In popular culture, these tendencies are clearly represented by films such as *Apocalipto* (2006) by Mel Gibson, *2012* (2009) by Roland Emmerich, and, more recently, *Ixcanul* (2015) by the Guatemalan director Jayro Bustamante.

16. I am aware of the studies of critics like Michael D. Carrasco, Kerry M. Hull, Denis Tedlock, and Michela Craveri, whose approach to the Maya written and verbal art have placed primary emphasis on the formal characteristics of this literary and cultural textual production in Mesoamerica. Hull and Carrasco state, "We feel it is no longer possible to regard the language in which history and myth are told as a transparent medium . . . language form is also marked in historically and regionally specific ways" (2012, 3), or "the important continuities and discontinuities that exist among literatures ranging from the Classic period to the present" (3). Although I agree with the attempts to place primary attention on form and language in Maya poetic production, I think that reducing the analysis to these formal elements may bring the danger of eclipsing the political force and urgency in the content of these literary works.

17. Among many others, see Falla (1978), Álvarez-Aragón et al. (2013), Bastos and Brett (2010), Bastos and Cumes (2007), Bastos and Camus (1993), Cojtí Cuxil (1997), Grandin (2000, 2004), Sanford (2003a, 2003b), Nelson (1999), Fischer and Brown (1996), Warren (1998), Mario R. Morales (1999), Wilson (1999), Hale (2006), Montejo (2005), Valle Escalante (2008), and Arias (1985, 2007).

18. There has been an ample discussion about Maya literature in Iximulew/ Guatemala. Among other studies, see Sam Colop (1994), Salazar Tetzagüic (1995), González (1997), Montejo (2005), Tedlock (2010), Hull and Carrasco (2012), Meza Márquez and Toledo Arévalo (2015), Craveri Slaviero (2004, 2011), Sánchez Martínez (2012), Urizar Mazariegos (2014), and more recently, Arias (2007, 2017), Chacón (2018), Worley (2016), Palacios (2016), and Burdette (2019). The majority of these studies have concentrated on narrative from the colonial and contemporary periods. My assumptions and conclusions in the book explicitly or implicitly reference and engage in dialogue with these studies to enrich my discussion.

19. The category of subalternity employed in this book is the one proposed by Ranajit Guha (1988, vii), which is understood as the general attribute to individuals or collectives subordinated in terms of class, race/ethnicity, caste, age, gender, job, or any other form of oppression.

20. See Keme (2018).

1. Kaqchikel Maya Identity

1. For example, Kaqchikel critic Manuel de Jesús Salazar Tetzagüic's *Rupach'uxik kina'oj qati't qamama' / Características de la literatura Maya kaqchikel* (Kaqchikel Maya Literary Characteristics, 1995) does not include a discussion of Morales Santos's and Lión's works. This absence is justified precisely by Salazar Tetzagüic's cultural reductionism of Maya literature. He defines it as "a full [Kaqchikel] linguistic manifestation that at every critical moment was able to take hidden paths to maintain itself in the face of the Spanish language, the language of the

invader" (20). For Salazar Tetzagüic, there is a battle between literatures produced in Indigenous languages against the invasion of Spanish. This perspective, however, does not consider the imposition of Spanish in schools that obliged many Indigenous people to lose their language.

2. For additional biographical information on Morales Santos, see Arturo Arias's chapter "A Brief History of Guatemalan Maya Literature's Emergence" in *Recovering the Lost Footprints* (2017).

3. Morales Santos's literary production is extensive. Please see the bibliography for a list of some of his most representative works.

4. A representative example in this critical enterprise is the study coordinated by Gladys Tobar Aguilar, Blanca Mendoza Hidalgo, and Nancy Maldonado de Masaya, titled *Critical Study of Francisco Morales Santos' Poetic Works: 1998 Winner of the National Literary Award, Miguel Angel Asturias* (2007). The study was conducted after Morales Santos was awarded the national literary prize in 1998.

5. In an interview, Morales Santos affirms his Kaqchikel identity, saying, "Yes, I am of [Kaqchikel] origins on both paternal and maternal sides. I tell you, some of my relatives still use traditional Kaqchikel dress and habitually communicate in the language" (qtd. in Nájera 1998, 4). At another time, the author said, "I was very conscious of my Indigenous origins, but not immersed in the culture. . . . We never talked about our identity with Luis [de Lión]. Perhaps because for us our origins were clear. Our concerns were more social and literary aesthetics" (Arias 2017, 45).

6. For an English translation of some of Morales Santos's poems, see *La tarea de relatar / The Task of Telling* (2000).

7. In addition to Morales Santos and Obregón, the group also included the poets Luis Alfredo Arango, Delia Quiñones, and Julio Fausto Aguilera. Nearly every member came from a rural area of the country, and because of this, their poetic production was considered by some critics to be "provincial." The group came into the public spotlight in 1970 with the anthology *Las plumas de la serpiente* (The Serpent's Feathers, 1970).

8. For some examples of Maya literatures from the pre-conquest period up to the present, see Tedlock (2010), Garza (1980), and Restall, Sousa, and Terraciano (2005).

9. Morales Santos uses the spelling "Caqchiquel" instead of "Kaqchikel," based on early orthography that originated before the establishment of the Academy of Maya Languages in Guatemala. I follow the author's spelling of the word when I cite the poem and the modern spelling when I analyze his work.

10. The modern K'iche' Maya spelling of this word is Q'uq'umatz, which means "Plumed Serpent." In the *Popol Wuj*, Q'uq'umatz is one of the creator gods, usually associated with the Milky Way.

11. The edition of the poem I use in this chapter is published by San Carlos de Guatemala University Press. I chose this edition based on Morales Santos's advice.

This edition, which apparently differs from the one used by Nájera in his analysis, has twenty-four rather than twenty-eight stanzas. According to the author, he did not authorize the changes, which were introduced after he submitted the book to the press; however, he feels that the other edition satisfactorily expresses his ideas.

12. Numbers in parentheses refer to page numbers.

13. In General Ríos Montt's seventeen months in power, his strategists planned the scorched earth operations that would decimate the Mayan regions of the country that were believed to be collaborating with the opposition. He proposed the "beans and bullets" campaign, in which he offered food (beans) to those who collaborated with the army, and bullets to those who refused or were considered "subversives." For more details on Ríos Montt's military strategies, see Comisión para el Esclarecimiento Histórico (1999, 2006).

14. For a report that details this event and the Río Negro community, see Johnston (2005) and Grandin (2004).

15. Víctor Jara (Chile, 1932–1973) was a singer and song writer from the so-called Committed Generation in Latin America. He was assassinated under the Augusto Pinochet dictatorship in Chile. His song, "Qué saco rogar al cielo?" (What Do I Get from Begging Heaven?), provides a social critique of the Roman Catholic Church's complicit role in repressive politics. The song concludes with a collective call to revolutionary action to bring about a new future.

16. On this topic, I am thinking of Mario Vargas Llosa, who interprets José María Arguedas's literary works and representation of Indigenous peoples in Peru as evoking "a desperate nostalgia for a lost world, a world that ended, destroyed in many ways" (1996, 273).

17. For a discussion about Mayarí de León's efforts to find her father's remains, see León (2014).

18. For more information about "El Proyecto," see https://proyectoluisdelion .org.

19. This debate has been thoroughly discussed by non-Indigenous scholars in Severo Martínez-Peláez's *La patria del criollo* (An Interpretation of Colonial Guatemala, 1970), and Carlos Guzmán Böckler and Jean Loup Herbert's *Guatemala, una interpretación histórico social* (Guatemala, A Socio-Historical Interpretation, 1970). I return to this discussion later in the chapter.

20. The reader familiar with Lión's novel, *Time Commences in Xibalbá*, will see the thematic parallels in that book and this story. In the novel, the characters are represented as destroying the world constituted by ladinos in order to reconstruct the world following the Maya worldview.

21. For studies that focus on Lión's short stories, see Velásquez de Mérida (2006) and Arias (2017). Arias and others have also produced important critical essays on Lion's narrative. See Arias (2007), Valle Escalante (2008), Shetemul (2003), and *Conversatorio* (1991).

22. See, for example, *Parnaso antigüeño* (1978), edited by Rigoberto Bran Azmitía. This text was required reading in Spanish-language and grammar classes at elementary schools in the Sacatepéquez region. The section containing Batres Montúfar's literary works can be found on pages 92–100.

23. Hunahpu is also the name of one of the Hero Twins from the K'iche' Maya *Popol Wuj*. Hunahpu and Xbalanque go to the underworld, Xib'alb'a, and engage in a battle with the Lords of Death. The twin brothers later become the moon and the sun. Hunahpu in Kaqchikel means "place of flowers." Its variant, "Hunajpu" (also written as "Jun Ajpu"), means "One Blowgun" and is related to a Maya glyph in the Long Count Calendar.

24. For more detailed information about Water Volcano's eruption, see "El volcán Junajpu" (Junajpu Volcano, 2014) by Paz Cárcamo. Pedro de Alvarado, along with his brothers Gonzalo and Jorge, had been commissioned by Hernán Cortés (who conquered the Mexica Empire in central Mexico) to conquer what is today Guatemala, El Salvador, and Honduras. Pedro and Gonzalo, after combating the Kaqchikel People in the region, ordered the foundation of "the City of the *Caballeros* [Gentlemen]" in 1527, which is today known as "Ciudad Vieja" (the Old City) in the Almolonga Valley in the Sacatepéquez region.

25. In addition to changing the name of the volcano, the Spanish also started the "Volcano's Celebration" in Ciudad Vieja, which reenacted the confrontation between the Spanish and their Indigenous Tlaxcalteca and Quahquecholteca allies against the Kaqchikel Maya. After simulating the bloody battles, the Spanish would then capture and imprison the Kaqchikel leader, Zinacan (also known as Ajpop Sotz'il Kaji' Imox), and stage the trial where he was condemned to death. According to Guillermo Paz Cárcamo, the " 'Volcano's Celebration' slowly stopped from being presented in public since instead of instilling fear in the Indigenous audience, they responded with pride. They publicly began to applaud the Kaqchikel resistance. The colonial Spanish authorities realized that the celebration could lead to a new form of Kaqchikel Maya resistance" (2014, s 16–17).

26. For a discussion about the eruptive forces of the landscape, see Anderson's *Disaster Writing* (2011).

27. Arturo Arias refutes my critical reading of Lión's novel where I argue that the Kaqchikel author proposes a Maya nationalism. For Arias, Lión's novel represents a "failed and chaotic spontaneous insurrection, which, nonetheless, is transgressive and represents the promise of future change that will permanently challenge coloniality" (2017, 89). I would insist, however, that Lión presents an Indigenous nationalist project. Instead of seeing a "failed, chaotic and spontaneous insurrection," my interpretation suggests that the Kaqchikel author knew very well that, within ladino hegemonic ideals of nationhood and citizenship, we as Indigenous peoples cannot live free of racism and marginalization and that we would continue to be interpreted as "a problem" for non-Indigenous peoples. In

other words, Lión knew that, for us, the "national, Guatemalan experience," or the colonial experience, represents humiliation. This led the Kaqchikel author to articulate—following Basil Davidson's (1992) approach—the basic principles of nationalism. Thus, for Lión, it was about thinking and imagining an alternative nationalist project where Indigenous peoples would feel pride in their identity, culture, and millenarian history. As we have been arguing in the reading of his works, these are recurring ideas and concerns for this Kaqchikel author.

28. A similar discursive strategy to the one proposed in this poem also appears in Lión's short story, "Tarzan of the Jungle" (1999). In the story, Lión appropriates the figure of the Tarzan presented on television to offer the "true" life of Tarzan, not in Africa, but in Guatemala where he struggles against foreigners to recover his dispossessed land.

29. For a discussion of an Indigenous intellectual insurgency and the role of Indigenous peoples in the revolutionary movements of the 1970s, see, among others, Falla (1978), Arias (1985), Bastos and Camus (1993), Konefal (2010), Warren (1998), and Grandin (2000, 2004). On the topic of racism in Guatemala, including among the Left, see Casaús Arzú (1998, 2007).

30. Of the two authors, Morales Santos had a better relationship with his father, Martín Morales Pérez. He dedicated the poem "My Father's Papers" to him. In the poem, as in *Mother*, Morales Santos highlights his parent's hard work and contribution to Guatemala's modernization. The poem references Indigenous forced labor policies legalized by Guatemalan presidents like Jorge Ubico, including "Truancy Law" (#1996) and the "Viability Law" (#1474). These decrees obligated all Indigenous peasants who did not own a certain minimum amount of land to work for a landowner on his farm for a certain number of days or to build roads without pay. Lión's father worked as a police officer during the Ubico period, which allowed Lión to obtain higher education at the university level.

31. It is important to mention here the work of the Sons and Daughters for Identity and Justice Against Oblivion and Silence in Guatemala (HIJOS in its Spanish acronym). This human rights organization emerged in 1999, three years after the Peace Accords were signed, to demand that the government respect human rights treaties and account for politically disappeared women, men, and children during the armed conflict. HIJOS began in Argentina in 1995, and it also has offices in Mexico and Colombia.

2. Strategic Essentialism against State Terrorism

1. I discuss these experiences in chapter 3 when I focus on the work of Q'anjob'al Maya poet, Sabino Esteban Francisco.

2. There are many studies that critically analyze the literary works of these authors, particularly their narrative. Among others, see Arias (2017),

Astvaldsson (2012), Caso (2010), Viereck Salinas (2007), Palacios (2016), Jossa (2007), Saldivia-Berglund (2003), Worley (2016), Sánchez Martínez (2012), Chacón (2018), and Thurston-Griswold (2007).

3. Another influential figure during the 1970s was the Q'eq'chi' Maya lawyer Antonio Pop Caal (1941–2002), who founded the Academy of Maya Languages in Guatemala in 1986. He gained fame in the country after participating in the XLI Americanists Conference that took place in Mexico in 1974. At that conference, Pop Caal presented a paper titled "Réplica de un indio a una disertación ladina" (An Indian's Response to a Ladino Proposal), which critiques settler colonialism in Iximulew and argues for the rights to recover Maya ancestral territories. His presentation was later included in the book *Utopia y Revolución* (Utopia and Revolution, 1981), edited by Guillermo Bonfil Batalla. Pop Caal became a fervent defender of Indigenous rights. Tragically, like Luis de Lión, he was brutally assassinated in 2002 for his political commitment.

4. The group took its name "RIN" from the Japanese language. According to Max Araujo, the term means "unity," "comradeship," "development," and "progress." For a history of this literary collective, see Méndez de la Vega (1986) and Zimmerman (1995, I: 316–26).

5. As stated earlier, the *Popol Wuj* represents the cornerstone of the Maya world and much of the Indigenista literature from the twentieth century. Miguel Ángel Asturias, who won the Nobel Prize in Literature in 1967 and was one of the founders of modern Latin American literature, translated one of the first versions of this book from French to Spanish. The book also served as an inspiration for the ladino author to write renowned books such as *Guatemalan Legends* (1929) and *Men of Maize* ([1949] 1969). Other Maya authors like Francisco Morales Santos, Victor Montejo, and, more recently, Humberto Ak'abal also produced rewritings of the K'iche' Maya sacred text. The first two created children's books, whereas Ak'abal wrote "paraphrases" of the text.

6. "Ucha'xik" derives from the K'iche' verb "cha,'" which means "to say"; "Ucha'xik" is the passive form of the verb and it literally means "his saying." Sam Colop's journalistic column was characterized by its critique of racism and colonialism that define Guatemalan dominant society. This column was widely read among the Maya intelligentsia. It is important to note here that Sam Colop's journalistic work was significant in large part because it opened the door for other Maya journalists. Today, the list of Maya journalists who write daily in some of the most important national newspapers include Estuardo Zapeta and Sandra Xinico B'atz' (both Kaqchikel); Victor Montejo (Pop'ti); Haroldo Shetemul (Achi); Francisca Gómez Grijalva, Irma Alicia Velasquez Nimatuj, and Maria Aguilar (all three are K'iche'), among others.

7. Sam Colop went to the United States with his then-spouse Irma Otzoy (K'iche'). While he studied in Buffalo, New York, Otzoy pursued graduate studies

in cultural anthropology at the University of Iowa and then her doctorate at the University of California, Davis.

8. For additional information about FEPMaya, see http://www.fepmaya .org/en/.

9. Yax' Te' Press, started by Fernando Peñalosa in 1995; Editorial Cultura, which is directed by Francisco Morales Santos and is part of the Ministry of Culture and Sports in Guatemala; and Cholsamaj Press have been some of the leading and active presses promoting the publication of Maya literature in Iximulew and the United States.

10. For a discussion of the literary dynamics during this period and some promi- nent authors, see Arias's first chapter in *The Lost Footprints* (2017).

11. The Zapatista Army of National Liberation (EZLN) is a Maya movement that emerged in Chiapas, Mexico, on January 1, 1994, as a response to the signing of the North American Free Trade Agreement (NAFTA), which was approved in December 1993 by the Mexican, Canadian, and U.S. governments. According to the EZLN, NAFTA is a death sentence for Indigenous peoples. Their struggle continues to this day.

12. Rigoberta Menchú's significant contribution as an activist and cultural icon has been amply studied. With regard to the controversies surrounding *I, Rigoberta Menchú*, see, among others, Gugelberger (1996), Stoll (1999), Arias (2001), Bever- ley (2004), Morales (2001), Valle Escalante (2009), and Grandin (2011).

13. Menchú has participated in various political spaces, including as a candi- date for the Guatemalan presidency on two occasions, in 2007 and 2011. She did not advance to the second round in either election.

14. With the popularity of the *testimonio* genre, many books were published in various parts of the continent. In Iximulew, Victor Montejo published his *Testi- mony: Death of a Guatemalan Village* in 1987. The book was published in Spanish in 1993 as *Testimonio, muerte de una comunidad indígena en Guatemala*. In addition to Menchú's and Montejo's testimonial narratives, the trilogy of testimonial accounts by Tzutuhil Maya Ignacio Bizarro Ujpán, compiled by James Sexton (see Bizarro Ujpán and Sexton, 1981, 1985, and 1992), was of particular importance. In the 1990s, the University of Rafael Landívar's Linguistic Institute began to promote literary publications in Maya languages. They even developed a literary contest. The literary works of, among others, Juan Yool Gomez (1990, 1994), and Juana Mactzul Batz (1991) came out of these efforts.

15. For these discussions, see chapter 4 in Montejo (1995).

16. The *testimonio* found important impetus in the 1970s after the Cuban pres- tigious literary award, Casa de las Americas, created a specific category for this genre. Such efforts emerged after the publication of Esteban Montejo's testimonial account *Biography of a Runaway Slave*, compiled by the literary critic and writer Miguel Barnet, published in 1966. Another testimonial account that set an important

precedent during this period was that of Bolivian Aymara activist Domitila Barrios de Chungara, *Let Me Speak!* (1977), edited by Brazilian filmmaker Moema Viezzer. The success of these books generated great interest in subaltern voices and created a space to narrate and authorize their experiences.

17. In Guatemala, the government has a semiautonomous publishing house that receives some funding for publications. This is the result of the so-called Ten Year Spring, which refers to Juan José Arévalo's and Jacobo Árbenz Guzmán's time in political power, 1944–1954. They were interested in promoting and supporting the arts and sports and created the Ministerio de cultura y deportes (Minister of Culture and Sports) to lead that effort. It is still in existence, but because of the armed conflict, it has received little funding. In recent years, Jimmy Morales's administration (2016–2020) reduced its budget, which has greatly affected its operations.

18. The bilingual K'iche'/Spanish version published by Cholsamaj Press is very different from the first edition. The poem "The Bats" that opens the original edition appears as the seventh one in Cholsamaj's edition. Moreover, either Ak'abal or the press decided to begin the book with the poem "Xalolilo lelele, A Pastoral Song," which in the original edition begins the second part of *Animal Gathering*. Cholsamaj's edition also divides the book into three parts: "Xalolilo lelele," which includes compositions from "Animal Gathering"; "Uk'ux kotz'i'j" (The Heart of a Flower); and "Ruxlab' tinimit" (The Fragrance of the Town). These last two parts include, in a different order, poems from "Xalolilo lelele," the second part of the original edition.

19. The "capitolocene" is a concept that Jason Moore employs to develop a critique of the "Anthropocene." Whereas the Anthropocene argues that the current environmental crisis we now call climate change has been caused by all human activity, the capitolocene instead argues that this crisis began to intensify with European colonization beginning in the 1450s. The constant extraction and exploitation of natural resources in tandem with Indigenous and Black slavery have resulted in a modernization that deepens the damage to the environment.

20. Nahualism is the Indigenous Mesoamerican belief in the transformation of humans into animals. According to this worldview, humans also have an animal spirit companion that is determined according to the Maya or Mexica calendar.

21. His first book was his epic poem *El Kanil, man of lightning: a legend of Jacaltenango, Department of Huehuetenango, Guatemala* published in 1982.

22. The reference to "Sat Kanh" is related to Maya prayers to *komam jahaw* and *yahaw sat kanh* (the heart of sky and heart of earth).

23. A *katun* or k'atun-cycle is a unit of time in the Maya calendar that equals twenty tunes or 7,200 days. A katun, in Gregorian time, is equal to and is renewed every twenty years.

24. In anthropological terms, a closed corporate community is defined as a peasant community that strongly emphasizes communal identity and has a defensive organization that resists all external contact and influence (Wolf 1986, 326).

25. These perspectives also affirm ladino critiques. Mario Roberto Morales (1999), following Nestor García Canclini's *Culturas híbridas* ("Hybrid cultures") (1990), also argues that globalization represents an "omnipotent" process that "cancels" and "hybridizes" Indigenous identities through a "cultural homogenization via economic globalization" (36). Regarding Maya youth, Morales suggests that "techno music," cable TV, videogames, and secondhand clothing contribute to erasing "the specific indigenous components (themselves already mestizo) of the structure of these juvenile identities" (343). For a critical analysis of Morales's approach, see chapter 4 of Valle Escalante (2009).

26. Carlos Newland references how, since the end of the nineteenth century, education has become an instrument to "illuminate and civilize the populations, soliciting that instruction be extended to women since, without her reform, the sons would not be well behaved. In general, civilization is synonymous of hard work and political stability, and barbarism is of laziness and anarchy. Thus, education must serve to better the economic productivity and adaptation of the individual to society" (1991, 337).

27. For a discussion of intercultural bilingual education in Iximulew, see chapter 5 of Valle Escalante (2009).

28. Marroquín's words are very similar to what Miguel Ángel Asturias (1999) proposed around the same period. He stated, "Why don't we . . . try to develop the world of the Indian, all of its virtues, all of the things we did not want to see, so we can elevate it without sacrifices within their beliefs and their culture? Once we elevate the Indian's culture, he himself will transculturate and will become a productive element of our culture" (139).

29. See, for example, http://www.bitzma.com/. The reader can listen to Tzutu B'aktun Kan's album "Tributo a los 20 Nahuales" (Tribute to the 20 Nahuals) at https://actitudmusic.bandcamp.com.

30. In addition to these young Otomí rockers in Mexico, we can add the Zapatistas, whose struggle from within the Lacandon jungle has used technology to develop one of the most sophisticated resistance campaigns against neoliberalism.

31. Edward Said states that these kinds of contacts and cultural exchanges are nothing new. He writes, "Cultures are not impermeable; just as Western science borrowed from Arabs, they had borrowed from India and Greece. Culture is never just a matter of ownership, of borrowing and lending with absolute debtors and creditors, but rather of appropriations, common experiences, and interdependencies of all kinds among different cultures. This is a universal norm" (1993, 217). These cultural exchanges, for Maya peoples, precede 1492 if we consider the commercial,

economic, and cultural exchanges between Indigenous nations in Mesoamerica and the U.S. Southwest before the arrival of Europeans.

32. The scholarship of Irma Alicia Velásquez Nimatuj (2011) and Greg Grandin (2000), among others, highlights the role of a Maya bourgeoisie in Quetzaltenango. In chapter 4, I explore the urban queer perspective in the poetic work of Manuel Tzoc.

3. Xib'alb'a and Globalism

1. For more information on the International Labor Organization, see https:// www.ilo.org/.

2. With this I am not suggesting that the Maya movement represents a contemporary political movement. In my view, we need to trace its origins to well before the twentieth century, because our struggles today display similarities to those that occurred in the colonial period, in particular in 1524 with the invasion of the Spanish Alvarado brothers of our ancestral territories. We must see our decolonial struggle as a historical continuation rather than a present-day manifestation. For studies that discuss the contemporary insurgency of the Maya movement, see Edgar Esquit Choy (2002), Montejo (2005), Fischer and Brown (1996), Bastos and Camus (1993), and Grandin (2000), among many others. These studies, however, trace the origins of the Maya movement either to the middle of the twentieth century or as far back as the 1880s with the Indigenous struggles against the implementation of liberal reforms in Guatemala.

3. The October Revolution refers to the popular uprising that overthrew dictator Jorge Ubico in 1944 and the U.S.-orchestrated coup d'état in 1954 that unseated President Jacobo Árbenz Guzmán. It is also known as the "Ten Years of Spring," marking the only years of representative democracy in Guatemala.

4. In Ab'aj/Piedra, there is a direct connection between Chávez and her Maya literary predecessors. The book is a beautiful song to our ancestors manifested through the metaphor of the "stone." Our persistence today, it suggests, is similar to the still standing ancestral sacred sites such as Tikal or Takalik Ab'aj. On this, Chávez's approach is similar to that of Victor Montejo, which I discussed in the previous chapter.

5. For the poetic works of these authors, see Valle Escalante (2010).

6. According to Foucault, once "disciplinary professions" are created, the metaphor of the prison can be extended to other institutions that serve to domesticate individuals. These may also include the school, psychiatric hospitals, and military institutions (300).

7. The construction of Xib'alb'a as a literary trope of the nation-state and (post)modernity is present in much of Guatemalan literature, including Miguel

Ángel Asturias's classic novel, *Men of Maize* ([1949] 1969), and Ronald Flores's *Los señores of Xiblablá* (2003). Maya texts that deal with Xib'alb'a include Luis de Lión's *Time Commences in Xibalbá* and Pablo García's *B'ixonik tzij kech juk'ulaj kaminaqib'*, which I discuss in the next section of this chapter.

8. By speaking of "postmodernity," I refer to the neoliberal economic policies based on extractivism in postwar Guatemala that has been implemented through agreements like the CAFTA-DR, approved in 2004.

9. Take, as an example, Martin Banús's op-ed "El indígena feo" (The Ugly Indian), published in the national newspaper *La Hora* (The Hour, 2014). In this article, Banús talks about how Indigenous peoples could be better off socially and economically "if in the last fifty years they had only conceived an average of two or three children per couple, as responsible and intelligent people do, especially during periods of crisis, they would be a truly admirable group of people." Based on this assumption, he uses "ugly Indians" to refer to people who are "socially irresponsible" and who, inexplicably, "have preferred to procreate as if they were bunnies and, along with their political vindications, they prefer to blame the national system for all of their problems."

10. The Trail of Tears is a name given to the forced relocation of Native American nations from southeastern parts of the United States following the Indian Removal Act of 1830. The removal included peoples from the Cherokee, Muscogee, Seminole, Chickasaw, and Choctaw Nations. For this particular historical event, see, among others, Jahoda (1976) and Perdue and Green (2005).

11. The Committed Generation refers to a generation of poets that emerged in the 1960s in Central American countries like Guatemala, El Salvador, and Nicaragua. They were influenced by Marxist-Leninist ideologies and the Cuban Revolution. They distanced themselves from previous literary movements like the Avant-Garde, *Modernismo*, and magical realism (e.g., the 1967 Nobel Prize winner, Miguel Angel Asturias) by writing literature that uses a "conversational style" and the popular language of the peasantry. In addition, many of the writers felt that writing poetry was not enough to change the existing conditions of the oppressed. Consequently many joined revolutionary movements in their struggles for freedom. Several of these writers, like Guatemalans Otto René Castillo, Roberto Obregón, and Luis de Lión, as well as the Salvadoran Roque Dalton, were assassinated for their efforts. For information about the Committed Generation, see Beverley and Zimmerman (1990).

12. As I mentioned in chapter 2, Morales Santos, Luis de Lión, and Humberto Ak'abal employed a poetics of brevity as a form of literary expression. By poetics of brevity I mean poems composed of two or three verses.

13. For a discussion of the representation of fear in contemporary Maya literature, including Esteban Francisco's works, see Urizar Marzariegos's MA thesis (2014).

4. Maya Feminism and Queer Poetics

1. Tommy Orange's novel *There There* (2018) has received a great deal of recognition for bringing the notion of urban Indigenous cultures into the mainstream conversation.

2. Cu Choc's work, particularly her collection *The Wheel*, has been widely analyzed. Among others, see Chacón (2007), Estrada (2014), Sitting (2009), Meza Márquez and Toledo Arévalo (2015), and Jiménez Estrada (2016).

3. For a discussion of Maya scribes and hieroglyphic writing, see Coe and Kerr (1998).

4. Friar Diego de Landa narrates how numerous books were burned because the Spanish believed that they contained "superstitions and lies of the devil." Witnessing how their memory was destroyed, the Maya felt "much affliction" ([1959] 1986, 105).

5. The line to "interrupt silence" is reminiscent of Humberto Ak'abal's poem "I Speak," in which he states, "Kinch'awik / che utz' apixik / ri uchi' / ri tz'inowik. / I speak / to cover / silence's mouth" (2006, 204).

6. The name is composed of the feminine adjective "Ix" (woman), the word "cheb'el" (brush), and "yax" (green/blue). Her name can be translated as the woman with green/blue brushes. She has also been referenced as Ix Cheel (Ixchel/Ix Chel) or the rainbow goddess (Tedlock 2010, 240), the Maya goddess of midwifery and healers.

7. *The Ritual of the Bacabs* is a Yucatec Maya manuscript from the eighteenth century. It includes information about various Maya ancestral deities and sacred prayers. The text was written in the Yucatec Maya language using the Latin alphabet. It was discovered by Frederic J. Smith between 1914 and 1915. William Gates, who gave it the title *The Ritual of the Bacabs,* later acquired the book. The original manuscript is now in the Princeton University library.

8. As we saw in chapter 2 with the works of Gaspar Pedro González and Victor Montejo, some Maya authors also adopted some of these assumptions.

9. Aura Cumes, for example, indicates that "we cannot negate the fact that Indigenous men have articulated their interests and accumulated power, in many ways, thanks to these forms of colonial domination" over women. Moreover, certain Indigenous sectors found "the Mayanist proposal innovative to fight against ladino racism. However, they were also looking for ways to redefine their own normative systems in which [Indigenous] men also maintain dominant power over [Maya women]" (Bastos and Cumes 2007, 168).

10. The Q'eq'chi word "Kaqla" means "rainbow," and the K'iche' Maya phrase "Uk'ux B'e" means "the heart of the path."

11. To the contributions of *The Maya Women of Kaqla* and *Uk'ux B'e* we can add the work of the collective *Komool* (brother or friend). This collective was

formed by Indigenous women who were guerrilla ex-combatants from the Guerrilla Army of the Poor (EGP) in the Ixil region. For a history of Komool, see Hernández-Alarcón et al. (2008) and Arias (2009, 2011, 2013).

12. Xchel, Xmucane, Xquic, and Xbalanque are Maya women who appear in Maya texts. Xchel (also spelled Ixchel or Ix Chel), as we mentioned earlier, appears in the sixteenth-century Maya Yucatec manuscript *The Ritual of the Bacabs* and is the goddess of colors, midwifery, and medicine. Xmucane appears in the *Popol Wuj*. She is one of the gods who participate in the creation of humankind. Xquic is the mother of the hero twins Hunahpu and Xbalanque in the *Popol Wuj*.

13. Sociologist Manuela Camus echoes MacLeod in stating that the activism of Indigenous women began in the 1970s, "when women become engaged with highland peasants and their aspirations for change, efforts that are blocked with the war in the 1980s" (2000/2001, 36). Aída Hernández (2001, 173) and Sylvia Marcos (2014, 16) place the origins of decolonial feminism in the same decade in Mexico and the rest of Latin America, respectively—emphasizing that some women's rights materialized in the 1990s with the emergence of the Zapatista Army of National Liberation in Chiapas, Mexico.

14. See Melani González (2016).

15. See Suncar (2015).

16. Guatemala's ex-president Otto Pérez Molina (2012–2015) and his vice president, Roxana Baldetti, for example, face corruption charges related to fraud and illicit financial gains.

17. For information about the Sepur Zarco case, see Velásquez Nimatuj (2019) and Guatemalan Human Rights Commission (2020).

18. See Vergano (2013).

19. Ideas of communitary feminism in Iximulew have been represented by the K'iche'/Xinka activist Lorena Cabnal. Echoing Paredes, Cabnal states, "There is not only a Western patriarchal system in Abya Yala (the Americas), but also we must affirm the existence of a millenary ancestral patriarchal system that has been formulated and constituted through Indigenous cosmological principles. These are then mixed with ethnic fundamentalism and essentialism. This patriarchal system has its own forms of expression, manifestation, and differentiated temporality from the Western one. Moreover, it existed at the moment of the penetration of the Western patriarchal system during colonization. Both became immersed, and throughout time, they constantly rematerialize, become resurgent, and renew themselves. This is what we call 're-functionalized patriarchy' from the perspective of communitarian feminism in Guatemala. However, our Aymara sisters in Bolivia (and in their specific case we hear it from Julieta Paredes) call the process 'patriarchal interlocking'" (qtd. in Gargallo 2014, 22).

20. Queer theory has generated debates in Latin America. Some scholars believe that the term "queer" does not properly represent diverse experiences of sexual

dissidence in the region. Others recognize its limitations but see its potentialities. I employ the word "queer" because Tzoc has consciously appropriated the term. Along with other artists, he participates in the editorial and artistic movement, *Cuirpoetikas*. For more information on this project, see https://queerpoeticas.wixsite .com. For the debates about queer theory in Latin America, see Falconí Trávez, Castellanos, and Viteri (2014) and González-Ortuño (2016).

21. Hernan Cortés and Friar Bernardino de Sahagún's views on sodomy have been recorded in the historical registers produced by European settlers. According to Bernal Díaz del Castillo, Cortés told the "Indians" that "they would also be cleaned from sodomy since they had many boys dressed as women, making money out of that damned profession" (2017, 87). Sahagún, for his part, stated, "The patient sodomite is abhorrent, heinous, and hideous. He deserves to be made fun of and laughed at; and the ugliness and stench of his heinous sin cannot occur due to the disgust it gives to men. In everything he shows himself to be effeminate and womanlike. In the way he walks or talks. Because of all of this, he deserves to be burned alive" (1981, 99–100).

22. For a discussion of diverse gender taxonomies in Maya languages, see Carrillo Can (2015).

23. Similar to Cu Choc's experience, Tzoc narrates that his parents decided not to teach their children the K'iche' Maya language, because they did not want them to suffer from the same racism they experienced in the city. They encouraged them to learn Spanish so they could "succeed" in society.

24. Personal communication, April 12, 2017.

25. For a discussion of Tzoc's artistic public performance, see Worley and Palacios (2019).

26. I use the acronym "2sLGBTQ+ community" to refer to nonconforming sexual identities in Guatemala and beyond.

27. In April 2017, members of the Guatemalan Congress proposed to penalize gay marriage and abortion legally. See Gramajo (2017).

28. The adjective "hueco" in Spanish means "hole," "empty," or "hollow." In Guatemala it is used to refer to gay people. It is commonly associated with ideas of cowardice and usually refers to men who display feminine affects. Moreover, "hueco" acquires a dehumanizing dimension, because it suggests that a person is empty, without feelings. The adjective has been used many times to justify verbal and physical violence, and even murder, against members of the gay community.

29. I am aware that the category "Two Spirit" has been employed within Indigenous communities, particularly in North America (see Driskill et al. 2011 and Jacobs et al. 1997); however, I share Daniel Brittany Chávez's critique where he argues that Two Spirit references "people that carry a female and male essence. This subjectivity does not problematize the complex roots of this bio-

political construct, or that Two can break with its literal binary or dichotomous meaning" (2015, 87). Chávez instead opts for the category *Niizh manitoag*, because it "opens gender and sexual identities to the pluriveralities that Indigenous Tribes represent." The term, Chávez concludes, "cannot be understood from colonized knowledges" (87). The discussions and debates about Two Spirit are complex and are not within the scope of this chapter. Despite its limitations, I opt to use the 2sLGBTQ+ acronym as a gesture to embrace sexual dissidence and as a way to suggest how Tzoc's ideas about queerness have been influenced by other prominent figures like Lemebel, Ginsberg, and the Queer Nation movement.

30. The warning reemerges again in poem "21" after the narrator describes a gay man approaching the reader: "Caution! Gay man in sight." If we get too close, we are told, we could turn into "a fag."

31. "Gallito Inglés" refers to a rare and exotic small type of rooster found in Guatemala and in many other countries in Latin America. The term is usually associated with the phallus.

32. The image of the "(o)" in the title may also be a reference to a vagina. However, the book does not highlight lesbian sexual activities.

33. The book does not include page numbers. For the citations, I use the numbering and titles of the poems, placing them in quotation marks and parentheses when I refer to them.

34. Gloria Trevi is a Mexican singer-songwriter, dancer, actress, television hostess, music video director, and businesswoman. Despite numerous controversies (she spent four years in prison for corruption charges that were later dropped), she has been a staunch defender of LGBTQ+ rights in her native Mexico. Her song "Todos me miran" has become a powerful and inspiring anthem to the lesbian, gay, bisexual, and transgender community.

35. With the word "mariquita," Lemebel plays on the pejorative adjective "marica" or "fag." In saying *marquita*, he turns the adjective into an endearing and embracing idea of dissident nonconforming minorities who have been repressed because of their queer sexual identities.

36. To learn more about Pedro Lemebel, see Holas-Véliz and Holas Allimant (2015).

Conclusion

1. For additional information about Ríos Montt's trial, see *Condenado por Genocidio* (2013) and *Sentencia por Genocidio* (2013).

2. *Utz Kaslemal* is a K'iche' Maya variation of the Quechua or Kichwa concept of Sumac Kawsay, which has been translated as "good living" or "living well." The concept comes from the Quechua worldview in the Andean region to describe

a way of doing things that is community-centric, ecologically balanced, and culturally sensitive. The concept gained political force among Indigenous rights movements in the Andean region toward the end of the 1990s, and its philosophical use has led to recognition of the rights of Mother Nature in political constitutions such as those in Bolivia and Ecuador.

Bibliography

Abram, David. 2013. "On Being Human in a More-Than-Human World." *Centers for Human and Nature.* http://www.humansandnature.org.

Achugar, Hugo. 1988. "The Book of Poems as a Social Act: Notes toward an Interpretation of Contemporary Hispanic American Poetry." In *Marxism and the Interpretation of Culture*, edited by Cary Nelson and Lawrence Grossberg, 651–62. Urbana: University of Illinois Press.

Aguirre Beltrán, Gonzalo. 1992. *El proceso de aculturación y el cambio socio-cultural en México.* México: Fondo de Cultura Económica.

Ahrens, J. M., and José Elías. 2015. "'No acepto el aborto, el matrimonio gay ni legalizar la marihuana.' Jimmy Morales. Ganador de la primera vuelta presidencial en Guatemala." *El país*, October 22. https://elpais.com.

Ak'abal, Humberto. [1990] 2008. *El Animalero / Animal Gathering.* Translated by Miguel Rivera. Guatemala: Editorial Piedra Santa.

Ak'abal, Humberto. 1993. *Guardián de la caída de agua.* Guatemala: Serviprensa Centroamericana.

Ak'abal, Humberto. 1995. *Hojas del árbol pajarero.* México: Editorial Praxis.

Ak'abal, Humberto. 1996a. *Ajkem Tzij / Tejedor de palabras.* Guatemala: Fundación Carlos Novella.

Ak'abal, Humberto. 1996b. *Hojas, solo hojas.* Guatemala: Artes Graficas.

Ak'abal, Humberto. 1996c. *Lluvia de luna en la cipresalada.* Guatemala: Artemis-Edinter.

Ak'abal, Humberto. 1997. *Retoño salvaje.* México: Editorial Praxis.

Ak'abal, Humberto. 1998. *Los cinco puntos cardinales.* Santafé de Bogotá: Organización de Estados Iberoamericanos.

Ak'abal, Humberto. 2004a. *Ajyuq' / El animalero.* Guatemala: Cholsamaj.

Ak'abal, Humberto. 2004b. *Raqonchi'aj / El grito.* Guatemala: Cholsamaj.

Ak'abal, Humberto. 2012. "Reflexiones de un poeta maya." *Revista D., Semanario de Prensa Libre*, no. 427 (September 30).

Ak'abal, Humberto, and Marie Louise Ollé. 2004. "Entretien avec Humberto Ak' abal." *Caravelle* 82: 205–23.

Alba Skar, Stacey. 2008. "Entrevista a Maya Cu Choc." *Hispámerica* 37, no. 111 (December): 53–59.

Alegría, Claribel, and Darwin Flakoll. [1966] 1982. *Cenizas de Izalco*. San José, Costa Rica: Editorial Universitaria Centroamericana.

Álvarez-Aragón, Virgilio, Carlos Figueroa Ibarra, and Arturo Taracena Arriola, eds. 2013. *Guatemala: Historia Reciente (1954–1996): Pueblos indígenas, actores políticos*. Guatemala: FLACSO.

Amrhein, Laura. 2006. "Xkeptunich: Terminal Classic Maya Cosmology, Rulership, and the World Tree." *Acta Mesoamericana* 23 (December): 121–34.

Anderson, Mark. 2011. *Disaster Writing: The Cultural Politics of Catastrophe in Latin America*. Charlottesville: University of Virginia Press.

Anglesey, Zoë. 1987. *Ixok Amar-Go: Poesía de mujeres centroamericanas por la paz / Central American Women's Poetry for Peace*. Penobscot, Maine: Granite Press.

Arias, Arturo. 1985. "El movimiento indígena en Guatemala (1970–1983)." In *Movimientos populares en Centroamérica*, edited by Daniel Camacho and Rafael Menjivar, 62–119. San José, Costa Rica: Asociación de los trabajadores de la cultura.

Arias, Arturo, ed. 2001. *The Rigoberta Menchú Controversy*. Minneapolis: University of Minnesota Press, 2001.

Arias, Arturo. 2007. *Taking Their Word: Literature and the Signs of Central America*. Minneapolis: University of Minnesota Press.

Arias, Arturo. 2009. "Letter from Guatemala: Indigenous Women on Civil War." *PMLA* 124, no. 5: 1874–77.

Arias, Arturo. 2011. "*Txitzi'n* for the *Poxnai*: Indigenous Women's Discourses on Revolutionary Combat." In *Meanings of Violence in Contemporary Latin America*, edited by Maria Helena Rueda and Gabriela Polit Dueñas, 11–35. London: Palgrave Macmillan.

Arias, Arturo. 2013. "Reconfiguring Guatemalan Historical Memory: The Lived Experience of Maya Women at War." *Oregon Review of International Law* 15, no. 2: 205–24. http://hdl.handle.net/1794/17862.

Arias, Arturo. 2017. *Recovering the Lost Footprints: Contemporary Maya Narratives*. New York: SUNY Press.

Arnedo, Miguel. 2001. "*Arte Blanco con Motivos Negros*: Fernando Ortiz's Concept of Cuban National Culture and Identity." *Bulletin of Latin American Research* 20, no. 1: 88–101.

Arvin, Maile, Eve Tuck, and Angie Morrill. 2013. "Decolonizing Feminism: Challenging Connections between Settler Colonialism and Heteropatriarchy." *Feminist Formations* 25, no. 1: 8–34.

Asturias, Miguel Ángel. [1946] 1969. *El Señor Presidente*. Buenos Aires: Editorial Losada.

Asturias, Miguel Ángel. [1949] 1969. *Hombres de maíz*. Buenos Aires: Editorial Losada.

Asturias, Miguel Ángel. 1999. "La tesis." In *1899/1999: Vida, obra y herencia de Miguel Ángel Asturias*, 136–39. France: Allca XX/Ediciones UNESCO.

Astvaldsson, Astvaldur. 2012. "Traducir la cultura: Reflexiones sobre la obra y el bilingüismo de Humberto Ak'abal." *Centroamericana* 22, nos. 1–2: 313–35.

Attwood, Bain, and Fiona Magowan, eds. 2001. *Telling Stories: Indigenous History and Memory in Australia and New Zealand.* Crows Nest, Australia: Allen and Unwin.

Avendaño, Nancy. 2001. "Encuentro con una voz." *Revista D., Semanario de Prensa.* no. 1061 (September 23): 12–13.

Banús, Martín. 2014. "El indio feo." Editorial, *La Hora,* November 11. http://lahora.gt.

Barnet, Miguel. [1966] 1980. *Biografía de Un Cimarrón.* Ciudad de La Habana: Editorial Letras Cubanas.

Barrios de Chungara, Domitila, and Moema Viezzer. 1977. *'Si me permiten hablar...' / Testimonio de Domitila, una mujer de las minas de Bolivia.* México: Siglo Veintiuno.

Barthes, Roland. 1974. "Introducción al análisis estructural de los relatos." In *Análisis estructural del relato,* 7–39. Buenos Aires: Editorial Tiempo Contemporáneo.

Bastos, Santiago, and Roddy Brett, eds. 2010. *El Movimiento Maya en la década después de la paz (1997–2007).* Guatemala City: F&G Editores.

Bastos, Santiago, and Manuela Camus. 1993. *Quebrando el silencio: Organizaciones del pueblo Maya y sus demandas (1986–1992).* Guatemala: FLACSO.

Bastos, Santiago, and Aura Cumes. 2007. *Mayanización y vida cotidiana: La ideología multicultural en la sociedad guatemalteca.* Guatemala: FLACSO / Centro de Investigaciones Regionales de Mesoamérica / Cholsamaj.

Beverley, John. 2004. *Testimonio: On the Politics of Truth.* Minneapolis: University of Minnesota Press.

Beverley, John, and Marc Zimmerman. 1990. *Literature and Politics in the Central American Revolutions.* Austin: University of Texas Press.

Bizarro Ujpán, Ignacio, and James D. Sexton. 1981. *Son of Tecún Umán: A Maya Indian Tells His Life Story.* Tucson: University of Arizona Press.

Bizarro Ujpán, Ignacio, and James D. Sexton. 1985. *Campesino: The Diary of a Guatemalan Indian.* Tucson: University of Arizona Press.

Bizarro Ujpán, Ignacio, and James D. Sexton. 1992. *Ignació: The Diary of a Mayan Indian from Guatemala.* Philadelphia: University of Pennsylvania Press.

Bonfil Batalla, Guillermo, ed. 1981. *Utopía y revolución: El pensamiento político contemporáneo de los indios en América Latina.* México: Editorial Nueva Imagen.

Brady, James, and Wendy Ashmore. 1999. "Mountains, Caves, Water: Ideational Landscapes of the Ancient Maya." In *Archaeologies of Landscape: Contemporary Perspectives,* edited by James Brady and Wendy Ashmore, 124–45. Malden, Mass.: Blackwell.

Bran Azmitía, Rigoberto. 1978. *Parnaso antigueño.* Guatemala: José de Pineda Ibarra.

Brett, Roddy. 2016. *The Origins and Dynamics of Genocide: Political Violence in Guatemala.* London: Palgrave Macmillan.

Burdette, Hannah. 2019. *Revealing Rebellion in Abiayala: The Insurgent Poetics of Contemporary Indigenous Literature.* Tucson: University of Arizona Press.

Cabezas, Omar. 1982. *La montaña es algo más que una inmensa estepa verde.* México: Siglo veintiuno editores.

Cabnal, Lorena. 2010. "Acercamiento a la construcción de la propuesta de pensamiento epistémico de las mujeres indígenas feministas comunitarias de Abya Yala." In *Feminismos diversos: El feminismo comunitario,* 10–25. Madrid: Asociación para la cooperación con el Sur.

Cabral, Amílcar. 1979. *Unity and Struggle: Speeches and Writings of Amilcar Cabral.* New York: Monthly Review Press.

Calabrese, Omar. 1999. *La era neobarroca.* Madrid: Editorial Catedra.

Camus, Manuela. 2000/2001. "Mujeres mayas: Sus distintas expresiones." *Revista INDIANA* 17/18: 31–56.

Caño, Daniel. 2011. *Stxaj no' anima / Oración salvaje.* Guatemala: Editorial Cultura.

Cardozo, Fernando Henrique, and Enzo Faletto. 1979. *Dependency and Development in Latin America.* Berkeley: University of California Press.

Carrillo Can, Isaac E. 2015. "El erotismo andróginx en la cosmovisión y lenguaje maya." In *Andar erótico descolonial,* edited by Raúl Moarquech Ferrera-Balanquet, 73–82. Buenos Aires: Ediciones del signo.

Casas, Bartolomé de las. 1958. *Apologética historia de las Indias,* 2 vols. Madrid: Biblioteca de Autores españoles-Ediciones Atlas.

Casaús Arzú, Marta Elena. 1998. *Uk'exwachixiik Ri Kaxlan Na'ooj Pa Iximuleew / La metamorfosis del racismo en Guatemala.* Guatemala: Editorial Cholsamaj.

Casaús Arzú, Marta Elena. 2007. *Guatemala: Linaje y racismo.* Guatemala: F&G Editores.

Caso, Nicole. 2010. *Practicing Memory in Central American Literature.* New York: Palgrave Macmillan.

Castillo, Otto René. 1982. *Informe de una injusticia: Antología poética.* San José, Costa Rica: Editorial Universitaria Centroamericana.

Castro Gómez, Santiago. 2008. "(Post)Coloniality for Dummies: Latin American Perspectives on Modernity, Coloniality, and the Geopolitics of Knowledge." In *Coloniality at Large, Latin America and the Postcolonial Debate,* edited by Mabel Moraña, Enrique Dussel, and Carlos A. Jáuregui, 259–85. Durham, N.C.: Duke University Press.

Césaire, Aimé. 1994. "Discourse on Colonialism." In *Colonial and Post-colonial Discourse,* edited by Patrick Williams and Laura Chrisman, 172–80. New York: Columbia University Press.

Chacón, Gloria. 2007. "Poetizas mayas: Subjetividades contra la corriente." *Cuadernos de Literatura* 11, no. 22: 94–106.

Chacón, Gloria. 2018. *Indigenous Cosmolectics: Kab'awil and the Making of Maya and Zapotec Literatures.* Chapel Hill: University of North Carolina Press.

Chacón, Gloria, and Juan Guillermo Sánchez Martínez, eds. 2016. "Los cinco puntos cardinales en la literature indígena contemporánea." *Dialogos: An Interdisciplinary Studies Journal* 19, no. 1.

Chatterjee, Partha. 1997. "Our Modernity." ccs.ukzn.ac.za/files/partha1.pdf.

Chávez, Adrián Inés. 1978. *Pop Wuj: Poema mito histórico Ki-ché.* Quetzaltenango, Guatemala: Centro editorial Vile.

Chávez, Daniel Brittany. 2015. "Devenir performerx: Hacia erótica soberana descolonial niizh manitoag." In *Andar erótico descolonial,* edited by Raúl Moarquech Ferrera-Balanquet, 83–98. Buenos Aires: Ediciones del signo.

Chávez, Rosa. 2005. *Casa Solitaria.* Guatemala: Oscar de León Palacios.

Chávez, Rosa. 2009a. *Ab'aj/Piedra.* Guatemala: Editorial Cultura.

Chávez, Rosa. 2009b. *Los dos corazones de Elena Kame.* Buenos Aires: Universidad Nacional de la Plata.

Chávez, Rosa. 2010a. *Quitapenas.* Guatemala: Catafixia.

Chávez, Rosa. 2010b. *Ri Uk'u'x Ri Ab'Aj / El corazón de la piedra.* Caracas: Monte Ávila Editores Latinoamericana.

Chávez, Rosa, and Camilla Camerlengo. 2014. *AWAS.* Guatemala: Catafixia.

Chinchilla, Norma Stoltz. 1998. *Nuestras utopías: Mujeres Guatemaltecas del siglo XX.* Guatemala: Agrupación de Mujeres Tierra Viva.

Chirix, Emma. 2010. *Ru rayb'al ri qach'akul / Los deseos de nuestro cuerpo.* Guatemala: Ediciones el Pensativo.

Christenson, Allen J. 2007. *Popol Vuh: The Sacred Book of the Maya.* Norman: University of Oklahoma Press.

Christenson, Allen J. 2012. "The Use of Chiasmus by the Ancient K'iche' Maya." In *Parallel Worlds: Genre, Discourse and Poetics in Contemporary, Colonial, and Classic Maya Literature,* edited by Kerry Hull and Michael Carrasco, 311–38. Boulder: University of Colorado Press.

Coe, Michael, and Justin Kerr. 1998. *The Art of the Maya Scribe.* New York: Harry N. Abrams.

Cojtí Cuxil, Demetrio. 1991. *La configuración del pensamiento político del pueblo Maya.* Quetzaltenango: Asociación de Escritores Mayances de Guatemala.

Cojtí Cuxil, Demetrio. 1997. *El Movimiento Maya (En Guatemala) / Ri Maya' Moloj Pa Iximulew.* Guatemala: Editorial Cholsamaj.

Comisión para el Esclarecimiento Histórico. 1999. *Guatemala: Memoria del silencio.* Guatemala: CEH.

Comisión para el Esclarecimiento Histórico. 2006. *Guatemala: Causas y orígenes del enfrentamiento armado interno.* Guatemala: F&G Editores.

Condenado por Genocidio: Sentencia condenatoria en contra de José Efraín Ríos Montt. 2013. Guatemala: F&G Editores.

Consejo del Pueblo Maya. 2014. *Proyecto Político: Un nuevo estado para Guatemala.* Guatemala: n.p.

Conversatorio: Homenaje imaginario a la obra literaria de Luis de Lión. 1991. Antigua, Guatemala: Galería Imaginaria.

Cook-Lynn, Elizabeth. 2000. "How Scholarship Defames the Native Voice . . . and Why." *Wicazo Sa Review* 15, no. 2 (Fall): 79–92.

Coordinación y Convergencia Nacional Maya Waqib' Kej. 2015. *Demandas y propuestas políticas de los pueblos Indígenas de Iximulew.* Guatemala: Coordinación y Convergencia Nacional Maya Waqib' Kej.

Cornejo Polar, Antonio. 2003. *Escribir en el aire: Ensayo sobre la heterogeneidad sociocultural en las literaturas Andinas.* 2nd ed. Lima: Latinoamericana Editores.

Craveri Slaviero, Michela. 2004. *El Arte Verbal K'iche': Las Funciones Poéticas De Los Textos Rituales Mayas Contemporáneos.* México, D.F.: Editorial Praxis.

Craveri Slaviero, Michela. 2011. "La literatura maya hoy y la construcción de las identidades: Procesos constantes de afirmación y de revitalización." *Revista de literaturas populares* 11, no. 2 (July–December): 392–409.

Cu Choc, Maya. 1997. "Poemaya." In *Novisimos: Maya Cu, Juan Carlos Lemus, Alfonso Porres, Fernando Ramos y Emilio Solano,* 69–102. Guatemala: Editorial Cultura.

Cu Choc, Maya. 2002. *La Rueda.* Guatemala: Editorial Cultura.

Cu Choc, Maya. 2005. *Recorrido: Poemas.* Guatemala: Maya Cú.

Cu Choc, Maya. 2011. "Tradición oral y escritura." In *Nosotras, las de la historia: Mujeres en Guatemala (siglos XIX-XXI),* edited by Ana Cofiño and Rosalinda Hernández Alarcón, 296–303. Guatemala: Asociación La Cuerda.

Cumes, Aura. 2012. "Mujeres indígenas, patriarcado y colonialismo: Un desafío a la segregación comprensiva de las formas de dominio." *Anuario Hojas de Warmi* 17: 1–16.

Dary, Claudia. 2013. "El estado y los indígenas: Del Indigenismo al multiculturalismo." In *Guatemala: Historia reciente (1954–1996), Tomo III: Pueblos indígenas: Actores políticos,* edited by Virgilio Álvarez Aragón, Carlos Figueroa Ibarra, Arturo Taracena, Sergio Tischler Visquerra, and Edmundo Urrutia, 105–67. Guatemala: FLACSO.

Davidson, Basil. 1992. *The Black Man's Burden: Africa and the Curse of the Nation-State.* New York: Times Books.

D'Emilio, John. 2006. "Capitalismo e Identidad Gay." *Revista Nuevo Topo* 2, no. 51 (April–May): 51–74.

Dennison, Jean. 2012. *Colonial Entanglements: Constituting a Twenty-First-Century Osage Nation.* Chapel Hill: University of North Carolina Press.

Díaz del Castillo, Bernal. 2017. *Historia verdadera de la nueva España.* Barcelona: Red ediciones S.L.

Dorfman, Ariel, and Armand Mattelart. [1972] 2003. *Para leer el pato Donald: Comunicación de masa y colonialismo.* México: Siglo veintiuno editore.

Driskill, Qwo-Li, Chris Finley, Brian Joseph Gilley, and Scott Lauria Morgensen, eds. 2011. *Queer Indigenous Studies: Critical Interventions in Theory, Politics, and Literature*. Minneapolis: University of Minnesota Press.

Drouin, Marc. 2011. *'Acabar hasta con la semilla': Comprendiendo el genocidio guatemalteco de 1982*. Guatemala: F&G Editores.

Ejército Zapatista de Liberación Nacional. 1996. "Cuarta declaración de la Selva Lacandona," January 1. http://palabra.ezln.org.mx.

Espinosa, Yuderkys, Diana Gómez Correal, and Karina Ochoa Muñoz, eds. 2014. *Tejiendo de otro modo: Feminismo, epistemología y apuestas descoloniales en Abya Yala*. Popáyan, Colombia: Editorial Universitaria del Cauca.

Esquit Choy, Edgar. 2002. *Otros poderes, nuevos desafíos: Relaciones interétnicas en Tecpán y su entorno departamental, 1871–1935*. Guatemala: Instituto de Estudios Interétnicos, USAC.

Estrada, Alicia Ivonne. 2014. "Ixoq Tzi'j: Palabra y cuerpo en *La rueda* de Maya Cu Choc." *Revista canadiense de Estudios Hispánicos* 39, no. 1 (October): 147–63.

Falconí Trávez, Diego, Santiago Castellanos, and María Amelia Viteri, eds. 2014. *Resentir lo 'queer' en América Latina: diálogos desde/con el sur*. Barcelona: Egales Editorial.

Falla, Ricardo. 1978. "El movimiento indígena." *Estudios Centroamericanos* 353: 438–61.

Falla, Ricardo. 1993. *Masacres de la selva: Ixcán, Guatemala (1975–1982)*. Guatemala: Universidad de San Carlos de Guatemala. Editorial Universitaria.

Falla, Ricardo. 2013. *El Popol Wuj: Una interpretación para el día de hoy*. Guatemala: AVANCSO.

Fanon, Frantz. [1961] 1971. *Los condenados de la tierra*. México: Fondo de cultura económica.

Favre, Henri. 1998. *El Indigenismo*. México, D.F.: Fondo de Cultura Económica.

Ferman, Claudia. 1993. *Política y posmodernidad: Hacia una lectura de la antimodernidad en Latinoamérica*. Miami, Fla.: Iberian Studies Institute.

Fischer, Edward. 1996. "Induced Culture Chance as a Strategy for Socioeconomic Development: The Pan-Maya Movement in Guatemala." In *Maya Cultural Activism in Guatemala*, edited by Edward Fischer and R. McKenna Brown, 51–73. Austin: University of Texas Press, Institute of Latin American Studies.

Fischer, Edward F., and R. McKenna Brown, eds. 1996. *Maya Cultural Activism in Guatemala*. Austin: University of Texas Press, Institute of Latin American Studies.

Flores, Ronald. 2003. *The Señores of Xiblablá*. Guatemala: Editorial Palo de Hormigo.

Florescano, Enrique. 1999. *Memoria indígena*. México, D.F.: Taurus.

Forster, Cindy. 2012. *La revolución indígena y campesina en Guatemala, 1970 a 2000*. Guatemala: Editorial Universitaria.

Forte, Maximilian, ed. 2002. *Indigenous Cosmopolitans: Transnational and Transcultural Indigeneity in the Twenty-First Century*. New York: Peter Lang.

Foucault, Michel. [1975] 1995. *Discipline and Punish: The Birth of the Prison*. New York: Vintage Books.

Francisco, Sabino Esteban. 2007. *Gemido de huellas / Sq'aqaw yechel aqanej*. Guatemala: Ministerio de Cultura y Deportes.

Francisco, Sabino Esteban. 2012. *Yetoq' Junjun b'Ijan Aq'Al / Con pedazo de carbón*. Guatemala: Ministerio de Cultura y Deportes, Editorial Cultura.

Francisco, Sabino Esteban. 2013. *Xik'ej K'al Xe'ej / Alas y raíces*. Guatemala: Editorial Catafixia.

Francisco, Sabino Esteban. 2017. *Sq'och Xajaw / La escalera de la Luna*. Guatemala: Editorial Cultura.

García, Pablo. 2009. *B'ixonik tzij kech juk'ulaj kaminaqib' / Canto palabra de una pareja de muertos*. Guatemala: F&G Editores.

García, Pablo. 2014. *Song from the Underworld*. Translated by Victoria Livingstone. El Cerrito, Calif.: Achiote Press.

García Canclini, Nestor. 1990. *Culturas híbridas: Estrategias para entrar y salir de la modernidad*. México: Grijalvo.

Gargallo, Francesca. 2014. *Feminismos desde Abya Yala: Ideas y proposiciones de las mujeres de 607 pueblos en Nuestra América*. México: Editorial Corte y Confección.

Garza, Mercedes de la, ed. 1980. *Literatura Maya*. Caracas: Biblioteca Ayacucho.

Gómez Grijalva, Dorotea. 2014. "Mi cuerpo es un territorio politico." In *Tejiendo de otro modo: Feminismo, epistemología y apuestas descoloniales en Abya Yala*, edited by Yuderkys Espinosa, Diana Gómez Correal, and Karina Ochoa Muñoz, 263–76. Popáyan, Colombia: Editorial Universitaria del Cauca.

González, Gaspar Pedro. 1992. *La otra cara: La vida de un maya*. Guatemala: Ministerio de Cultura y Deportes.

González, Gaspar Pedro. 1995. *A Mayan Life*. Rancho Palos Verdes, Calif.: Fundación Yax Te'.

González, Gaspar Pedro. 1996. *Sb'eyb'al jun naq Maya' Q'anjob'al. (La otra cara)*. Rancho Palos Verdes, Calif.: Ediciones Yax Te'.

González, Gaspar Pedro. 1997. *Kotz'ib': Nuestra literatura Maya*. Rancho Palos Verdes, Calif.: Fundación Yax Te'.

González, Gaspar Pedro. 1998a. *El retorno de los mayas*. Guatemala: Fundación Myrna Mack.

González, Gaspar Pedro. 1998b. *The Return of the Maya*. Rancho Palos Verdes, Calif.: Yax Te' Foundation.

González, Gaspar Pedro. 1998c. *Sq'anej Maya' / Palabras mayas*. Rancho Palos Verdes, Calif.: Fundación Yax Te'.

González, Gaspar Pedro. 2001. *The Dry Season: Q'anjob'al Maya Poems*. Translated by R. McKenna Brown. Cleveland, Ohio: Cleveland State University Poetry Center.

González, Gaspar Pedro. 2010. *The 13th B'aktun: A New Era.* Translated by Robert Sitler. Berkeley, Calif.: North Atlantic Books.

González, Gaspar Pedro. 2014. *Xumakil / Botón en Flor / Budding.* Philadelphia: Yax Te' Books.

González, Melani. 2016. "Continúan crímenes: Aparecen dos mujeres descuartizadas." *Guatevisión,* September 12. http://www.guatevision.com.

González, Otto-Raúl. 1978. "Poesía contemporánea de Guatemala: Los poetas de 'Nuevo Signo.'" *Cuadernos Americanos* 27, no. 221: 174–87.

González Casanova, Pablo. 1963. "Sociedad plural, colonialismo interno y desarrollo." *América Latina* 3: 15–32.

González-Ortuño, Gabriel. 2016. "Teorías de la disidencia sexual: De contextos populares a usos elitistas. La teoría queer en América latina frente a las y los pensadores de disidencia sexogenérica." *De Raíz Diversa. Revista Especializada en Estudios Latinoamericanos* 3, no. 5 (January–June): 179–200.

Gordon, Lewis R. 2000. *Existentia Africana: Understanding Africana Existential Thought.* New York: Routledge.

Gramajo, Jessica. 2017. "Diputados piden castigar el aborto y el matrimonio gay." *Prensa Libre,* April 27. http://www.prensalibre.com.

Grandin, Greg. 2000. *The Blood of Guatemala: A History of Race and Nation.* Durham, N.C.: Duke University Press.

Grandin, Greg. 2004. *The Last Colonial Massacre: Latin America in the Cold War.* Chicago: University of Chicago Press.

Grandin, Greg. 2011. *Who Is Rigoberta Menchú?* New York: Verso.

Grupo de Mujeres Mayas Kaqla. 2004. *La palabra y el sentir de las mujeres mayas de kaqla.* Guatemala: Grupo de Mujeres Mayas Kaqla.

Guatemalan Human Rights Commission. 2020. "Sepur Zarco, Sexual Slavery Case." http://www.ghrc-usa.org.

Guatemalan Truth Commission Report. 2012. *Memory of Silence: The Guatemalan Truth Commission Report.* New York: Palgrave Macmillan.

Gugelberger, Georg M., ed. 1996. *The Real Thing: Testimonial Discourse and Latin America.* Durham, N.C.: Duke University Press.

Guha, Ranajit. 1988. *Elementary Aspects of Peasant Insurgency in Colonial India.* Delhi: Oxford University Press.

Guha, Ranajit. 1996. "The Small Voice of History." In *Subaltern Studies: Writings on South Asian History,* Vol. 9, edited by Shahid Amin and Dipesh Chakrabarty, 1–12. Delhi: Oxford University Press.

Gutiérrez, Gustavo. 1971. *Teología de la liberación; perspectivas.* Lima: CEP.

Guzmán Böckler, Carlos. 1986. *Donde enmudecen las conciencias: Crepúsculo y aurora en Guatemala.* México: Secretaria de educación.

Guzmán Böckler, Carlos, and Jean-Loup Herbert. 1971. *Guatemala: Una interpretación histórico-social.* México: Siglo veintiuno editores.

Halberstam, Judith. 2011. *The Queer Art of Failure*. Durham, N.C.: Duke University Press.

Hale, Charles R. 2006. *Más que un Indio: Racial Ambivalence and Neoliberal Multiculturalism in Guatemala*. Santa Fé, N.Mex.: School for American Research Press.

Harlow, Barbara. 1987. *Resistance Literature*. New York: Methuen.

Hernández, Aída. 2001. "Entre el etnocentrismo feminista y el esencialismo étnico: Las mujeres indígenas y sus demandas de género." *Debate Feminista* 24 (October): 206–30.

Hernández Alarcón, Rosalinda, Andrea Carrillo Samayoa, Jacqueline Torres Urízar, Ana López Malina, and Ligia Z. Peláez Aldana. 2008. *Memorias rebeldes contra el olvido / Paasantzila Txums'al Ti' sotzeb' al K'u'l*. Guatemala: La Cuerda / AVANCSO.

Hill, Robert, and Judith Maxwell, eds. 2006. *The Kaqchikel Chronicles: The Definitive Edition*. Austin: University of Texas Press.

Holas-Véliz, Sergio, and Israel Holas Allimant. 2015. "Farewell Sweet Ladybird: A Manifesto and Three Chronicles by Pedro Lemebel (1952–2015)." *Cordite: Poetry Review*, May 1. http://cordite.org.au.

Houston, Stephen, and Andrew Scherer. 2010. "La ofrenda máxima: El sacrificio humano en la parte central del área maya." In *El sacrificio humano en la tradición religiosa mesoamericana*, edited by Leonardo López Luján and Guilhem Oliver, 167–91. México, D.F.: Instituto Nacional de Antropología e Historia.

Houston, Stephen, and Karl Taube. 2010. "La sexualidad entre los antiguos mayas." *Arquelogía Mexicana. (La sexualidad en Mesoamérica)* 18, no. 104 (July–August): 38–45.

Hull, Kerry, and Michael Carrasco, eds. 2012. *Parallel Worlds: Genre, Discourse and Poetics in Contemporary, Colonial and Classic Maya Literature*. Boulder: University Press of Colorado.

"In Our Own Words: A Conversation with Gaspar Pedro González." 2006. *Journal of the South and Meso American Indian Center* 10, no. 2 (Summer): 22–24.

"Investigación sobre feminicidio en Guatemala." 2005. *Cuadernos de Guatemala*, nos. 7 and 8 (October).

Jacobs, Sue-Ellen, Wesley Thomas, and Sabine Lang, eds. 1997. *Two-Spirit People: Native American Gender Identity, Sexuality, and Spirituality*. Urbana: University of Illinois Press.

Jahoda, Gloria. 1976. *The Trail of Tears*. New York: Holt, Rinehart and Winston.

Jiménez Estrada, Vivian. 2016. "Contemporary Expressions of Maya Indigenous Knowledge: Politics and Poetry in Ixim Ulew." *Dialogos: An Interdisciplinary Studies Journal* 19, no. 1 (Spring): 89–104.

Jocón González, María Estela. 2005. *Fortalecimiento de la participación política de las mujeres mayas*. Guatemala: Asociación Maya Uk'u'x B'e.

Johnston, Barbara Rose. 2005. "Chixoy Dam Legacy Issues Study." Center for Political Ecology. http://www.centerforpoliticalecology.org.

Jossa, Emanuela. 2007. "The Colors of the Earth: Nature and Landscape in the Poetry of Joy Harjo and Humberto Ak'abal." *Journal of the Southwest* 49, no. 4 (Winter): 585–601.

Keme, Emil' (Emilio del Valle Escalante). 2018. "Arech kak'asi'k le Abiayala rajawaxik ne kakam le Americas. Utzukuxik jun ajwaralikil winaq chi kab'e chi naj / Para que Abiayala viva, las Américas debèn morir. Hacia una Indigeneidad transhemisférica / For Abiayala to Live, the Americas Must Die: Toward a Trans-Hemispheric Indigeneity." *Native American and Indigenous Studies Journal* 5, no. 1: 1–68.

Knowlton, Timothy. 2015. "The Maya Goddess of Painting, Writing and Decorated Textiles." *PARI Journal* 16, no. 2: 31–41.

Konefal, Betsy. 2010. *For Every Indio Who Falls: A History of Maya Activism in Guatemala, 1960–1990.* Albuquerque: University of New Mexico Press.

"La comunidad LGBTI de Guatemala pide respeto y denuncia a los diputados por tortura." 2017. *La conexión USA.com,* May 17. http://www.laconexionusa.com.

Landa, Diego de. [1959] 1986. *Relación de las cosas de Yucatán.* México: Editorial Porrua.

Lemebel, Pedro. 2001. "Hablo por mi diferencia." In *A corazón abierto: Geografía literaria de la homosexualidad en Chile,* edited by Juan Pablo Sutherland, 35–39. Chile: Editorial Sudamericana.

Lemus, Juan Carlos. 2004. "Ak'abal: 'No, gracias.' El poeta explica por qué rechaza el Premio Nacional de Literatura." *Latinoamerica Online,* January 25. http://www.latinoamerica-online.info/.

León, Mayarí. 2014. "Nos hace falta indignación por nuestros intelectuales y artistas asesinados." *Literamérica: Lugar de encuentro para la creación periodística, literaria y fotográfica,* May 28. https://literamerica.wordpress.com.

León Díaz, José Luis de (Luis de Lión). 1966. *Los zopilotes.* Guatemala: Editorial Landívar.

Liano, Dante. 1997. *Visión crítica de la literatura guatemalteca.* Guatemala: Editorial Universitaria.

Ligorred Peramon, Francesc. 1997. *U Mayathanoob ti dzib' / Las voces de la escritura.* Yucatán: Ediciones de la Universidad Autónoma de Yucatán.

Lincoln, Kenneth. 1982. "Native American Literatures: 'Old Like Hills, Like Stars.'" In *Three American Literatures,* edited by Houston Baker Jr., 80–167. New York: Modern Languages Association.

Lión, Luis de. 1985. *El tiempo principia en Xibalbá.* Guatemala: Serviprensa centroamericana.

Lión, Luis de. 1996. *El tiempo principia en Xibalbá.* Guatemala: Artemis y editer.

Lión, Luis de. 1997. "Poemas para el correo." *El Periódico* (Guatemala), May 18, 12–13.

Lión, Luis de. [1994] 2009. *Poemas del Volcán de Agua, los poemas míos.* Guatemala: Editorial Cultura.

Lión, Luis de. 1998. *Poemas del Volcán de Fuego.* Guatemala: Bancafé.

Lión, Luis de. 1999. *La puerta del cielo y otras puertas.* Guatemala: Artemis Edinter.

Lión, Luis de. 2002. *El libro de José: Didáctica de la palabra.* Guatemala: Magna Terra Editores.

Lión, Luis de, ed. 2007. *Una experiencia poética: Taller de poesía infantil.* Guatemala: Editorial Cultura.

Lión, Luis de. 2012. *Time Commences in Xibalbá.* Translated by Nathan C. Henne. Tucson: University of Arizona Press.

López, Luis Enrique. 1997. "La diversidad étnica, cultural y lingüística latinoamericana y los recursos humanos que la educación require." *Revista Iberoamericana de Educación* 13 (January–April): 47–98.

MacLeod, Morna. 2011. *Nietas del fuego, creadoras del alba: Luchas político-culturales de mujeres mayas.* Guatemala: FLACSO.

MacLeod, Morna. 2013. "Pueblos indígenas y revolución: Los (des)encuentros entre indianistas y clasistas." In *Guatemala: Historia reciente (1954–1996), Tomo III: Pueblos indígenas: Actores politicos,* edited by Virgilio Álvarez Aragón, Carlos Figueroa Ibarra, Arturo Taracena, Sergio Tischler Visquerra, and Edmundo Urrutia, 25–58. Guatemala: FLACSO.

Mactzul Batz, Juana. 1991. *!Keqab'ij Pachun Tz'ij!* Guatemala: Instituto de Lingüística, Universidad Rafael Landívar.

Marcos, Sylvia. 2014. "Feminismos en camino descolonial." In *Mas allá del feminismo: caminos para andar,* edited by Margarita Millán, 15–34. Cord, México: Red de feminismos descoloniales.

Marroquín, Alejandro D. 1972. "Panorama del indigenismo en Guatemala." *América indígena* 23, no. 2 (April–June): 291–317.

Martínez, Francisco Mauricio. 2007. "Entrevista a Francisco Morales Santos." *El diario del Gallo. Blog sobre literatura guatemalteca.* http://diariodelgallo.word press.com.

Martínez Peláez, Severo. 1970. *La patria del criollo.* Guatemala: Universidad de San Carlos de Guatemala.

Marx, Karl. 1964. *Economic and Philosophic Manuscripts of 1844.* New York: International Publishers.

Memmi, Albert. 1965. *The Colonizer and the Colonized.* Boston: Beacon Press.

Menchú, Rigoberta, and Elizabeth Burgos. 1983. *Me llamo Rigoberta Menchú y así me nació la conciencia.* México, D.F.: Siglo Veintiuno Editores.

Menchú, Rigoberta, Gianni Minà, and Dante Liano. 1998. *Rigoberta Menchú, la nieta de los Mayas.* Madrid: El País-Aguilar.

Méndez de la Vega, Luz. 1986. *La poesía del Grupo RIN-78.* Guatemala: Grupo Literario Editoria RIN-78.

Meza Márquez, Consuelo, and Aida Toledo Arévalo. 2015. *La escritura de poetas mayas contemporáneas producida desde excéntricos espacios identitarios.* Aguascalientes, México: Universidad Autónoma de Aguascalientes.

Mignolo, Walter. 1989. "Literacy and Colonization: The New World Experience." In *1492–1992: Re/Discovering Colonial Writing,* edited by Rene Jara and Nicholas Spadaccini, 51–86. Minneapolis, Minn.: Prisma Institute.

Mignolo, Walter. 1995. *The Darker Side of the Renaissance: Literacy, Territoriality, and Colonization.* Ann Arbor: University of Michigan Press.

Mignolo, Walter. 2000. *Local Histories / Global Designs: Coloniality, Subaltern Knowledges, and Border Thinking.* Princeton, N.J.: Princeton University Press.

Mignolo, Walter. 2011. *The Darker Side of Western Modernity: Global Futures, Decolonial Options.* Durham, N.C.: Duke University Press.

Moi, Toril. 2001. *Sexual Textual Politics: Feminist Literary Theory.* London: Routledge.

Moller, Jonathan, and Ricardo Falla. 2004. *Our Culture Is Our Resistance: Repression, Refuge, and Healing in Guatemala.* New York: PowerHouse.

Momaday, Scott. 2011. *La casa hecha de alba.* Alicante, España: Appaloosa Editorial.

Mongia, Padmini. 1996. *Contemporary Postcolonial Theory: A Reader.* London: St. Martin's Press.

Montejo, Victor. [1982] 2001. *El Q'anil, Man of Lightning.* Tucson: University of Arizona Press.

Montejo, Victor. 1987. *Testimony: Death of a Guatemalan Village.* Willimantic, Conn.: Curbstone Press.

Montejo, Victor. 1992. *Brevisima relación testimonial de la continua destrucción del Mayab' (Guatemala).* Providence: Guatemala Scholars Network.

Montejo, Víctor. 1993. *Testimonio: muerte de una comunidad indígena en Guatemala.* Guatemala: Editorial Universitaria.

Montejo, Victor. 1995. *Sculpted Stones / Piedras labradas.* Translated by Victor Perera. Willimantic, Conn.: Curbstone Press.

Montejo, Victor. 1999. *Voices from Exile: Violence and Survival in Modern Maya History.* Norman: University of Oklahoma Press.

Montejo, Victor. 2005. *Maya Intellectual Renaissance: Identity, Representation, and Leadership.* Austin: University of Texas Press.

Montejo, Victor. 2006. *The Bird That Cleans the World.* Translated by Wallace Kaufman. Willimantic, Conn.: Curbstone Press.

Montejo, Victor. 2014. *Pixan, el cargador del espíritu.* El Pedregal, Guatemala: Editorial Piedra Santa.

Montenegro, Gustavo Adolfo. 2002. "Esto es como un sueño: Entrevista con Humberto Ak'abal." *Página de Literatura Guatemalteca*, November 2. http://www.literaturaguatemalteca.org.

Montenegro, Gustavo Adolfo. 2004. "Luis de Lión: 'Yo siempre tuve un cielo.'" *Revista D., Prensa Libre*, no. 1196 (May 9): 8–11.

Montenegro, Gustavo Adolfo. 2009. "Poeta Francisco Morales recibirá mañana reconocimiento Emeritissimum, de la Universidad de San Carlos." *Prensa Libre*, September 30. http://www.prensalibre.com.

Moore, Jason. 2017. "The Capitalocene, Part I: On the Nature and Origins of Our Ecological Crisis." *Journal of Peasant Studies*: 1–38.

Morales, Mario Roberto. 1999. *La articulación de las diferencias ó el sindrome de Maximón: Los discursos literarios y políticos del debate interétnico en Guatemala.* Guatemala: Facultad Latinoamericana de Ciencias Sociales.

Morales, Mario Roberto. 2000. "Sujetos interétnicos y moda posmo en xela." *Siglo Veintiuno*, July 19. http://www.sigloxxi.com.

Morales, Mario Roberto, ed. 2001. *Stoll-Menchú: La invención de la memoria.* Guatemala: Consucultura.

Morales, Mario Roberto. 2003. "A fuego lento: El dilema identitario de los ladinos." *Siglo Veintiuno*, November 4. http://www.sigloxxi.com.

Morales, Mario Roberto. 2012. "El indio por el indio: Una versión crítica del mestizaje indígena de Guatemala." *PublicoGT*, February 5. http://publicogt.com.

Morales Santos, Francisco. 1961. *Agua en el silencio.* Guatemala: La Antigua Guatemala.

Morales Santos, Francisco. 1963. *Ciudades en el llanto.* Guatemala: La Antigua Guatemala.

Morales Santos, Francisco. 1968. *Nimayá.* Guatemala: Nuevo Signo.

Morales Santos, Francisco. 1988. *Madre, nosotros también somos historia / Nan, Ri Oj Xuquje Oj Ajer Tzij k'Wi Chi Taq b'Ix.* Guatemala: Comunidad de Escritores de Guatemala.

Morales Santos, Francisco. 2000. *La tarea de relatar / The Task of Telling.* Translated by Joan Lindgren. Portland, Ore.: Trask House Books.

Morales Santos, Francisco. 2008. *Asalto al cielo: Antología personal (1967–1994).* Guatemala: Magna Terra Editores.

Moraña, Mabel, ed. 1998. *Indigenismo hacia el fin del milenio: Homenaje a Antonio Cornejo-Polar.* Pittsburgh, PA: Instituto Iberoamerican de Literatura Internacional.

Moreton-Robinson, Aileen. 2000. *Talkin' Up to the White Woman: Indigenous Women and Feminism.* Queensland, Australia: University of Queensland Press.

Morris, Warren Frederick. 2002. *Escaping Alienation: A Philosophy of Alienation and Dealienation.* Lanham, Md.: University Press of America.

Moya, Ruth. 1997. "Interculturalidad y reforma educativa en Guatemala." *Revista Iberoamericana de Educación* 13 (February–April): 129–55.

Muñoz, Mario. 1996. *De amores marginals: 16 cuentos mexicanos.* Veracruz: Universidad veracruzana.

Nájera, Francisco. 1988. "Un poema-testimonio de Francisco Morales Santos." In *Madre, nosotros también somos historia, Francisco Morales Santos,* 1–25. Guatemala: Editorial Universitaria.

Nelson, Diane M. 1999. *A Finger in the Wound: Body Politics in Quincentennial Guatemala.* Berkeley: University of California Press.

Newland, Carlos. 1991. "La educación elemental en Hispanoamérica: Desde la independencia hasta la centralización de los sistemas educativos nacionales." *Hispanic American Historical Review* 71, no. 2 (May): 335–64.

Nuevo Signo. 1970. *Las plumas de la serpiente: Antología poética del grupo Nuevo Signo.* Guatemala: Ediciones Nuevo Signo.

Oliver, Kelly. 2009. *Animal Lessons: How They Teach Us to Be Human.* New York: Columbia University Press.

Ong, Walter. 1989. *Orality and Literacy: The Technologizing of the Word.* London: Routledge.

Orange, Tommy. 2018. *There There.* New York: Alfred A. Knopf.

Organización Internacional del Trabajo. 1989. "Convenio número 169, sobre pueblos indígenas y tribales." *Organización internacional del trabajo,* July 27. https://www.ilo.org.

Palacios, Rita. 2016. "A Poetics of Weaving in the Work of Humberto Ak'abal." *Dialogos: An Interdisciplinary Studies Journal* 19, no. 1 (Spring): 105–18.

Paredes, Julieta. 2010. *Hilando fino desde el feminismo comunitario.* La Paz: Comunidad de Mujeres Creando / DED-Bolivia.

Paz Cárcamo, Guillermo. 2014. *Kaji' Imox / El camino del pueblo kaqchikel.* Guatemala: Cholsamaj.

Perdue, Theda, and Michael D. Green. 2005. *The Cherokee Removal: A Brief History with Documents.* Boston: Bedford/St. Martin's.

Pop Caal, Antonio. 1981. "Réplica del indio a una disertación ladina." In *Utopía y revolución: El pensamiento político contemporáneo de los indios en América Latina,* edited by Guillermo Bonfil Batalla, 145–52. México: Editorial Nueva Imagen.

Postema, Gerald. 1991. "On the Moral Presence of Our Past." *McGill Law Journal* 4: 1153–80.

Queer Nation. 1990. "Queer Nation Manifesto: History Is a Weapon." http://www.historyisaweapon.com.

"Quetzalí: La primera reina indígena trans de Guatemala que busca la igualdad." 2017. *El periódico,* September 24. http://www.elperiodico.com.

Rama, Ángel. 1984. *La ciudad letrada.* Hanover, N.H.: Ediciones del norte.

Rangel Romero, Pablo D. 2013. "La dimensión internacional de la lucha indígena, 1970–2010." In *Guatemala: Historia reciente (1954–1996), Tomo III: Pueblos indígenas: Actores políticos,* edited by Virgilio Álvarez Aragón, Carlos Figueroa

Ibarra, Arturo Taracena, Sergio Tischler Visquerra, and Edmundo Urrutia, 169–212. Guatemala: FLACSO.

Restall, Matthew, Lisa Sousa, and Kevin Terraciano. 2005. *Mesoamerican Voices: Native-Language Writings from Colonial México, Oaxaca, Yucatan, and Guatemala.* Cambridge: Cambridge University Press.

Reuque Paillalef, Rosa Isolde, and Florencia Mallon. 2002. *Una flor que reenace: Autobiografía de una dirigente Mapuche.* Santiago: Centro de Investigaciones Diego Barros Arana.

Rifkin, Mark. 2011. *When Did Indians Become Straight? Kinship, the History of Sexuality, and Native Sovereignty.* New York: Oxford University Press.

Rifkin, Mark. 2012. *The Erotics of Sovereignty: Queer Writing in the Era of Self-Determination.* Minneapolis: University of Minnesota Press.

Rothenberg, Daniel, ed. 2012. *Memory of Silence: The Guatemalan Truth Commission Report.* New York: Palgrave Macmillan.

Rothschild, Friedrich Salomon. 1962. "Laws of Symbolic Mediation in the Dynamics of Self and Personality." *Annals of New York Academy of Sciences* 96: 774–84.

Rueckert, William. 1996. "Literature and Ecology: An Experiment in Ecocriticism." In *The Ecocriticism Reader: Landmarks in Literary Ecology,* edited by Cheryll Glotfelty and Harold Fromm, 105–23. Athens: University of Georgia Press.

Sachse, Frauke, and Allen J. Christenson. 2005. "Tulan and the Other Side of the Sea: Unraveling a Metaphorical Concept from Colonial Guatemalan Highland Sources." *Mesoweb.* http://www.mesoweb.com.

Sahagún, Bernardino. 1981. *El México antiguo.* Caracas: Biblioteca Ayacucho.

Said, Edward. 1993. *Culture and Imperialism.* New York: Alfred A. Knopf.

Said, Edward. 2000. "Secular Criticism." In *The Edward Said Reader,* edited by Moustafa Bayoumi and Andrew Rubin, 218–42. New York: Vintage Books.

Salazar Tetzagüic, Manuel de. 1995. *Rupach'uxik Kina'oj Qati't Qamama' / Características de la literatura maya kaqchikel.* Guatemala: Cholsamaj.

Saldivia-Berglund, Marcela. 2003. "Representación y etnicidad: Hacia una interpretación de la poesía maya actual en Guatemala: Ajkem tzij: tejedor de palabras de Humberto Ak'abal." *Latin American Indian Literatures Journal* 19, no. 1 (Spring): 49–83.

Sam Colop, Luis Enrique. 1979. *La copa y la raíz.* Guatemala: Editorial San Antonio.

Sam Colop, Luis Enrique. 1980. *Versos sin refugio.* Guatemala: Editorial San Antonio.

Sam Colop, Luis Enrique. 1991. *Jub'aqtun omay kuchum k'aslemal / Cinco siglos de encubrimiento.* Guatemala: Cholsamaj.

Sam Colop, Luis Enrique. 1994. "Maya Poetics." PhD diss., State University of New York at Buffalo, New York.

Sam Colop, Luis Enrique. 2001. *Popol Wuj: Versión poética del texto en K'iche'.* Guatemala: Cholsamaj.

Sam Colop, Luis Enrique. 2011. *Popol Wuj*. Guatemala: F&G Editores.

Sam Colop, Luis Enrique. 2012. "Poetics in the Popol Wuj." In *Parallel Worlds: Genre, Discourse and Poetics in Contemporary, Colonial and Classic Maya Literature*, edited by Kerry Hull and Michael Carrasco, 283–309. Boulder: University of Colorado Press.

Sánchez Martínez, Juan Guillermo. 2012. *Memoria e Invención en la poesía de Humberto Ak'abal*. Quito: Ediciones Abya-Yala / Universidad Politécnica Salesiana.

Sanford, Victoria. 2003a. *Buried Secrets: Truth and Human Rights in Guatemala*. New York: Palgrave Macmillan.

Sanford, Victoria. 2003b. *Violencia y genocidio en Guatemala*. Guatemala: F&G Editores.

Schlesinger, Stephen C., and Stephen Kinzer. 1982. *Fruta amarga: La CIA en Guatemala*. México: Siglo veintiuno editores.

Scott, James C. 1985. *Weapons of the Weak: Everyday Forms of Peasant Resistance*. New Haven, Conn.: Yale University Press.

Sentencia por genocidio y delitos contra los deberes de Humanidad contra el Pueblo Maya Ixil. 2013. Guatemala: Editorial serviprensa centroamericana.

Shetemul, Haroldo. 2003. "La novela de la indianidad: Análisis sociológico de *El tiempo principia en Xibalbá* de Luis de Lión." MA thesis, Facultad de Humanidades, Departamento de letras, Universidad de San Carlos de Guatemala.

Sigal, Peter. 2000. *From Moon Goddesses to Virgins: The Colonization of Yucatecan Maya Sexual Desire*. Austin: University of Texas Press.

Sitting, Ann. 2009. "Contemporary Guatemalan Mayan Women Write an Identity Based on Respect, Interconnectedness, Love and Peace." *Letras Femeninas* 35, no. 2: 153–72.

Smith, Linda Tuhiwai. 1999. *Decolonizing Methodologies: Research and Indigenous Peoples*. London: Zed Books.

Smith, Paul Chaat. 2009. *Everything You Know about Indians Is Wrong*. Minneapolis: University of Minnesota Press.

Spivak, Gayatri Chakravorty. 1988. "Can the Subaltern Speak?" In *Marxism and the Interpretation of Culture*, edited by Cary Nelson and Lawrence Grossberg, 271–313. Basingstoke: Macmillan Education.

Spivak, Gayatri Chakravorty. 1996. "Subaltern Studies: Deconstructing Historiography?" In *The Spivak Reader*, edited by Donna Landry and Gerald MacLean, 203–37. London: Routledge.

Stavenhagen, Rodolfo. 1968. *Clases, colonialismo y aculturación*. Guatemala: Editorial J. de Pineda Ibarra, Ministerio de Educación.

Stoll, David. 1999. *Rigoberta Menchú and the Story of All Poor Guatemalans*. Boulder, Colo.: West Review Press.

Stuart, David. 2011. *The Order of Days: The Maya World and the Truth about 2012*. New York: Harmony Books.

Suncar, Joel. 2015. "Localizan cuerpo de mujer decapitada en la Zona 6." *Prensa Libre*, July 29. http://www.prensalibre.com.

Swann, Brian. 1988. "Introduction: Only the Beginning." In *Harper's Anthology of Twentieth- Century Native American Poetry*, edited by Duane Niatum, ix–xxxii. New York: Harper & Row.

Taracena, Arturo. 1999. *Invención criolla, sueño ladino, pesadilla indígena*. Guatemala: CIRMA.

Tarica, Estelle. 2008. *The Inner Life of Mestizo Nationalism*. Minneapolis: University of Minnesota Press.

Taussig, Michael. 2002. "Culture of Terror—Space of Death: Roger Casement's Putumayo Report and the Explanation of Torture." In *Genocide: An Anthropological Reader*, edited by Alexander Laban Hinton, 164–91. Malden, Mass.: Blackwell.

Tedlock, Dennis. 2010. *2000 Years of Mayan Literature*. Berkeley: University of California Press.

Thurston-Griswold, Henry Charles. 2007. "La novelización del testimonio en La otra cara, de Gaspar Pedro González." *Hispania* 90, no. 4 (December): 681–87.

Tischler Visquerra, Sergio. 2001. *Guatemala 1944: Crisis y revolución. Ocaso y quiebre de una forma estatal*. Guatemala: F&G Editores.

Tobar Aguilar, Gladys, Blanca Mendoza Hidalgo, and Nancy Maldonado de Masaya. 2007. "Estudio crítico de la obra del poeta Francisco Morales Santos, Premio Nacional de Literatura: Miguel Ángel Asturias." Informe de investigación de cultura, pensamiento e identidad de la sociedad guatemalteca. Guatemala: Universidad de San Carlos de Guatemala.

Toledo, Mario Monteforte. 2004. "El caso Ak'abal." In *El Grito / Raquonchi'aj*, edited by Humberto Ak'abal, 11–16. Guatemala: Cholsamaj.

Tonnssen, Morten, and Kadri Tüür. 2014. "The Semiotics of Animal Representations." In *The Semiotics of Animal Representations*, edited by Morten Tonnssen and Kadri Tüür, 7–30. Amsterdam: Rodopi.

Tzoc, Manuel. 2006. *Esco-p(o)etas para una muerte en ver(sos) b-a . . . l . . . a*. Guatemala: Folio 114.

Tzoc, Manuel. 2009. *De textos insanos*. México: Santa Muerte Cartonera.

Tzoc, Manuel. 2011. *Gay(o)*. Guatemala: Milenacaserola.

Tzoc, Manuel. 2011. *El ebrio mar y yo*. Guatemala: S.O.P.A.

Tzoc, Manuel. 2013. *El jardín de los infantes locos y la escafandra de oro*. En colaboración con Cecilia Porras Sáenz. Guatemala: Editorial Catafixia.

Tzoc, Manuel. 2016. *Constante huida: Crimen de un corazón que no recuerdo y/o pronunicamientos del habla tartamuda*. Guatemala: Editorial Catafixia.

Urizar Mazariegos, Julio A. 2014. "Aproximación a las representaciones del miedo en la obra poética de cinco escritores mayas contemporáneos guatemaltecos." Tesis de licenciatura, Facultad de Humanidades, Departamento de letras, Universidad de San Carlos de Guatemala.

Vail, Gabrielle, and Andrea Stone. 2002. "Representations of Women in Postclassic and Colonial Maya Literature and Art." In *Ancient Maya Women*, edited by Tracy Ardren, 203–28. New York: Rowman & Littlefield.

Valle Escalante, Emilio del. 2008. *Nacionalismos mayas y desafíos postcoloniales en Guatemala: Colonialidad, modernidad y políticas de la identidad cultural*. Guatemala: FLACSO.

Valle Escalante, Emilio del. 2009. *Maya Nationalism and Postcolonial Challenges in Guatemala: Coloniality, Modernity, and Identity Politics*. Santa Fé, N.Mex.: School for Advanced Research.

Valle Escalante, Emilio del, ed. 2010. *U'k'ux kaj, u'k'ux ulew: Antología de poesia maya guatemalteca contemporanea*. Pittsburgh, PA: Instituto Iberoamericano de Literatura Internacional.

Van Akkeren, Ruud. 2007. *Visión indígena de la conquista*. Guatemala: Serviprensa, 2007.

Vargas Llosa, Mario. 1996. *La utopía arcaica: José María Arguedas y las ficciones del indigenismo*. México: Fondo de cultura económica.

Velásquez de Mérida, Sonia Catalina. 2006. "Luis de Lión: La lucha del Héroe. Acercamiento psicocrítico a su narrativa breve." Tesis de licenciatura, Facultad de Humanidades, Departamento de letras, Universidad de San Carlos de Guatemala.

Velásquez Nimatuj, Irma Alicia. 2011. *La pequeña burguesía indígena comercial de Guatemala: Desigualdades de clase, raza y género*. 2nd ed. Guatemala: AVANCSO/Cholsamaj.

Velásquez Nimatuj, Irma Alicia. 2019. *"La justicia nunca estuvo de nuestro lado": Peritaje cultural sobre conflicto armado y violencia sexual en el caso Sepur Zarco, Guatemala*. Bilbao: Universidad del País Vasco.

Vergano, Dan. 2013. "Beheaded Maya Massacre Victims Found." *National Geographic*, September 13. http://news.nationalgeographic.com.

Viereck Salinas, Roberto. 2007. "Oralidad, escritura y traducción: Hacia una caracterización de la nueva poesía indígena de México y Guatemala." *Latin American Indian Literatures Journal* 23, no. 1 (Spring): 1–26.

Villa Rojas, Alfonso. 1995. *Estudios etnológicos: Los mayas*. México: Universidad Autónoma de México.

Villoro, Juan. 2007. "Premio de Literatura Indígena B'atz para Leoncio Pablo García Talé y Miguel Angel Oxlaj Cúmez." *Istmo: Revista virtual de estudios literarios y culturales centroamericanos*. October 15. http://istmo.denison.edu.

Vogler, Thomas. 2003. "Poetry Witness: Writing the Real." In *Witness and Memory: The Discourse of Trauma*, edited by Ana Douglass and Thomas Vogler, 173–206. New York: Routledge.

Warren, Kay B. 1998. *Indigenous Movements and Their Critics: Pan-Maya Activism in Guatemala*. Princeton, N.J.: Princeton University Press.

Warrior, Robert Allen, ed. 2014. *The World of Indigenous North America*. London: Routledge.

West, Cornell. 1993. "The New Cultural Politics of Difference." In *The Cultural Studies Reader*, edited by Simon During, 256–70. London: Routledge.

Wilson, Richard. 1999. *Resurgimiento Maya en Guatemala: Experiencias Q'eqchi'es*. Antigua, Guatemala: Centro de Investigaciones Regionales de Mesoaméricacirma.

Wolf, Eric. 1986. "The Vicissitudes of the Closed Corporate Peasant Community." *American Ethnologist* 13: 325–29.

Wolfe, Patrick. 1999. *Settler Colonialism and the Transformation of Anthropology: The Politics and Poetics of an Ethnographic Event*. London: Cassell.

Wolfe, Patrick. 2006. "Settler Colonialism and the Elimination of the Native." *Journal of Genocide Research* 8, no. 4: 387–409.

Womack, Craig. 1999. *Red on Red: Native American Literary Separatism*. Minneapolis: University of Minnesota Press.

Worley, Paul. 2016. "Pan-Maya and 'Trans-Indigenous': The Living Voice of the Chilam Balam in Victor Montejo and Leslie Marmon Silko." *Studies in American Indian Literatures* 28, no. 1 (Spring): 1–20.

Worley, Paul M., and Rita M. Palacios. 2019. *Unwriting Maya Literature: Ts'íib as Recorded Knowledge*. Tucson: University of Arizona Press.

Xiquin, Calixta Gabriel (Caly Domitila Kanek). 1990. "Guatemala: Participación de la mujer en la historia maya." *Boletín del Grupo Internacional de Trabajo sobre Asuntos Indígenas (IWGIA)* 10, nos. 3–4: 127–38.

Xiquin, Calixta Gabriel (Caly Domitila Kanek). 1996. *El Hueso de La Tierra*. Guatemala: Libros San Cristóbal.

Xiquin, Calixta Gabriel. 2002. *Tejiendo Los Sucesos En El Tiempo / Weaving Events in Time*. Rancho Palos Verdes, Calif.: Yax Te' Foundation.

Xiquin, Calixta Gabriel. 2008. *La Cosmovisión Maya y Las Mujeres: Aportes Desde El Punto de Vista de Una Ajq'il (Guía Espiritual) Kaqchikel*. Guatemala: Editorial Cultura.

Yañez, Daniela. 2016. "Angela Davis: 'Tenemos mucho que aprender de los actos revolucionarios del pueblo mapuche.'" *Mapuexpress*, July 21. http://www.mapuexpress.org.

Yool Gómez, Juan. 1990. *Ri' Xta Coyopá*. Guatemala: Instituto de Lingüística, Universidad Rarael Landivar.

Yool Gómez, Juan. 1994. *Rub'is Jun Mayab' / Tristeza de Un Maya*. Antigua, Guatemala: Proyecto Lingüístico Francisco Marroquín.

Zimmerman, Marc. 1995. *Literature and Resistance in Guatemala: Textual Modes and Cultural Politics from El Señor Presidente to Rigoberta Menchú 2v*. Athens: Ohio University Center for International Studies.

Zimmerman, Marc, and Raúl Rojas. 1998. *Voices from the Silence: Guatemalan Literature of Resistance*. Athens: Ohio University Center for International Studies.

Index